THE LIMITS OF FISCAL, MONETARY, AND TRADE POLICIES

International Comparisons and Solutions

THE LIMITS OF FISCAL, MONETARY, AND TRADE POLICIES

International Comparisons and Solutions

Jonathan E Leightner
Georgia Regents University, USA

World Scientific

NEW JERSEY · LONDON · SINGAPORE · BEIJING · SHANGHAI · HONG KONG · TAIPEI · CHENNAI

Published by

World Scientific Publishing Co. Pte. Ltd.

5 Toh Tuck Link, Singapore 596224

USA office: 27 Warren Street, Suite 401-402, Hackensack, NJ 07601

UK office: 57 Shelton Street, Covent Garden, London WC2H 9HE

Library of Congress Cataloging-in-Publication Data
Leightner, Jonathan E. (Jonathan Edward), 1957–
  The limits of fiscal, monetary, and trade policies : international comparisons and solutions / by Jonathan E Leightner (Georgia Regents University, USA).
    pages cm
  Includes bibliographical references and index.
  ISBN 978-9814571876
  1. Fiscal policy. 2. Monetary policy. 3. Commercial policy. 4. Saving and investment. I. Title.
  HJ192.5.L45 2015
  339.5--dc23
                                                                    2014009135

British Library Cataloguing-in-Publication Data
A catalogue record for this book is available from the British Library.

Cover illustration © Luke Leightner, lukeleightner@hotmail.com

The cover art depicts a mixture of a board game and reality. In the board game, a person wins when none of the other players can pay him the rent they owe him. In reality, building a hotel is a mistake if there are too few people who can afford its rent.

In-House Editors: Dipasri Sardar/Chye Shu Wen/Rajni Gamage

Typeset by Stallion Press
Email: enquiries@stallionpress.com

Printed in Singapore

DEDICATION

I dedicate this book to Justice and to all those who advance her kingdom in their families, villages, cities, provinces, nations, and world. To those who promote trust, hope, and love.

To those who advance trust by eliminating the taking and giving of bribes, who enforce standardized weights and measures, who condemn and prosecute those who deceive. To those who oppose the scheming of those with more power to steal from the poor and less fortunate via legal or illegal means. To those who stop pyramid schemes. To those who stop deceptive derivatives. To those who condemn fat sheep who take more than their share and then muddy the waters and trample the pastures ruining them for the weak.

To those who give hope by establishing governments and states that recognize that a few pennies from a poor widow involve more sacrifice than bags of gold from the rich. To those who create social systems where the owners of land and capital cannot squeeze what they own for every penny of value that it produces; instead the poor and the needy have access to part of the bounty. To those who pay their workers and creditors in a timely manner instead of holding their pay in order to earn interest.

To those who advance love by healing the sick, mending the broken-hearted and proclaiming liberty to the captives. To those who see an abandoned baby squirming in its birthing blood without its umbilical cord tied and who take that baby, wash it, feed it, cloth it, and allow it to thrive. To those who see their workers, not as means to greater profit, but as people of divine worth. To those who instead of ignoring the beggar at their front gate do something to make his or her life better. To those who work against discrimination. To those who love their neighbors as themselves where "neighbor" is defined broad enough to include an enemy who has been robbed and beaten and who is lying by the side of the road dying.

I dedicate this book to Justice and to the trust, hope, and love that are required for it to pour forth as a mighty river.

CONTENTS

List of Figures   ix

List of Tables   xv

About the Author   xvii

Acknowledgments   xix

Chapter 1: Introduction   1

Chapter 2: Banking Policy   11

Chapter 3: Monetary Policy   23

Chapter 4: Fiscal Policy   35

Chapter 5: Trade Policy   63

Chapter 6: Currency Policy   97

Chapter 7: China and Export Versus Consumption-Driven Growth   137

Chapter 8: Income Distribution   171

Chapter 9: Conclusion   187

Appendix 1: Reiterative Truncated Projected Least Squares   197

Appendix 2: Additional Figures for Chapter 4   229

Appendix 3: Additional Figures for Chapter 5   241

Appendix 4: Additional Information for Chapter 8   255

Appendix 5: Additional Tables for Chapter 9   267

References   273

Index   281

LIST OF FIGURES

Figure 1.1:   The World's Holdings of Foreign Reserves   4
Figure 1.2:   Holdings of Foreign Reserves by the Countries with
               the most in 2011   6
Figure 3.1:   USA ∂GDP/∂Money Data Seasonally Adjusted   27
Figure 3.2:   Japan ∂GDP/∂Money Data Seasonally Adjusted   29
Figure 3.3:   UK ∂GDP/∂Money   31
Figure 3.4:   Brazil ∂GDP/∂Money Data Not Seasonally Adjusted   32
Figure 3.5:   Russian Federation ∂GDP/∂Money Data Not
               Seasonally Adjusted   33
Figure 4.1:   ∂(Nominal GDP)/∂(Nominal Government
               Consumption) for Japan: Seasonally Adjusted   44
Figure 4.2:   ∂(Nominal GDP)/∂(Nominal Government
               Consumption) for the UK: Seasonally Adjusted   47
Figure 4.3:   ∂(Nominal GDP)/∂(Nominal Government
               Consumption) for the USA: Seasonally Adjusted   48
Figure 4.4:   ∂(Nominal GDP)/∂(Nominal Government
               Consumption) for Brazil: Not Seasonally Adjusted 49
Figure 4.5:   ∂(Nominal GDP)/∂(Nominal Government
               Consumption) for the Russian Federation: Not
               Seasonally Adjusted   51
Figure 4.6:   ∂(Nominal GDP)/∂(Nominal Government
               Consumption) for Cyprus: Not Seasonally Adjusted 53
Figure 4.7:   ∂(Nominal GDP)/∂(Nominal Government
               Consumption) for Germany: Seasonally Adjusted   54
Figure 4.8:   ∂(Nominal GDP)/∂(Nominal Government
               Consumption) for Greece: Not Seasonally Adjusted 56

Figure 4.9:	∂(Nominal GDP)/∂(Nominal Government
Consumption) for Ireland: Not Seasonally
Adjusted	57

Figure 4.10:	∂(Nominal GDP)/∂(Nominal Government
Consumption) for Italy: Seasonally Adjusted	59

Figure 4.11:	∂(Nominal GDP)/∂(Nominal Government
Consumption) for Spain: Seasonally Adjusted	60

Figure 5.1:	Gains and Losses from Trade	65

Figure 5.2:	Exporter Devaluation — Price in the Importing
Country's Currency [Also Importer Devaluation
If All the Arrows are Reversed and "1"s and "2"s
Switched.]	67

Figure 5.3:	Exporter Devaluation — Price in the Exporting
Country's Currency [Also Importer Devaluation
If All the Arrows are Reversed and "1"s and "2"s
Switched.]	68

Figure 5.4:	Exporter Suppresses Wages	69

Figure 5.5:	Importer Suppresses Wages	70

Figure 5.6:	∂GDP/∂Exports for Japan: Seasonally Adjusted	80

Figure 5.7:	∂GDP/∂Exports for the UK	81

Figure 5.8:	∂GDP/∂Exports for the USA	82

Figure 5.9:	∂GDP/∂Exports for Brazil: Not Seasonally Adjusted	83

Figure 5.10:	∂GDP/∂Exports for the Russian Federation	84

Figure 5.11:	∂GDP/∂Exports for Germany: Seasonally Adjusted	85

Figure 5.12:	∂GDP/∂Exports for Greece: Not Seasonally Adjusted	86

Figure 5.13:	∂GDP/∂Exports for Ireland	87

Figure 5.14:	∂GDP/∂Exports for Italy	88

Figure 5.15:	∂GDP/∂Exports for Spain: Seasonally Adjusted	89

Figure 6.1:	S(M) and D(X)	98

Figure 6.2:	S(M), D(X), and D(total)	100

Figure 6.3:	An Increase in the Global Glut of Savings	101

Figure 6.4:	China's Currency — the Renminbi (RMB)	102

Figure 6.5:	Using a Fixed Exchange Rate to Increase China's
Exports	103

Figure 6.6:	The Thai Baht, November 1984–December 1996	105

Figure 6.7:	Results of Soros' Speculative Attack against
the Thai Baht	106

Figure 6.8: ∂(Exports)/∂(Reserves) for Japan: Exports Measured
               in Yen, Reserves Measured in SDRs   122
Figure 6.9: ∂(Exports)/∂(Reserves) for the USA: Exports
               Measured in Dollars, Reserves Measured in SDRs   124
Figure 6.10: ∂(Exports)/∂(Reserves) for the UK: Exports
               Measured in Pounds, Reserves Measured in SDRs   125
Figure 6.11: ∂(Exports)/∂(Reserves) for Brazil: Exports
               Measured in Reais, Reserves Measured in SDRs   127
Figure 6.12: ∂(Exports)/∂(Reserves) for Russia: Exports
               Measured in Rubles, Reserves Measured in SDRs   128
Figure 6.13: ∂(Exports)/∂(Reserves) for Europe: Exports
               Measured in Euros, Reserves Measured in SDRs   129
Figure 6.14: ∂(Exports $-$ Imports)/∂(Reserves) for Europe:
               Exports $-$ Imports Measured in Euros, Reserves
               Measured in SDRs   130
Figure 6.15: ∂(Exports $-$ Imports)/∂(Reserves) for the USA:
               Exports $-$ Imports Measured in Dollars, Reserves
               Measured in SDRs   131
Figure 6.16: ∂(Exports $-$ Imports)/∂(Reserves) for the UK:
               Exports $-$ Imports Measured in Pounds, Reserves
               Measured in SDRs   132
Figure 6.17: ∂(Exports $-$ Imports)/∂(Reserves) for Japan:
               Exports $-$ Imports Measured in Yen, Reserves
               Measured in SDRs   133
Figure 6.18: ∂(Exports $-$ Imports)/∂(Reserves) for Brazil:
               Exports $-$ Imports Measured in Reais, Reserves
               Measured in SDRs   134
Figure 6.19: ∂(Exports $-$ Imports)/∂(Reserves) for Russia:
               Exports $-$ Imports Measured in Rubles, Reserves
               Measured in SDRs   135
Figure 7.1:   The Lorenz Curve and the Gini Coefficient   139
Figure 7.2:   Change in GPP due to a Change in Ratio of Wages
               to Profits and Rent: Provinces Moving toward
               Consumption-Driven Growth   147
Figure 7.3:   Change in GPP due to a Change in the Ratio of
               Wages to Profits and Rent: Provinces Moving away
               from Consumption-Driven Growth   148

Figure 7.4:   Ratio of Wages to Profits and Rent: Provinces
               Moving toward Consumption-Driven Growth   150
Figure 7.5:   Ratio of Wages to Profits and Rent: Provinces
               Moving away from Consumption-Driven Growth   151
Figure 7.6:   Ratio of Consumption to Gross Provincial Product:
               Provinces Moving toward Consumption-Driven
               Growth   156
Figure 7.7:   Ratio of Consumption to Gross Provincial Product:
               Provinces Moving away from Consumption-Driven
               Growth   157
Figure 7.8:   Ratio of Net Exports to Gross Provincial Product:
               Provinces Moving toward Consumption-Driven
               Growth   158
Figure 7.9:   Ratio of Net Exports to Gross Provincial Product:
               Provinces Moving away from Consumption-Driven
               Growth   159
Figure 7.10:   Effect of China's Rising Interest Rates on the
               International Currency Market   165
Figure 8.1:   Labor's Share of Income: Non-Euro(17) Countries   174
Figure 8.2:   Labor's Share of Income: Euro(17) Countries   175
Figure 8.3:   The Change in Investment due to a Change in the
               Consumption/Savings Ratio: USA and UK   179
Figure 8.4:   The Change in Investment due to a Change in the
               Consumption/Savings Ratio: Spain and Italy   180
Figure 8.5:   The Change in Investment due to a Change in the
               Consumption/Savings Ratio: Estonia   181
Figure 8.6:   The Change in Investment due to a Change in the
               Consumption/Savings Ratio: Finland   182
Figure 8.7:   The Change in Investment due to a Change in the
               Consumption/Savings Ratio: Germany   183
Figure A1.1:   The Intuition Behind RTPLS   200
Figure A1.2:   Projecting to the Upper Frontier   205
Figure A1.3:   Projecting to the Lower Frontier   206
Figure A1.4:   The First 100 Observations: A Single More Complex
               Simulation   217

Figure A1.5: The First 100 Observations after Eliminating Effect
              of X_2 and X_3: The Elimination of the Effect of X_2
              and X_3 Based on OLS Using All 800 Observations   218
Figure A1.6: Using RTPLS When $\partial Y/\partial X$ is Negative   226
Figure A2.1: ∂(Nominal GDP)/∂(Nominal Government
              Consumption) for Austria: Not Seasonally Adjusted   230
Figure A2.2: ∂(Nominal GDP)/∂(Nominal Government
              Consumption) for Belgium: Not Seasonally Adjusted   231
Figure A2.3: ∂(Nominal GDP)/∂(Nominal Government
              Consumption) for Estonia: Not Seasonally Adjusted   232
Figure A2.4: ∂(Nominal GDP)/∂(Nominal Government
              Consumption) for Finland: Not Seasonally Adjusted   233
Figure A2.5: ∂(Nominal GDP)/∂(Nominal Government
              Consumption) for France: Seasonally Adjusted   234
Figure A2.6: ∂(Nominal GDP)/∂(Nominal Government
              Consumption) for Luxembourg: Not Seasonally
              Adjusted   235
Figure A2.7: ∂(Nominal GDP)/∂(Nominal Government
              Consumption) for Malta: Not Seasonally Adjusted   236
Figure A2.8: ∂(Nominal GDP)/∂(Nominal Government
              Consumption) for Netherlands: Seasonally Adjusted   237
Figure A2.9: ∂(Nominal GDP)/∂(Nominal Government
              Consumption) for Portugal: Not Seasonally Adjusted   238
Figure A2.10: ∂(Nominal GDP)/∂(Nominal Government
              Consumption) for Slovakia: Not Seasonally Adjusted   239
Figure A2.11: ∂(Nominal GDP)/∂(Nominal Government
              Consumption) for Slovenia: Not Seasonally Adjusted   240
Figure A3.1: ∂GDP/∂Exports for Austria: Not Seasonally
              Adjusted   242
Figure A3.2: ∂GDP/∂Exports for Belgium: Not Seasonally
              Adjusted   243
Figure A3.3: ∂GDP/∂Exports for Cyprus: Not Seasonally
              Adjusted   244
Figure A3.4: ∂GDP/∂Exports for Estonia: Not Seasonally
              Adjusted   245

Figure A3.5:   ∂GDP/∂Exports for Finland: Not Seasonally
              Adjusted   246
Figure A3.6:   ∂GDP/∂Exports for France: Not Seasonally Adjusted   247
Figure A3.7:   ∂GDP/∂Exports for Luxembourg   248
Figure A3.8:   ∂GDP/∂Exports for Malta: Not Seasonally Adjusted   249
Figure A3.9:   ∂GDP/∂Exports for the Netherlands   250
Figure A3.10: ∂GDP/∂Exports for Portugal   251
Figure A3.11: ∂GDP/∂Exports for Slovakia: Not Seasonally
              Adjusted   252
Figure A3.12: ∂GDP/∂Exports for Slovenia   253

LIST OF TABLES

Table 3.1:	∂GDP/∂Money	25
Table 4.1:	∂GDP/∂G Estimates	38
Table 5.1:	∂GDP/∂Exports	75
Table 6.1:	∂Exports/∂(Foreign Reserves)	111
Table 6.2:	∂(Exports $-$ Imports)/∂(Foreign Reserves)	116
Table 7.1:	∂GPP/∂(Wages/(Profits $+$ Rents)) and the Ratio of Wages/(Profits $+$ Rents)	144
Table 7.2:	C/GPP and (Exports $-$ Imports)/GPP Ratios	152
Table 8.1:	Gini Coefficients	172
Table 9.1:	The Maximum then Minimum Annual Averages of the ∂GDP/∂G, ∂GDP/∂X, and ∂GDP/∂Money Results: 1981–2012	188
Table A1.1:	The Mean $|e|$, 5,000 Simulations for Each Case	211
Table A1.2:	The Standard Error of $|e|$, 5,000 Simulations for Each Case	212
Table A1.3:	A More Complex Simulation	219
Table A4.1:	Labor's Share of Income	258
Table A4.2:	∂I/∂(C/S) Estimates	262
Table A5.1:	∂GDP/∂G Annual Averages: 1981–2012	268
Table A5.2:	∂GDP/∂X Annual Averages: 1981–2012	270
Table A5.3:	∂GDP/∂Money Annual Averages: 1981–2012	272

ABOUT THE AUTHOR

Jonathan E. Leightner is a Professor of Economics at Georgia Regents University. He is an applied macroeconomist who has journal publications on the effectiveness of fiscal, monetary, and currency policies in many different countries including China, Japan, Thailand, and the USA. He also has publications on technology transfer to Japan, income distribution in South Korea, and Thailand's 1997 financial crisis. He has published his research in *Applied Economics Letters, China & World Economy, Frontiers of Economics in China, Journal of Development Studies,* and the *Journal of Economic Issues* among many others. He has been a visiting professor for John Hopkins University in Nanjing, China; Chulalongkorn University in Bangkok, Thailand; and for Seikei University in Tokyo, Japan. His most recent research focuses on the causes and consequences of financial crises; on the relationships between economics, religion, and morality; and on how to eliminate the influence of unknown, immeasurable, and omitted variables when conducting regression analysis.

ACKNOWLEDGMENTS

I appreciate the many hours that Yumiko Deevey spent searching for and downloading data, translating Japanese, and finding citations for me. I would also like to thank Kunihiro Fujio, her father, who provided research assistance from Japan. I appreciate Pam Jackson and Mark Thompson for checking the entire manuscript for errors. I would like to thank Dennis Appleyard for teaching me international economics 27 years ago and for checking Chapters 5 and 6 for errors in international economics. Any remaining errors in the book are my fault.

This book was made possible by Tomoo Inoue writing a computer program that quickly conducts the RTPLS process. Tomoo Inoue also deserves credit for running the computer simulations presented in Appendix 1. I owe a debt to C.A. Knox Lovell who first came up with the idea that observations at the top of a scatter plot are associated with the most favorable omitted variables — the key intuition underlying the statistical technique used in this book.

Finally, I would like to acknowledge the patience of my wife, Sandra, for whom I have done no home repairs for the last six months while I have spent every spare minute writing this book.

Chapter 1

INTRODUCTION

The Main Argument

In 2007–2008, a speculative bubble in the US housing market exploded sending the US economy, and soon thereafter the European economy, into crisis. Unemployment skyrocketed. For example, unemployment in the USA jumped from 4.6% in 2007 to 9.6% in 2010 and then fell to 8.1% in 2012. The United Kingdom's unemployment rate of 5.4% in 2007 rose to 7.9% in 2010 and then has stayed in the range of 7.9–8.1% between 2010 and 2012. Italy's unemployment, which was 6.2% in 2007, has continued to rise hitting 10.8% in 2012. Spain's unemployment, which was 8.3% in 2007, has continued to rise hitting 25.2% in 2012 (http://www.bls.gov/flscomparelf/lfcompendiur). In response to this crisis, central banks have increased their money supplies by unprecedented amounts (Lauricella *et al.*, 2012; Mead and Hilsenrath, 2013). Meanwhile, concerned about growing budget deficits, governments are cutting spending and increasing taxes. As the resulting fiscal austerity makes the recession worse and as the effects of increasing the money supply diminish, governments (especially European governments) cling to the hope that internal devaluations (a euphemism for cutting wages and reducing labor power) will result in increased exports and a return to export-driven growth.

China's stated government goals stand in stark contrast to these trends. China does not want to return to an export-driven growth model; instead, it wants to establish a domestic consumption-driven growth model. According to Orlik (2013), manufacturing wages in China have risen by 71% between 2008 and 2013 while average private sector wages rose 12.3% in 2011

1

and 14% in 2012. However, to successfully establish a consumption-driven growth model, China must do more than just allow wages to rise. China must solve some major problems in its health care, pension, banking, and court systems; furthermore, China needs to address problems due to corruption, its growing inequality, and insufficient competition.

Which strategy is best — is it best to embrace the European goal of restarting export-driven growth via internal devaluations or is it best to embrace China's current goal of establishing a domestic consumption-driven growth model? The economic future of the world depends on how this question is answered. The correct answer to this question depends on the fundamental cause of the current crisis.

This book will show that the fundamental cause of the current crisis is a global surplus of savings which is either (1) sitting idle, (2) seeking a return by earning rents or by deception in contrast to seeking a return by expanding production, or (3) funding speculative bubbles. Successful production expanding investment requires two things: (1) there must be savings to fund the investment and (2) there must be the reasonable hope that what that investment produces can be sold. In other words, there must be sufficient consumption to provide a reason to invest. There is a global surplus of savings because there is currently insufficient consumption to justify production expanding investment.

The European approach to the crisis — internal devaluations that reduce wages — reduces worldwide consumption and, thus, the reason to invest. Internal devaluations will make the worldwide crisis worse. Granted if Spain, for example, can reduce its wages more than all other countries, then Spain will probably be able to drive its economy off of increased exports; however, the world will lose more than Spain gains due to a net fall in worldwide consumption and a net increase in the global surplus of savings. China has the right idea — what the world needs is more consumption, not less.

Consider some key elements of the above thesis.

A Global Surplus of Savings

US corporate cash holdings fell from US$1.53 trillion in 2007 to US$1.39 trillion in 2008 but jumped to US$2.05 trillion of cash and other liquid assets by June of 2011 which is the highest amount of US corporate cash since 1963 (Monga, 2011; see also Casselman, 2012 and Chasan, 2013). "Corporate cash holdings are now €2 trillion (US$2.64 trillion) across the euro zone and an extraordinary £750 billion (US$1.19 trillion) in the UK" (Fidler, 2012). The Institute of International Finance estimated that in January 2012 "corporations in the USA, the euro zone, the UK, and Japan held some US$7.75 trillion in cash, or near equivalents, an unprecedented sum" (Fidler, 2012).

Meanwhile, according to Simon Tilford (chief economist at the Centre for European Reform) "the ratio of investment to gross domestic product (GDP) in Europe is at a 60-year low" (Fidler, 2012). According to the rating agency Standard & Poor's, US corporations cut investment by an estimated US$175 billion between 2009 and 2011 which boosted their cash reserves (Gara, 2012). Instead of investing their cash in expanding production, US corporations "announced plans to buy back US$117.8 billion of their own shares in February [2013], the highest monthly total in records that date back to 1985." In 2013, "companies in the S&P 500 index are expected to pay at least US$300 billion in dividends . . . which would top last year's record of US$282 billion" (Demos *et al.*, 2013). It is as if corporations are willing to sit on their cash, use their cash to buy back their own stock, or use their cash to pay greater dividends; in other words, they are willing to do anything with their cash except invest it in expanding production.

Banks are also accumulating cash reserves. By the end of 2012, US bank deposits hit a record US$10.6 trillion; meanwhile, the loan-to-deposit ratio has fallen from 95% in 2007 to 72%. Since 2008, outstanding loans at US thrifts and banks have fallen 5.3% (Sidel, 2013). Commercial Japanese bank deposits at the Central Bank of Japan increased 113% between March and November 2013. Furthermore, the loan to deposit gap for Japanese commercial banks has widened by 8% per year on average for the last 10 years. "Loans at Japanese banks amounted to 69% of deposits at the end of October" 2013 (Dvorak and Warnock, 2013a). Deposits are up while loans are down in spite of interest rates approaching 0%.

One of the primary ways that governments save is by accumulating foreign reserves. Figure 1.1 shows that world holdings of foreign reserves increased relatively steadily from 5.55 trillion in 1976 to 37.87 trillion in 2001. In 2001, the world dramatically increased its accumulation of foreign

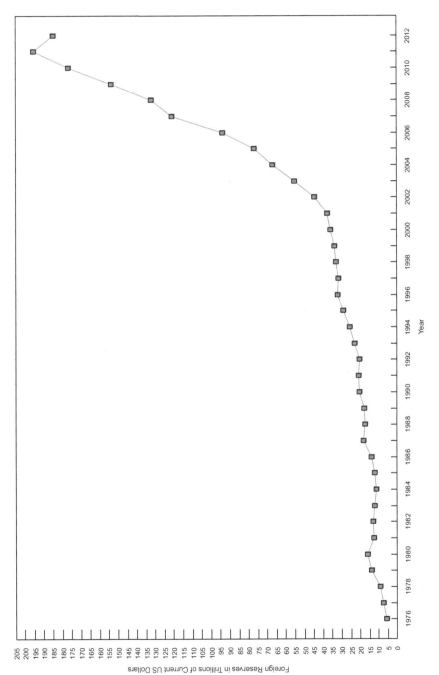

Figure 1.1:   The World's Holdings of Foreign Reserves

reserves. By 2011, foreign reserves were 195.41 trillion, although they fell in 2012 to US$184.92 trillion. In the 35 years between 1976 and 2011, world holdings of foreign reserves grew 34-fold.

Figure 1.2 shows the holdings of foreign reserves by the eight countries that held the most foreign reserves in 2011. Between 1979 and 1994, the USA had the most foreign reserves. These reserves slowly grew to US$294 billion in 2008, jumped to 404 billion in 2009, grew to 537 billion in 2011, and then plummeted to 139 billion in 2012. China's foreign reserves were 172 billion in 2000 but grew to US$3,663 billion by September 2013 for a 20.3-fold increase in 13 years. Japan's holdings of foreign reserves increased from 80 billion in 1992 to 1,227 billion in 2012 for a 14-fold increase in 20 years. Governments, corporations, and banks have all increased their savings in the last two decades.

The Qualitative Difference between a Return from Investment Based on Owning versus a Return Based on Expanding Production

If I earn a return from owning something — a house, a business, treasury bonds, or foreign currency — then my return is someone else's loss.[1] The renter of my house loses the money that I gain. The person who sold me the business loses the future income stream from the business. The government loses the interest they pay on the Treasury bonds. In contrast, if I earn a return based on expanded production, then the total wealth generated in the world has increased and there is the possibility that everyone gains. Admittedly, the line between earning a return from owning and earning a return from expanding production can be blurred because the money I paid for a treasury bond might be used to build a new road that increases the production capabilities of my country. However, this distinction is still useful especially in a world where there is currently very little investment in expanding production and a large amount of investment that aims at earning a return from rent. Many experts trace the beginning of the crisis

---

[1]A part of my return is compensation for my bearing risk; however, usually the return from owing a given item far exceeds the historical risk from owning that type of item as evidenced by the cost of insuring that item being far less than the return that I earn.

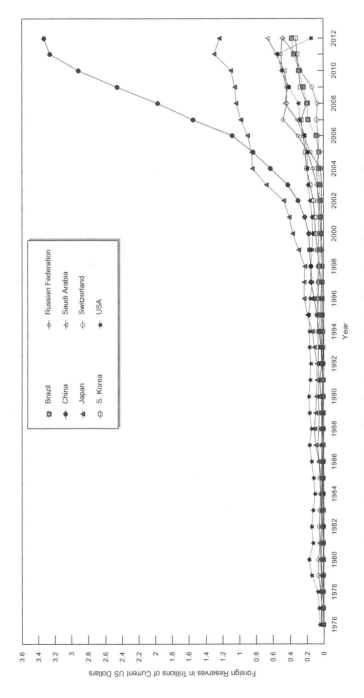

Figure 1.2:   Holdings of Foreign Reserves by the Countries with the most in 2011

to the selling of mortgage derivatives. Those who bought these derivatives were attempting to earn a return from owning.

Most governments welcome long-term capital flows because these flows tend to build factories that increase the host country's productive capabilities and GDP. Many of these same governments are scared of short-term capital flows because these flows tend to focus on getting a return from owning something and can quickly enter or leave a country destabilizing its economy. In a world with insufficient consumption to justify additional productive investment, an increasing percent of total investment is "rent seeking."

Consumption-Driven Growth Worked in the Past

Consider two examples of successful consumption-driven growth: the USA and Japan. Rosenberg (2003) tells how car production and sales in the USA in the 1920s led to investments in industries to make tires, auto parts, plate glass, steel, roads, traffic lights, gas stations, and, ultimately, suburbs. "With suburbanization came increased spending on new housing. Many of the new homes would be electrified and have telephones and radios. Thus, investment spending in electric power, telephone, and communications industries took off" (Rosenberg, 2003, p. 4).

The Japanese government, beginning in the late 1950s, purposefully targeted improving Japan's income distribution as a major goal of government policy. This led to the ratio of the wage bill to profits increasing from 0.902 to 3.065 between 1952 and 1981 (Leightner, 1992). The average real personal income for Japan's urban workers and farmers nearly doubled between 1955 and 1959 (Ozawa, 1985). These changes led to Japan enjoying several waves of consumption-driven growth.

> TV sets, which were used in only 16% of [Japanese] households in 1958, were used in as many as 91% by 1963. The popular consumer durables in the early 1950s were relatively low-income products such as radios, fluorescent lamps, bicycles, electric fans, and sewing machines. The later 1950s saw a growth in demand for monochrome TV sets, washing machines, and automatic rice cookers. The demand for more sophisticated high-income goods such as color TVs, refrigerators, air conditioners, and automobiles expanded phenomenally throughout the 1960s, but especially in the latter years of the decade.
>
> Consumer demand for clothing similarly underwent a qualitative change: synthetic fiber or blended fiber products became increasingly popular as many of

them had a permanent press feature. And tastes for fashion-oriented clothing, too, developed significantly. Many of these consumer goods are time saving in nature for housewives and created more leisure time. On average, the Japanese housewife spent 11 hours per day on household chores before the war but less than 8 hours at the end of the 1960s. Innovations in the consumer goods sector, therefore, in turn created new demands for leisure-related goods and services (Ozawa, 1985, pp. 233–234).

Outline of the Rest of the Book

The core of the world's economic problems today is a surplus of savings. This savings is not being invested in expanding production because there is insufficient consumption to justify production expanding investment. The primary solution to this problem is to increase consumption providing a reason to invest the surplus savings in production expanding ways. China is the only major country today that is actively and openly embracing consumption-driven growth.[2] In contrast, Europe, as directed by the International Monetary Fund (IMF), is attempting to reduce wages and labor power in order to restart export-driven growth. The European approach is counter-productive.

The rest of the book develops the details of the above thesis as it relates to the experience of Brazil, China, Japan, the Russian Federation, Thailand, the United Kingdom, the USA, and the 17 countries that use the Euro. Chapter 2 examines banking policy. Chapters 3–5 theoretically and empirically examine the effects of changes in the money supply (M-1), government spending (G), and exports (X) on GDP. The estimates of $\partial GDP/\partial M\text{-}1$, $\partial GDP/\partial G$, and $\partial GDP/\partial X$ in these chapters[3] show that the effectiveness of monetary, fiscal, and trade policies are falling by a noticeable amount

---

[2]Japan has also talked about "consumption-driven growth"; however, the Japanese government's plan to increase the national sales tax in early 2014 is contrary to such a model.

[3]The notation "$\partial Y/\partial X$" means the "change in Y due to a one unit change in X." In other words, $\partial Y/\partial X$ is the slope of the line (or the derivative of the line) showing the relationship between Y and X. In Chapter 7, I use annual data for China from China's Statistical Yearbook. For all other chapters, I use quarterly data from the IMF. I always use the maximum amount of data available. I use a statistical technique, explained in Appendix 1, which is designed to capture the influence of variables that are not explicitly included in the analysis (omitted variables). This technique produces a separate slope estimate for each observation making it possible to see how $\partial Y/\partial X$ is changing over time.

for most of the countries examined. This result means that the methods currently being employed to solve the crisis are becoming less and less effective. Furthermore, I find that in many cases, the negative effects of cutting the money supply, government spending, and exports exceed the positive effects of increasing these items. This implies that to undo the damage caused by cutting government spending under austerity, Spain, for example, would have to increase government spending much more than they cut it.

The empirical estimates in Chapter 6 show that, since 1995, countries have not been able to successfully increase GDP by accumulating additional foreign currency in an effort to depress their exchange rates and increase exports. Chapter 7 presents a detailed analysis of what China has already done, is currently doing, and still needs to do to implement a consumption-driven growth model. Chapter 8 examines the effects of income distribution on growth. Chapter 9 concludes by arguing that the effectiveness of fiscal, monetary, and trade policies would be enhanced by embracing a consumption-driven growth model.

Chapter 2

BANKING POLICY

Utility maximization theory is one of the foundation models of economics. According to this theory, people choose to maximize their personal benefit subject to a budget constraint. If all people are given the freedom to choose, they will each maximize their personal benefit, resulting in a maximum of social well-being given the current income distribution. This theory works best when applied to individual decisions that do not affect other people and when applied to relatively short time frames. If what maximizes my utility produces pollution that makes someone else sick, then social well-being may not be maximized. Furthermore, since utility maximization is subject to a budget constraint, how income is distributed will affect who benefits the most from their choices and the total amount of benefit produced. These are important issues, but the issue I want to focus on here is the time frame used for utility analysis.

Utility theory implicitly assumes the time frame of the chooser. If the chooser is addicted to crack cocaine and, thus, is only focusing on his desperate need to get a fix in the next few minutes, then he will make choices that maximize his benefit over the next few minutes; however, these choices may not be in his long-term best interest. Indeed, in the long run, he is likely to regret the choices he makes in the next few minutes. In contrast, if someone focuses on a time frame that encompasses the remainder of her life, then she will make optimal decisions for the rest of her life if her assumptions about the future hold true. However, the future is uncertain, as the world economic crisis that started in 2008 has well demonstrated. Thus, someone who considers the time frame that encompasses the rest of her life must factor in the uncertainty of the future.

Most people get more immediate benefit from consuming their income than from saving it (the miser who takes joy in his huge stacks of coin which he will never use is the exception, not the rule). When most of us save, we do it for the benefit of the person we will become. The fact that many of us, as we get older, regret not having saved more in our youth, implies that our younger selves either discounted our futures or made mistakes. The interest rate is the price of the trade-off between the present and the future — it is what the market says we should be paid for not consuming today so that we can consume more in the future. The role of banks is to take money from those who wish to save (and thereby earn interest) and give it to those who want to spend more than their current income and are willing to pay the going interest rate to do so. The market interest rate will be the interest rate that equates the quantity of money that people want to save with the quantity that other people want to borrow.

However, the previous statement ignored the gap between the savings and lending interest rates that provides income for the bank. Most governments want their banks to finance the maximum amount of production expanding investment possible. Thus, these governments would like to minimize the gap between savings and lending interest rates. In contrast, banks want to maximize profits which can be achieved with a much larger gap between the savings and lending interest rates than what the government wants. Theoretically, the gap between the savings and lending interest rates should also reflect the short-term nature of most savings versus the longer-term nature of most investments.

If there are so many banks that any one bank cannot affect the interest rate (i.e., if the loanable funds market fits the economic model of pure competition), then the gap between the savings and lending gap should be as small as it possibly can be. However, financial liberalization, which has swept over the globe in the 1980s and 1990s, has led to a tremendous consolidation of financial institutions, moving the market further away from the purely competitive ideal. Leightner and Lovell (1998) show that financial liberalization in Thailand increased the ability of banks to increase profits much more than it increased the financing of production increasing investment. Financial liberalization does this in several ways — some of which make it possible for banks to earn fees, move long-term investments off of their personal accounting books, and/or take advantage of other participants having imperfect information.

Financial Liberalization and its Consequences

In most countries, the number of financial institutions is falling while the size and power of the remaining financial institutions is increasing. For example, in 1984, there were 17,914 commercial banks or savings institutions in the USA; however, in 2012, the number had decreased to 7,083 for a 60% decline (http://www2.fdic.gov/hsob/HSOBRpt.asp). Between 1996 and 2006, the number of banks has fallen from 80 to 43 in Argentina, from 87 to 40 in Brazil, from 27 to 12 in Hong Kong, from 61 to 46 in India, from 65 to 35 in Indonesia, from 148 to 124 in Japan, from 29 to 16 in South Korea, from 34 to 21 in Malaysia, from 27 to 8 in Mexico, from 22 to 11 in Peru, and from 15 to 8 in Singapore. Meanwhile, the share of total assets held by the three largest banks (the three-firm concentration ratio) increased between 1996 and 2006 from 0.35 to 0.6 in Brazil, from 0.4 to 0.6 in Chile, from 0.65 to 0.85 in Hong Kong, from 0.35 to 0.55 in Indonesia, from 0.25 to 0.5 in South Korea, from 0.55 to 0.65 in Mexico, and from 0.6 to 0.9 in Singapore (Olivero *et al.*, 2009).

These changes have occurred in the context of the world embracing financial liberalization — a reduction in the regulations and rules that governments use to monitor and control their financial institutions. Presumably, financial liberalization frees up banks to innovate, and the resulting advances in technology are good for the entire world. The financial crisis that began in the USA in 2007–2008 has led to this presumption being questioned. The US Senate's Financial Crisis Report states that the crisis was "the result of high risk, complex financial products; undisclosed conflicts of interests; and the failure of regulators, the credit rating agencies, and the market itself to rein in the excesses of Wall Street" (US Senate, 2011, p. 1). These "high risk, complex financial products" were developed under financial liberalization and include CDOs (Collateralized Debt Obligations), CDS (Credit Default Swaps), ABX (Asset-backed Securities Index), and RMBS (Residential Mortgage Backed Securities Indices) — all of which played important roles in the financial crisis.

Consider CDOs. When I purchased my house in the 1990s, my bank told me that I could afford a house that cost three times as much. When this revelation did not change my mind, the bank representative patiently explained to my wife and I that Americans increase their net worth by purchasing the most expensive houses that they can. We were told that because all US houses were increasing in value, buying a more expensive house would make me ultimately wealthier. The bank also informed us that our mortgage might be sold on a secondary market. We insisted on buying the house we had selected which cost one-third of our limit, and the bank did not sell our mortgage on the secondary market. The bank knew our mortgage was solid and that it was a good investment for the bank.

If, however, we had been persuaded by the bank to buy the most expensive house we could "afford," the bank probably would have sold our mortgage on the secondary market. In this case, the more expensive the house we purchased, the larger the fee the bank would get from writing our mortgage. Therefore, the bank has a financial incentive to push home buyers into the most expensive houses possible. Our mortgage could have then been bundled with other mortgages into a CDO. The mortgages in the CDO would be layered and the different layers given different credit ratings and then sold to investors. Theoretically, the bundling of many mortgages together reduces the overall risk. However, in reality, banks had the incentive to make loans to everyone, whether they were good risks or not, because the bank earned the fees no matter how risky the loan.

Many of the mortgages included in these bundles did not even meet minimum underwriting standards. Richard M. Bowen III testified to the Financial Crisis Inquiry Commission that he was promoted to Business Chief Underwriter for Correspondent Lending in the Consumer Lending Group of Citigroup in early 2006 and that in this role he was in charge of 220 underwriters. By mid-2006, he discovered that 60% of the US$90 billion of mortgages going through his office were "defective" (not underwritten to policy) and that this defective rate increased to "over 80%" in 2007 (Bowen, 2010, pp. 1–2).

The US Senate's Financial Crisis Report argues that US banks sometimes work contrary to their client's interests.

> In the case of Goldman Sachs, the practices included exploiting conflicts of interest with the firm's clients. For example, Goldman used CDS and ABX contracts to

place billions of dollars of bets that specific RMBS securities, baskets of RMBS securities, or collections of assets in CDOs would fall in value, while at the same time convincing customers to invest in new RMBS and CDO securities. In one instance, Goldman took the entire short side of a $2 billion CDO known as Hudson 1, selected assets for the CDO to transfer risk from Goldman's own holdings, allowed investors to buy the CDO securities without fully disclosing its own short position, and when the CDO lost value, made a $1.7 billion gain at the expense of the clients to whom it had sold the securities . . . . In another instance, Goldman marketed a CDO known as Abacus 2007-AC1 to clients without disclosing that it had allowed the sole short party in the CDO, a hedge fund, to play a major role in selecting the assets. The Abacus securities quickly lost value, and the three long investors together lost $1 billion, while the hedge fund profited by about the same amount. (p. 319).

When lauding the virtues of free markets, economists usually assume perfect information — the seller knows his or her true cost of production and the buyer knows the true value of what he or she is purchasing. If there are many buyers and many sellers in such a world (and several other assumptions are also true), the market produces an efficient outcome. Clearly, the preceding examples show that there is not perfect information in banking and that some banks were seeking to earn a return from deception. The local bank that makes a mortgage loan has the most complete information — that bank knows the local real estate market, how different neighborhoods vary, which neighborhoods are associated with the best schools, etc. However, pre-crisis bankers ignored all that information because they could make a fast dollar by pushing buyers to buy the most expensive house possible and then selling the resulting mortgage on the secondary market to investors who had no idea what the true risks were. What is the solution to this problem? Some would argue for more regulation or more paper work; however, a simpler solution that produces the best information is to make banks hold on to all the mortgages they originate. In other words, make CDOs, RMBSs, ABXs, etc., illegal.

The bigger the bank, the bigger and more complex the financial instruments it can create and the higher the fees it can collect. This results in bank profits being positively related to the size of the bank. This, in turn drives many mergers and acquisitions resulting in the number of banks in the USA decreasing by 60%, as mentioned above. If these consolidations were driven by cost savings, then they might be good for society; however, if they are driven by returns to market power or returns from deception, then they are definitely bad for society. Leightner (2006) found that very small Thai banks were able to provide loans and buy securities at a much lower average total cost than large banks. This implies that there are diseconomies to scale for banks in the provision of loans and securities, and, thus, relatively small banks are best for society. Leightner (2006) points out that this result is consistent with most empirical studies of banks around the world. His study further shows the average price Thai banks receive increases much faster than the average cost increases. Thus, he concludes that banks have a profit incentive to get as big as possible, even though relatively small banks are best for society. The reason that average price increases as banks get bigger and bigger is that larger banks can earn more money off of fees, like the fees earned by selling mortgages on the secondary market, and these fees are more profitable than the making and holding of standard loans and the holding of standard securities (the things that directly finance growth).

The notion that extremely large banks are "too big to fail" compounds these problems. If a bank manager believes that his bank is too big to fail, then he has the incentive to do extremely risky things that would pay off with high profits if they succeed since, if they fail, the government will bear the loss. In this case, the bank manager only considers the upside of risks. Furthermore, the Thai case demonstrates that public trust in the entire banking system is a "public good." If one bank breaks the public trust, then customers tend to flee all banks in that country's banking system creating a system-wide banking crisis (Alam and Leightner, 2001). Indeed, there are some economic models of crises that are built on massive bank runs (Diamond and Dybvig, 1983; Diamond, 2007). Clearly, the government's goal of having a stable financial system that finances growth is inconsistent with bank managers taking excessive risks because they believe they can avoid all negative consequences due to being too big to fail.

All of the above analysis is already in the existing literature, which is much more vast and detailed than what I have cited. This book's most important contribution lies in its tracing these and other problems back to a global surplus of savings. Why did the banking system create investment funds like CDOs and its siblings? The answer to this question is the return from investing in production expansion was less than the return from earning fees from making risky mortgages and selling them on a secondary market. Yes, the government needs to change the underlying structure of the US financial system so that the conflicts of interests and the deception that played such an important role in the US banking crisis cannot happen again. However, these types of structural changes are only addressing half of the problem. The other half of the problem is why is the return from investing in production expansion so low?

The return from investing in production expansion is so low because the supply of loanable funds (savings) has increased as the rich get richer while the demand for loanable funds has fallen because there is insufficient consumption to provide a reason to invest the savings in ways that would increase production. In such a world, savings seek a return from owning things or from deception, like bundled mortgages, instead of from expanding production. Consider specifically how the global surplus of savings affected the banking systems of Thailand, Cyprus, and Ireland.

Thailand

From 1986 to 1994, Thailand was one of the fastest growing countries in the world, had successfully maintained a fixed exchange rate since November 4, 1984, and was a favorite country for foreign investment. However, by 1993, the Thai government was very concerned because wages in Thailand were rising while wages in Cambodia, Laos, Vietnam, Myanmar, and southern China were not rising. Wages in Malaysia were also rising but not as fast as Thailand's. The Thai government was concerned that Thai businesses would move to neighboring countries in order to reduce their costs.

Although the Thai government's response to this concern may bewilder many westerners, the ancient Chinese philosopher Confucius would have applauded it. The Thai government decided to help its neighbors grow. Top Thai officials organized meetings of government officials and business leaders in the major cities of Thailand. I attended one of those meetings. At the meeting, the Thai government told Thai businessmen that they wanted Thai business to invest in Thailand's neighbors. The Thai government also promised to do whatever it took to make such investment successful; it offered to help with negotiations, to provide foreign exchange, to give tax incentives, etc. At the meeting I attended in Chiang Mai, the Thai officials suggested building gas pipelines from Myanmar to Thailand, building dams and hydro-electric plants in Laos, and setting up manufacturing plants in Vietnam and southern China. On the surface, it looks as if the Thai government was encouraging exactly what they feared — Thai firms moving to Thailand's neighbors where wages were lower. However, the Thai government was actually trying to become the patron of Indo-China. The theory was that if Thailand helped its neighbors grow, then Thailand's neighbors would be obligated to be loyal to Thailand and not do anything that would hurt Thailand. The whole region could grow together like one big, happy family with Thailand in the lead.

A good patron also provides financing for growth. Thus, Thailand set up the Bangkok International Banking Facility (BIBF) in 1993. The BIBF in essence eliminated Thailand's capital controls (laws that restrict how much foreign money can come in and/or go out of a country). The goal of the BIBF was to attract large inflows of money from Japan, the USA, and Europe which would be lent to Thailand's neighbors. However, interest rates in Thailand were approximately 5% higher than they were in the rest of the world and much higher than they were in Thailand's neighbors. Consequently, the BIBF was able to attract huge inflows of foreign savings; however, that savings preferred to stay in Thailand where its return was higher (Leightner, 1999, 2007b).

More foreign savings came flooding into Thailand than could be productively used and speculative bubbles were the result. Jittrapanun and Prasartset (2009) estimate that these bubbles resulted in excess supply in relationship to market demand becoming 150% in iron and steel, 192% in motor cars, 195% in petrochemicals, 200% in metropolitan Bangkok housing, and 300% in private hospitals. When investors take out loans to build factories, or houses, or office buildings that are far in excess of market demand, then they have difficulty selling what the investment produces and, thus, they have difficulty re-paying their loans. A banking crisis is the result.

In 1996, the Bangkok Bank of Commerce ran into some major problems that involved a political scandal, a major bank official stealing two suitcases full of money from the bank and fleeing to Canada, and a failed cover-up by Thailand's central bank. In the spring of 1997, Somprasong Land Company defaulted on a US$3 million interest payment on some European Debentures. On March 3, 1997, the Thai government suspended trade of all financial company stocks and bonds on the stock exchange of

Thailand, increased reserve requirements for all financial institutions, and shut down 10 weak finance and securities companies.

These events, as well as some others, provided the ammunition for currency speculators, like George Soros, to launch a speculative attack on the Thai baht. The Thai government's defense of the Thai baht consumed most of Thailand's foreign reserves — Thailand's foreign reserves were approximately 36 billion in December 1996 but were between 1 and 5 billion on July 2, 1997 when Thailand gave up its fixed exchange rate. The Thai baht fell from 25 baht per dollar on July 1, 1997 to 54 baht per dollar in January 1998. On August 19, 1997, Thailand took out a US$17.2 billion loan from the IMF and the World Bank. The conditions that Thailand accepted in exchange for the IMF/World Bank loan included the IMF's typical austerity measures plus a promise not to rescue any more Thai financial institutions.

By May 1998, 56 of Thailand's 91 finance and securities companies had been shut down and 7 more had been taken over by the government. About 4 of Thailand's 15 commercial banks were also taken over by the Thai government. In the course of taking over these financial institutions, the Thai government fired all of their senior leadership and wrote down their capital to 1/1,000th of its previous value. The Thai government also announced if the remaining financial institutions did not get their non-performing loans under control, then they would be treated in the same way.

Under this threat, bank managers decreased the amount of new loans they made to almost zero. A severe credit crunch resulted. Many firms that owed money to Thailand's financial institutions stopped paying on their loans and started stock piling cash because they knew that their chances of getting new loans was almost nil. This made the non-performing loan problem of banks worse. Some borrowers leveraged the desperation of banks to get their non-performing loans under control by asking the banks for bribes, write-downs of part of the principle that they owed, and/or lower interest rates. The resulting incidence of "strategic non-performing loans" became epidemic. The Thai government rewrote Thailand's bankruptcy code so that the bankruptcy process that previously took four or five years could be completed in one year. However, the bankruptcy court that heard the first major case under the new rules threw the case out of court because the company was technically not bankrupt — they had the money to pay back their loans, they just were not doing it.

The Thai financial crisis also led to the political rise of Thaksin Shinawatra, massive street protests, a mob of protesters taking over Bangkok's biggest international airport, a coup against Thaksin, more protesters taking over the central business area of Bangkok, Thaksin's sister being elected prime minister, and another round of massive street protests in Bangkok as I was finishing this book in December 2013. In other words, the consequences of Thailand opening its doors to the global surplus of savings in 1993 were still being felt in Thailand in 2013, 20 years later (Leightner, 1999; 2002a; 2002b; 2007b).

Cyprus

Due to Cyprus' relatively low corporate tax rate and the strong legal protections that come with being a European Union country, many foreigners (especially Russians) put their savings into Cyprus' banks (Alpert, 2013). This has led to Cyprus' banking sector being eight times the size of the country's GDP; Cyprus' banks had more savings than domestic production expanding investments could absorb. Therefore, these banks invested in assets that would earn rent, like Greek government bonds. Apparently, as the Greek economy fell into crisis and many foreigners were exiting Greek bonds, Cyprus' banks were buying Greek government bonds because they were bargain priced and because Cyprus' banks did not believe that the European Union would allow the value of those bonds to decline. When the values of Greek bonds were drastically decreased, Cyprus' banks were severely damaged. Cyprus' financial sector accounts for 45% of Cyprus' economy (Stevis *et al.*, 2013); thus, the entire economy was at risk.

The European Central bank, the International Monetary Fund (IMF), and the European Commission proposed a tax on deposits under €100,000 of 6.75% and a tax of 9.9% on deposits above that limit. Cyprus' government rejected this proposal causing much fear that Cyprus would be forced to abandon its use of the euro. Ultimately, a deal was accepted that preserved the total value of deposits under €100,000, but will cause much steeper losses for deposits exceeding €100,000. How steep these losses will be are currently unknown; however, some estimate that they will range from 60 to 100% (Jenkins, 2013). As a consequence of this crisis, most Cyprus' businesses are now operating on a "cash only" basis (Persianis *et al.*, 2013).

Ireland

Like Thailand between 1986 and 1996, Ireland was viewed as a great success before its crisis. Due to demographic factors, rising education levels, and a surge in female labor force participation, Irish employment rose from 1.1 million to 2.1 million between the late 1980s and 2007. Meanwhile, labor productivity increased and economic growth averaged 6.3% per year between 1987 and 2007.

> This exceptional economic growth allowed the Irish government to achieve a holy grail that was the envy of politicians around the world: They lowered tax rates and raised public spending year in and year out and yet economic growth delivered sufficient tax revenues to generate a string of budget surpluses (Whelan, 2013, p. 3).

However, a housing bubble funded by an inflow of European savings destroyed Ireland's exceptional economic performance.

The first stage of establishing the European Monetary Union (EMU) was to allow the free movement of capital between member states, and this stage was to be implemented between July 1, 1990 and December 31, 1993. This free movement of capital allowed European savings to enter Ireland causing mortgage interest rates, which prior to the EMU were in excess of 10%, to fall to less than 5%. European savings sought out Ireland's real estate market because of Ireland's economic success, growing population, rising incomes, and initial low per capita housing stock. According to estimates made by Somerville (2007), Ireland had the smallest per capita housing stock in the European Union as of 2000. As a result of these forces, Ireland's housing prices quadrupled between 1996 and 2007; by way of comparison, US housing prices only doubled during that time frame.

Ireland's total stock of houses grew from 1.2 million in 1991 to 1.4 million in 2000 and then to 1.9 million in 2008. After 2002, per capita new house completions surged to four times higher in Ireland then they were in the USA. Indeed, new "house completions went from 19,000 in 1990 to 50,000 in 2000 to a whopping 93,000 in 2006" (Whelan, 2013, p. 6).

> After 2003, the rapid expansion of property lending was largely financed with bonds issued to international investors. From less than €15 billion in 2003, international bond borrowings of the six main Irish banks rose to almost €100 billion (well over half of GDP) by 2007" (Whelan, 2013, p. 11).

In other words, what financed Ireland's real estate bubble was the global surplus of savings.

Whelan (2013) clearly sees the role that foreign savings played in Ireland's crisis; however, he places the primary blame for the crisis on Irish government policies.

> Some in Ireland blame the low interest rates associated with euro membership for the housing bubble and resulting crash. I think the weight of blame is better placed on domestic fiscal and regulatory policy. While the authorities may not have been able to do much about the low interest rates brought by euro membership, they had the power to place limits on mortgage lending (limiting multiples of income or requiring large down-payments) and to restrict the exposure of individual financial institutions to property development. In addition, rather than "lean against" the property bubble, Ireland's government provided a host of tax-based incentives that encouraged property speculation (pp. 27–28).

Whether or not Whelan is correct in placing the primary blame on the Irish government, my thesis remains unaltered. In the wake of these crises, everyone is talking about how governments could have better regulated their economies, and I admit that the regulation issues are extremely important to address. However, no one seems to be talking about how the global surplus of savings continues to plague our world and what should be done to eliminate it. We need to fix the regulation issues and seriously address the global surplus of savings.

Chapter 3

MONETARY POLICY

Correctly using traditional statistical techniques to analyze the effectiveness of changes in monetary, fiscal, and trade policy in today's world would require the construction and justification of a worldwide macroeconomic model that included every force that can affect gross domestic product (GDP) and all the ways that nations are inter-connected, especially through trade and financial flows. Such a model would have to capture all changes in technologies, in resource endowments, and in relative prices (including interest rates and exchange rates). Creating such a model is not possible.

Fortunately, Leightner (2002a), Leightner and Inoue (2007 and 2012b), and Inoue *et al.* (2013) developed Reiterative Truncated Projected Least Squares (RTPLS), a technique that captures the influence of omitted variables without having to measure, model, or find proxies for them. Furthermore, RTPLS produces reduced form estimates of the slope without having to build macroeconomic models. RTPLS produces a separate slope estimate for every observation which makes it possible to see how the estimated relationship is changing over time. See Appendix 1 of this book for a detailed explanation of RTPLS. Chapters 3–5 include RTPLS estimates of the change in GDP due to a change in the money supply (∂GDP/∂Money),[1]

---

[1] "∂" simply means "the change in." $\partial Y/\partial X$ is the "change in Y due to a one unit change in X" which is the same as the slope. When $\partial Y/\partial X$ is calculated, the change in X considered is made as small as possible in order to increase accuracy. In the language of calculus, "$\partial Y/\partial X$" is the total derivative, holding nothing constant (unless otherwise explicitly stated). "$\partial Y/\partial X$" should not be confused with the partial derivative that is calculated holding all other explanatory variables constant. A 99% confidence interval is calculated for most of the $\partial Y/\partial X$ estimates in this book by applying the Central Limit Theorem to a given estimate along with

due to a change in government spending (∂GDP/∂G), and due to a change in exports (∂GDP/∂X), using the maximum amount of quarterly data available from the IMF for Japan, the United Kingdom, the USA, Brazil, the Russian Federation, and the 17 countries of the European Union (as of January 2013). Unfortunately, there was insufficient quarterly data to include China and India in this analysis.

There are several different ways to calculate the money supply: M-0 is currency and coin in circulation, M-1 is M-0 plus traveler's checks and checkable deposits, M-2 is M-1 plus time deposits that are less than US$100,000 plus savings and money market deposits. Where possible, I used M-1 data.[2] Estimates for ∂GDP/∂Money for the 17 countries of the European Union were not made because these countries gave up independent monetary policy when they adopted the euro.

Table 3.1 lists the RTPLS estimates for ∂GDP/∂Money for the first quarter of 1970 to the fourth quarter of 2012. Figure 3.1 shows the ∂GDP/∂Money estimates and money supply for the USA from 1980 to 2012. The line for the money supply shows the US Federal Reserve System's (FED's) unprecedented increase in the money supply from 2008 through 2012 which has been named "quantitative easing" and which is a major response of the US government to the current crisis. Much of this quantitative easing has been done by the FED purchasing bonds — by paying new coin and currency for these bonds, the FED puts additional coin and currency into circulation which also causes checkable deposits to increase through a money expansion process. Note that as the FED has increased the money supply, ∂GDP/∂Money has fallen. Table 3.1 shows that ∂GDP/∂Money fell from 10.89 in the fourth quarter of 2007 to 6.79

---

the two estimates before it and the two estimates after it, as explained in Appendix 1. This 99% confidence interval means that we can be 99% sure that the true average value for $\partial Y/\partial X$ for those five estimates lies between the upper and lower limits of the confidence interval.

[2]The IMF had overlapping GDP and M-1 data for the first quarter of 1991 to the fourth quarter of 2012 for Brazil, for the second quarter of 1955 to the fourth quarter of 2012 for Japan, and for the first quarter of 1959 to the first quarter of 2013 for the USA. Unfortunately, the IMF did not have M-1 data for the Russian Federation and for the UK. For the Russian Federation, I used the IMF's M-2 data between the second quarter of 1995 and the fourth quarter of 2012. For the UK, I used the IMF's M-0 data for the second quarter of 1969 to the first quarter of 2006.

Table 3.1: ∂GDP/∂Money

	Japan	UK	USA		Japan	UK	USA	Brazil	Russia
1970 Q1	3.36	9.41	8.36	1981 Q1	3.69	7.30	8.96		
1970 Q2	3.35	9.27	8.36	1981 Q2	3.60	7.28	8.91		
1970 Q3	3.41	9.13	8.28	1981 Q3	3.60	7.45	9.09		
1970 Q4	3.34	8.89	8.19	1981 Q4	3.53	7.20	8.93		
1971 Q1	3.22	8.76	8.23	1982 Q1	3.59	7.85	8.78		
1971 Q2	3.03	8.80	8.15	1982 Q2	3.55	7.81	8.81		
1971 Q3	2.90	8.94	8.13	1982 Q3	3.52	7.78	8.71		
1971 Q4	2.82	8.78	8.12	1982 Q4	3.50	7.45	8.46		
1972 Q1	2.86	9.05	8.08	1983 Q1	3.52	7.94	8.32		
1972 Q2	2.89	8.67	8.15	1983 Q2	3.55	7.83	8.30		
1972 Q3	2.85	8.64	8.03	1983 Q3	3.59	7.90	8.37		
1972 Q4	2.77	8.12	7.98	1983 Q4	3.69	7.46	8.42		
1973 Q1	2.77	8.62	8.10	1984 Q1	3.69	7.98	8.49		
1973 Q2	2.79	8.23	8.08	1984 Q2	3.76	7.94	8.53		
1973 Q3	2.82	8.20	8.12	1984 Q3	3.73	7.85	8.62		
1973 Q4	2.92	7.72	8.12	1984 Q4	3.67	7.45	8.59		
1974 Q1	2.93	7.92	8.06	1985 Q1	3.72	8.06	8.51		
1974 Q2	3.02	7.97	8.15	1985 Q2	3.78	8.14	8.38		
1974 Q3	3.09	7.75	8.18	1985 Q3	3.82	8.17	8.22		
1974 Q4	3.10	7.24	8.23	1985 Q4	3.83	7.72	8.10		
1975 Q1	3.04	7.72	8.22	1986 Q1	3.82	8.29	8.03		
1975 Q2	3.08	7.64	8.17	1986 Q2	3.73	8.30	7.76		
1975 Q3	3.08	7.61	8.28	1986 Q3	3.74	8.23	7.56		
1975 Q4	3.06	7.31	8.42	1986 Q4	3.58	7.78	7.24		
1976 Q1	3.03	7.76	8.46	1987 Q1	3.55	8.54	7.24		
1976 Q2	3.04	7.50	8.46	1987 Q2	3.50	8.57	7.25		
1976 Q3	3.05	7.38	8.48	1987 Q3	3.55	8.59	7.31		
1976 Q4	3.06	7.20	8.45	1987 Q4	3.60	8.16	7.45		
1977 Q1	3.12	7.62	8.42	1988 Q1	3.60	8.84	7.42		
1977 Q2	3.20	7.37	8.50	1988 Q2	3.53	8.72	7.40		
1977 Q3	3.25	7.40	8.53	1988 Q3	3.66	8.66	7.46		
1977 Q4	3.19	6.86	8.50	1988 Q4	3.55	8.28	7.57		
1978 Q1	3.24	7.21	8.46	1989 Q1	3.59	9.04	7.74		
1978 Q2	3.17	7.12	8.58	1989 Q2	3.66	9.01	7.96		
1978 Q3	3.19	7.01	8.63	1989 Q3	3.62	8.98	7.98		
1978 Q4	3.15	6.58	8.73	1989 Q4	3.88	8.43	7.93		
1979 Q1	3.15	6.94	8.73	1990 Q1	3.63	9.28	8.00		
1979 Q2	3.18	7.01	8.65	1990 Q2	3.77	9.19	8.04		
1979 Q3	3.18	6.99	8.71	1990 Q3	3.90	9.24	7.99		
1979 Q4	3.22	6.68	8.81	1990 Q4	3.91	8.70	7.94		
1980 Q1	3.21	7.24	8.82	1991 Q1	3.92	9.45	7.85	0.16	
1980 Q2	3.42	7.18	8.82	1991 Q2	3.86	9.36	7.78	2.62	
1980 Q3	3.58	7.21	8.62	1991 Q3	3.87	9.35	7.74	3.55	
1980 Q4	3.70	6.91	8.86	1991 Q4	3.76	8.85	7.58	5.14	

(*Continued*)

Table 3.1:   (Continued)

	Japan	UK	USA	Brazil	Russia		Japan	UK	USA	Brazil	Russia
1992 Q1	3.80	9.75	7.36	8.29		2003 Q1	1.41	8.10	9.35	4.50	1.11
1992 Q2	3.75	9.57	7.33	8.82		2003 Q2	1.13	7.97	9.14	4.91	1.03
1992 Q3	3.74	9.38	7.18	9.73		2003 Q3	1.11	7.87	9.21	5.03	1.17
1992 Q4	3.67	8.88	7.02	8.42		2003 Q4	1.10	7.43	9.28	4.18	1.02
1993 Q1	3.68	9.64	6.98	11.18		2004 Q1	1.11	8.00	9.25	4.50	0.91
1993 Q2	3.62	9.44	6.81	11.67		2004 Q2	1.09	7.84	9.28	4.72	0.97
1993 Q3	3.56	9.38	6.69	13.23		2004 Q3	1.07	7.77	9.28	4.51	1.15
1993 Q4	3.47	8.86	6.65	9.90		2004 Q4	1.06	7.42	9.32	4.08	1.04
1994 Q1	3.55	9.50	6.68	9.79		2005 Q1	1.05	7.84	9.52	4.23	0.92
1994 Q2	3.49	9.32	6.77	8.90		2005 Q2	1.04	7.92	9.57	4.57	0.96
1994 Q3	3.52	9.23	6.80	8.11		2005 Q3	1.02	7.76	9.75	4.62	1.05
1994 Q4	3.44	8.74	6.91	5.94		2005 Q4	1.02	7.35	9.89	3.98	0.95
1995 Q1	3.40	9.40	6.99	9.19		2006 Q1	1.01	7.90	10.03	4.24	0.87
1995 Q2	3.34	9.34	7.04	9.69	−0.38	2006 Q2	1.01		10.22	4.37	0.85
1995 Q3	3.14	9.24	7.14	9.45	0.07	2006 Q3	1.01		10.37	4.22	0.89
1995 Q4	3.15	8.67	7.31	6.94	0.19	2006 Q4	1.04		10.46	3.68	0.78
1996 Q1	3.01	9.36	7.43	8.08	0.04	2007 Q1	1.03		10.58	3.97	0.67
1996 Q2	2.96	9.21	7.63	8.63	0.16	2007 Q2	1.03		10.76	4.03	0.67
1996 Q3	2.89	9.11	7.84	8.61	0.45	2007 Q3	1.04		10.80	3.85	0.73
1996 Q4	2.86	8.57	8.07	8.02	0.57	2007 Q4	1.02		10.89	3.06	0.72
1997 Q1	2.86	9.19	8.25	5.70	0.37	2008 Q1	1.03		10.80	3.79	0.66
1997 Q2	2.81	9.09	8.43	6.14	0.40	2008 Q2	1.02		10.81	4.09	0.72
1997 Q3	2.78	9.07	8.54	6.16	0.67	2008 Q3	1.00		10.33	4.05	0.81
1997 Q4	2.67	8.52	8.58	5.33	0.61	2008 Q4	0.98		9.22	3.54	0.81
1998 Q1	2.61	9.21	8.64	5.45	0.38	2009 Q1	0.93		9.27	3.79	0.69
1998 Q2	2.54	9.06	8.73	5.66	0.49	2009 Q2	0.94		8.83	3.90	0.71
1998 Q3	2.51	8.91	8.84	5.68	0.68	2009 Q3	0.93		8.80	3.94	0.78
1998 Q4	2.47	8.50	8.88	4.97	0.84	2009 Q4	0.94		8.76	3.61	0.70
1999 Q1	2.39	9.06	8.97	5.34	1.03	2010 Q1	0.95		8.75	3.73	0.61
1999 Q2	2.29	8.75	9.05	5.80	1.20	2010 Q2	0.94		8.77	3.95	0.64
1999 Q3	2.20	8.74	9.21	5.64	1.58	2010 Q3	0.94		8.64	3.88	0.67
1999 Q4	2.16	8.00	9.19	4.63	1.46	2010 Q4	0.92		8.44	3.63	0.65
2000 Q1	2.16	8.86	9.40	5.06	1.49	2011 Q1	0.88		8.22	3.82	0.59
2000 Q2	2.13	8.64	9.66	5.32	1.45	2011 Q2	0.86		8.07	4.11	0.63
2000 Q3	2.07	8.42	9.75	5.06	1.59	2011 Q3	0.87		7.47	4.10	0.68
2000 Q4	2.13	7.81	9.96	4.28	1.41	2011 Q4	0.87		7.42	3.82	0.64
2001 Q1	2.04	8.48	9.79	4.65	1.30	2012 Q1	0.87		7.28	4.01	0.56
2001 Q2	1.94	8.44	9.77	4.88	1.31	2012 Q2	0.86		7.19	4.15	0.60
2001 Q3	1.88	8.30	9.14	4.73	1.46	2012 Q3	0.85		6.96	4.00	0.66
2001 Q4	1.78	7.55	9.37	4.14	1.28	2012 Q4	0.83		6.79	3.60	0.63
2002 Q1	1.54	8.12	9.39	4.61	1.18						
2002 Q2	1.48	8.00	9.48	4.65	1.20						
2002 Q3	1.47	8.02	9.54	4.22	1.38						
2002 Q4	1.43	7.49	9.40	3.68	1.22						

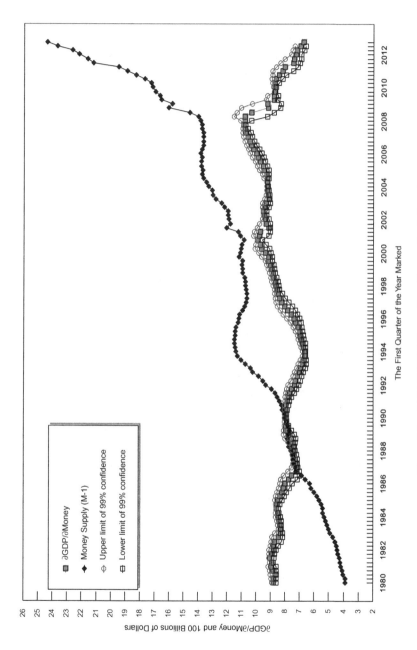

Figure 3.1: USA ∂GDP/∂Money Data Seasonally Adjusted

in the fourth quarter of 2012 for a 37.6% decrease. A value for ∂GDP/ ∂Money of 6.79 means that for every dollar increase in the money supply, GDP increased by US$6.79.

Note that the ∂GDP/∂Money line in Figure 3.1 is almost the mirror image of the money supply line. This means that every time the FED has increased the money supply, ∂GDP/∂Money fell. Every time the FED has decreased the money supply, ∂GDP/∂Money rose. This means that the negative effects on GDP of cutting the money supply are greater than the positive effects on GDP of increasing the money supply. For example, in the third quarter of 1994 when the FED increased the money supply, ∂GDP/∂Money was 6.80, but after cutting the money supply for several quarters in a row, ∂GDP/∂Money was 8.43 in the second quarter of 1997. The negative effects of cuts in the money supply are 24% greater than the positive effects of raising the money supply.

On June 19, 2013, Ben Bernanke (the chair of the US FED in 2013) announced that soon the FED would begin "tapering" some of its quantitative easing policies. He suggested that the FED might scale back its monthly purchases of securities from US$85 billion to US$65 billion in the September 2013 policy meeting and that it might end all new purchases by the middle of 2014. These announcements caused major concern in financial markets worldwide. Ben Bernanke has NOT talked about shrinking the FED's balance sheet which has grown from US$870 billion of assets in August 2007 to US$3,529 billion of assets on July 31, 2013 (i.e., quantitative easing has resulted in a quadrupling of the FED's assets). However, if the FED was to sell some of the assets it has purchased since August 2007, Figure 3.1 implies that those sales will reduce GDP much more (24% more?)[3] than the purchases increased it.

Table 3.1 and Figure 3.2 show that Japan's ∂GDP/∂Money peaked in the first quarter of 1991 at 3.92 and that it had fallen to 0.83 as of the fourth quarter of 2012 for a 78.8% fall in effectiveness. Leightner (2013a) uses OECD data on Japan's consumer price index (CPI, which is a measure of inflation for goods consumers purchase) and an index for M-1 to show

---

[3]This could deviate from the 24% if the money expansion process through the banking system due to the FED purchases of bonds is not the same as the money expansion process for the FED's selling of bonds.

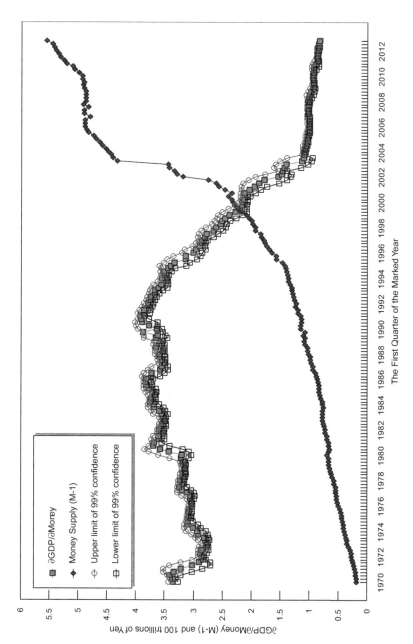

Figure 3.2: Japan ∂GDP/∂Money Data Seasonally Adjusted

that Japan's ∂CPI/∂M-1 fell by 73.8% between the third quarter of 1993 and the first quarter of 2013. This is bad news for Japan's current Prime Minister, Shinzo Abe, who campaigned on the promise to increase Japan's money supply by however much it takes to change Japan's deflation into 2% inflation (Dvorak and Warnock, 2013b). Furthermore, if Japan's problems that started in the early 1990s and that persist to today are a harbinger of the world's future, then monetary authorities should be seriously concerned.

Table 3.1 and Figure 3.3 show that ∂GDP/∂Money for the United Kingdom (UK) peaked in the first quarter of 1992 at 9.75 and had fallen to 7.90 by the first quarter of 2006 for a 19% fall in effectiveness. Unfortunately, the IMF does not provide money supply data for the UK after the first quarter of 2006. Although the IMF data provided for the UK was supposedly seasonally adjusted, Figure 3.3 clearly shows seasonal patterns.[4] The seasonal patterns shown in Figure 3.3 reveal that increases in the UK's money supply are correlated with smaller multiplier values for ∂GDP/∂Money than decreases in the UK's money supply are. Figure 3.4 shows a similar phenomenon for Brazil. Brazil's ∂GDP/∂Money peaked at 13.23 in the third quarter of 1993 and fell to 4.00 by the third quarter of 2012 for a 70% decline in effectiveness. Figure 3.5 shows that the Russian Federation's ∂GDP/∂Money peaked in the third quarter of 2000 at 1.59 and had fallen to 0.66 as of the third quarter of 2012 for a 58% decline in effectiveness.

The decline in the effectiveness of monetary policy appears to have begun with the current crisis in the USA (Figure 3.1), but it began long before the current crisis in Japan, the UK, Brazil, and Russia (Figures 3.2–3.5). A declining ∂GDP/∂Money for many years fits with this book's argument that the core cause of the world's current problems is insufficient consumption which has been building due to increased income inequality for many years. The primary path by which increases in the money supply

---

[4]In contrast, the IMF provided data for the USA and Japan were seasonally adjusted and do not show seasonal patterns. If the seasonal patterns in a series of data are due to inaccuracies in the collection of the data, then seasonally adjusting the data would probably increase the accuracy of RTPLS estimates; however, if seasonal patterns reflect what is really happening in the economy, then eliminating them will reduce the influence of some omitted variables which may increase or decrease the accuracy of RTPLS estimates depending on how these omitted variables affect the dependent and independent variables. See Appendix 1 for more information.

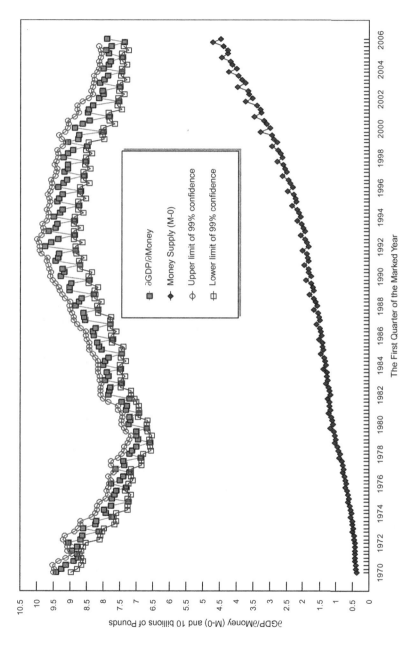

Figure 3.3: UK ∂GDP/∂Money

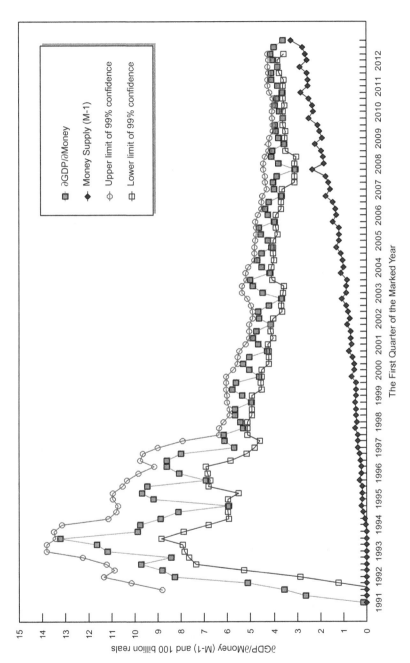

Figure 3.4:   Brazil ∂GDP/∂Money Data Not Seasonally Adjusted

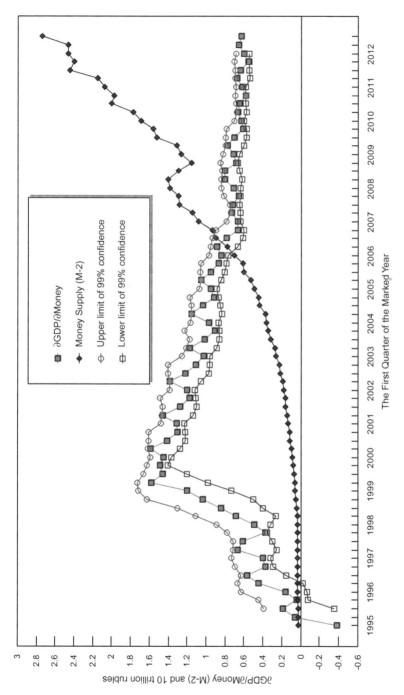

Figure 3.5: Russian Federation $\partial GDP/\partial Money$ Data Not Seasonally Adjusted

affect GDP (in a Keynesian model) is by lowering interest rates which makes borrowing money for investment and consumption cheaper. To the extent that increases in the money supply causes consumption to increase, monetary policy can address the core problem, but not in the best way. If firms perceive that consumption is increasing due to increased consumer debt, then they are less likely to invest in expanding production than they would if they perceive that consumption is increasing due to rising consumer income. Rising consumption due to rising consumer income is perceived as more sustainable than rising consumption due to rising consumer debt (Hilsenrath and Simon, 2011).

Two conditions are necessary for firms to invest. First, there must be savings to fund the investment. This is not a problem in the world today because there is a surplus of savings. Second, firms must believe that what their investments produce will be sold. In other words, there must be sufficient consumption to justify the investment. If there is insufficient consumption, then increasing the money supply in order to drive down interest rates will not increase investment in tools, machinery, and factories that will produce more goods. In this case, savings will either sit idle, be invested in owning something in order to gain a return from rent, seek a return from deception, or fund speculative bubbles (Casselman, 2012; Chasan, 2013; Dvorak and Warnock, 2013a; Fidler, 2012; Frangos, 2013; Gara, 2012; Monga, 2011; Sidel, 2013).

Chapter 4

FISCAL POLICY

In Chapter 3, I showed that the effectiveness of monetary policy is declining and has been declining for many years prior to the current crisis. If, as argued in this book, the fundamental problem in the world's economy today is insufficient consumption to justify additional investment leading to a surplus of savings (savings sitting idle, funding speculative bubbles, or seeking a return from rent or deception), then no matter how low monetary policy drives the interest rate, production increasing investment will not increase. No matter how cheap you make additional investment, additional investment is not rational if you will be unable to sell what the additional investment produces. In this chapter, I examine the effectiveness of fiscal policy. Unlike monetary policy, government spending is a form of final demand and, thus, has the potential to replace consumption as a buyer of the goods that additional investment produces. However, for the past two decades, inequality in most countries has been increasing causing consumption to fall. Governments, wanting to remain in power, have been increasing government spending in order to replace the falling consumption. This has led to growing government deficits. Growing government deficits tend to dampen business expectations causing investment to decline. This chapter will show that the effectiveness of fiscal policy, like monetary policy, has been declining noticeably.

For the empirical estimates of this chapter, I downloaded quarterly data on gross domestic product (GDP) and government consumption (G) from the IMF's database for as many quarters (Q) as possible. The last chapter did not include an examination of the effects of changing the money supply on countries using the euro because these countries cannot control their money supplies; however, they do control their fiscal policies. Thus, this chapter examines the effects of fiscal policy on each of the countries using euros separately, in addition to examining the effects of fiscal policy in the USA, UK, Japan, Brazil, and the Russian Federation.[1]

One of the most important ways to calculate GDP is to add up the final expenditures of all final buyers. This approach entails adding together personal consumption expenditures (C), gross domestic investment in tools, machinery, buildings and the change in inventories (I), Government purchases of final goods and services (G), and net exports (X − M). Given this equation, GDP = C + I + G + X − M, one might expect an increase in G to produce an equal increase in GDP, causing ∂GDP/∂G to equal 1. However, a ∂GDP/∂G = 1 is not what most macroeconomic models predict. The classical model of economics predicts ∂GDP/∂G = 0 because any increase in G would cause interest rates to rise sufficiently to cause consumption and investment (C + I) to fall by an amount equal to the increase in G. The classical model assumes that both the supply and demand for labor are

---

[1]The European data used began in the first quarter of 1964 for Austria, 1980 for Belgium, 1995 for Cyprus, 1993 for Estonia, 1970 for Finland and France, 1960 for Germany, 2000 for Greece, 1997 for Ireland, 1970 for Italy, 1995 for Luxembourg, 1992 for Malta, 1977 for the Netherlands and Portugal, 1993 for Slovakia, 1995 for Slovenia, and 1970 for Spain. The data set for each of these countries extended to the fourth quarter of 2012 except for Cyprus, Estonia, Ireland, and Luxembourg which ended in the third quarter of 2012, and for Portugal which ended in the fourth quarter of 2011. For each of these European countries, the data switched from the national currencies of these countries to the euro midway through the data set. To do the estimations for these European countries, the data listed in the national currencies were translated into euros by dividing them by the following conversions which were downloaded from http://ec.europa.eu/economy_finance/euro/adoption/conversion/ — Belgium (40.3399), Germany (1.95583), Estonia (15.6466), Ireland (0.787564), Greece (340.750), Spain (166.386), France (6.55957), Italy (1936.27), Cyprus (0.585274), Luxembourg (40.3399), Malta (0.429300), Netherlands (2.20371), Austria (13.7603), Portugal (200.482), Slovenia (239.640), Slovakia (30.1260), and Finland (5.94573).

The non-European data used extended from the first quarter (unless otherwise noted) of 1991 for Brazil, 1955 (Q2) for Japan, 1994 for the Russian Federation, 1955 for the UK, and 1948 for the USA. The data set for these countries ended in the fourth quarter of 2012, except for the USA whose data extended to the first quarter of 2013. The data used for both GDP and G were nominal data (not corrected for inflation). The data for France, Germany, Italy, Japan, the Netherlands, Spain, the UK, and the USA were seasonally adjusted. The data for the rest of the countries were not seasonally adjusted. A separate analysis was conducted for each country.

a function of the real wage and the labor market is always in equilibrium, thus there is never unemployment.

A simple Keynesian model can be created from the Classical model merely by eliminating the Classical assumption of labor market equilibrium. By eliminating this single Classical assumption, the Keynesians produce a model where $\partial GDP/\partial G$ would be much greater than one. In a simple Keynesian model, when the government purchases something (G increases), the government purchase generates income for the seller who spends (C increases) part of his income on something else which increases the income for the person who sold to him, who spends part of that income on something else (causing C to increase even more), setting into motion a process that multiplies the effects of the initial government purchase. If the percent of additional income a person consumes is called the "marginal propensity to consume" (MPC), then the person who sold to the government spends G(MPC). The person who sold to the person who sold to the government spends $[G(MPC)]MPC = G(MPC)^2$. To get the total change in consumption, we would need to add $G(MPC) + G(MPC)^2 + G(MPC)^3 + \cdots + G(MPC)^n$. This is a mathematical series which converges to the following equation: $\partial GDP/\partial G = \partial G[1/(1 - MPC)]$. If people spend 90% (MPC $= 0.9$) of additional income they receive, then $[1/(1 - 0.9)] = 10$ meaning that every additional dollar that the government spends would cause GDP to rise by US$10. However, this simple explanation made many assumptions that do not hold in reality. More complex Keynesian models include forces such as increases in income that increase taxes, imports, and investment; increases in interest rates that affect consumption and investment; and increases in inflation that affect production, consumption, and investment. Given these complicating factors and an MPC of 90%, Keynesian models tend to predict a multiplier between 1 and 10.

A Classical macroeconomic model predicts $\partial GDP/\partial G = 0$ and a Keynesian model predicts $\partial GDP/\partial G > 1$. Fortunately, the analytical technique (Reiterative Truncated Projected Least Squares (RTPLS)) used in this book does not require the assumption of a theoretical macroeconomic model. If this chapter's empirical results show $\partial GDP/\partial G = 0$, then they support the Classical model; if they show $\partial GDP/\partial G > 1$, then they support the Keynesian model. Table 4.1 presents the empirical results of this chapter

Table 4.1: $\partial GDP/\partial G$ Estimates

	Japan	UK	USA	Brazil	Rus.	Austr.	Belg.	Cypr.	Eston.	Finl.	Franc.	Germ.	Greec.	Irel.	Italy	Lux.	Malta	Neth.	Port.	Slova.	Slove.	Spain
1981 Q1	6.92	4.40	6.03			4.53	3.59			4.32	3.88	4.40			5.21			3.69	4.67			5.92
1981 Q2	6.90	4.36	5.93			4.84	3.37			4.56	3.87	4.55			5.30			3.69	4.78			5.90
1981 Q3	6.81	4.38	6.04			5.08	3.49			4.67	3.89	4.53			5.15			3.72	5.12			6.08
1981 Q4	6.68	4.47	5.88			5.25	3.54			5.07	3.92	4.62			5.23			3.77	5.08			5.89
1982 Q1	6.76	4.40	5.74			4.47	3.69			4.30	3.89	4.49			5.23			3.78	5.15			5.97
1982 Q2	6.73	4.39	5.76			4.77	3.46			4.57	3.92	4.62			5.33			3.66	5.44			5.98
1982 Q3	6.69	4.47	5.69			5.02	3.63			4.69	3.88	4.58			5.29			3.66	5.05			5.99
1982 Q4	6.84	4.50	5.59			5.14	3.61			5.11	3.89	4.61			5.11			3.62	5.43			5.95
1983 Q1	6.65	4.39	5.61			4.45	3.68			4.24	3.90	4.60			5.18			3.69	5.22			5.97
1983 Q2	6.61	4.41	5.68			4.76	3.42			4.54	3.95	4.73			5.11			3.75	5.27			5.79
1983 Q3	6.61	4.56	5.73			5.05	3.67			4.72	3.97	4.65			5.12			3.75	5.52			5.85
1983 Q4	6.69	4.57	6.00			5.25	3.98			4.98	3.98	4.72			5.26			3.74	5.54			5.90
1984 Q1	6.70	4.63	5.97			4.52	3.92			4.32	3.99	4.76			5.29			3.95	5.45			6.04
1984 Q2	6.74	4.54	5.94			4.76	3.59			4.58	3.96	4.65			5.29			3.89	5.63			6.02
1984 Q3	6.81	4.49	5.95			5.03	3.40			4.70	3.95	4.80			5.26			3.94	5.83			5.98
1984 Q4	6.80	4.54	5.93			5.22	4.08			5.05	3.94	4.69			5.18			3.94	5.71			6.10
1985 Q1	6.95	4.56	5.88			4.40	3.96			4.18	3.95	4.69			5.13			3.95	5.75			6.11
1985 Q2	6.97	4.77	5.85			4.73	3.67			4.47	3.97	4.74			5.22			3.89	5.75			5.93
1985 Q3	7.00	4.75	5.82			5.07	3.90			4.49	4.01	4.79			5.23			3.89	5.58			5.94
1985 Q4	6.96	4.80	5.77			5.18	3.89			4.81	4.02	4.74			5.26			3.98	5.58			5.94
1986 Q1	7.01	4.71	5.79			4.33	4.03			4.09	4.01	4.76			5.29			3.99	6.64			6.01
1986 Q2	7.12	4.69	5.72			4.75	3.73			4.31	4.05	4.76			5.37			3.99	6.73			6.22
1986 Q3	7.02	4.73	5.69			4.97	4.00			4.50	4.07	4.79			5.34			3.97	6.79			6.22
1986 Q4	6.80	4.78	5.70			5.12	3.86			4.82	4.05	4.86			5.26			3.87	6.93			6.00
1987 Q1	6.86	4.80	5.71			4.34	4.04			4.05	4.05	4.74			5.19			3.73	6.95			6.06
1987 Q2	6.87	4.82	5.76			4.75	3.75			4.38	4.08	4.76			5.15			3.82	6.91			5.88
1987 Q3	6.93	4.93	5.82			4.98	4.04			4.32	4.10	4.76			5.05			3.82	6.91			5.92
1987 Q4	7.17	4.94	5.85			5.15	3.99			4.85	4.13	4.83			5.06			3.85	6.94			5.98

(Continued)

Table 4.1: (*Continued*)

	Japan	UK	USA	Brazil	Rus.	Austr.	Belg.	Cypr.	Eston.	Finl.	Franc.	Germ.	Greec.	Irel.	Italy	Lux.	Malta	Neth.	Port.	Slova.	Slove.	Spain
1988 Q1	7.18	4.97	5.87			4.56	4.22			4.31	4.14	4.81			4.99			3.86	6.07			6.00
1988 Q2	7.11	5.01	5.95			4.85	3.99			4.58	4.16	4.84			4.99			3.89	6.06			6.10
1988 Q3	7.16	5.16	6.02			5.07	4.38			4.50	4.20	4.86			5.02			3.90	6.17			6.14
1988 Q4	7.28	5.10	5.99			5.21	4.36			5.06	4.24	4.88			5.05			3.96	6.19			5.97
1989 Q1	7.34	5.13	6.07			4.65	4.44			4.44	4.27	5.00			5.03			4.02	6.19			5.87
1989 Q2	7.21	5.19	6.04			4.90	4.20			4.71	4.29	5.06			5.08			4.02	5.88			5.87
1989 Q3	7.24	5.14	6.06			5.17	4.56			4.62	4.30	5.08			5.08			4.05	5.97			5.91
1989 Q4	7.33	5.13	6.03			5.31	4.48			5.03	4.35	5.19			5.12			4.07	5.93			5.91
1990 Q1	7.31	5.13	6.01			4.78	4.60			4.32	4.35	5.13			5.04			4.09	5.85			5.94
1990 Q2	7.43	5.13	6.03			4.96	4.30			4.42	4.34	5.15			4.92			4.10	5.95			5.74
1990 Q3	7.54	5.04	6.03			5.23	4.58			4.39	4.29	5.31			4.82			4.10	5.81			5.68
1990 Q4	7.16	4.96	5.87			5.40	4.51			4.46	4.23	5.46			4.70			4.15	5.82			5.73
1991 Q1	7.31	4.94	5.79	3.60		4.71	4.52			3.83	4.22	5.26			4.85			4.09	5.30			5.70
1991 Q2	7.35	4.85	5.85	3.80		4.97	4.20			3.86	4.19	5.04			4.84			4.10	5.30			5.64
1991 Q3	7.33	4.77	5.91	3.87		5.28	4.44			3.78	4.20	5.04			4.85			4.08	5.24			5.53
1991 Q4	7.20	4.79	5.96	4.72		5.39	4.36			3.81	4.21	5.06			4.88			4.10	5.28			5.39
1992 Q1	7.22	4.77	5.98	5.70		4.73	4.53			3.71	4.24	5.03			4.94		4.41	4.04	5.26			5.30
1992 Q2	7.13	4.76	6.02	5.84		4.98	4.18			3.77	4.16	5.00			4.93		4.70	4.03	5.26			5.27
1992 Q3	7.08	4.69	6.01	5.69		5.19	4.47			3.66	4.08	4.89			4.90		5.12	3.97	5.23			5.24
1992 Q4	6.93	4.72	6.07	5.78		5.25	4.33			3.77	4.00	4.89			4.87		4.23	3.98	5.21			5.38
1993 Q1	6.95	4.79	6.12	5.71		4.53	4.35		5.07	3.83	3.93	4.90			4.90		4.36	3.95	5.02	5.02		5.21
1993 Q2	6.86	4.93	6.17	5.71		4.79	4.14		4.71	3.93	3.86	4.90			4.91		4.38	3.97	5.05	4.74		5.13
1993 Q3	6.78	4.94	6.19	5.70		5.03	4.41		4.95	3.91	3.87	4.97			4.92		4.52	3.98	4.97	5.20		5.08
1993 Q4	6.77	4.96	6.24	5.62		5.06	4.37		4.12	3.99	3.87	5.00			5.02		4.15	3.94	5.11	4.33		5.16
1994 Q1	6.83	4.97	6.31	4.63	3.92	4.58	4.55		4.27	3.89	3.89	4.93			5.01		3.81	4.01	5.06	5.02		5.24
1994 Q2	6.65	5.07	6.38	5.26	4.37	4.76	4.34		4.26	4.05	3.95	4.99			5.12		4.36	4.02	5.14	5.57		5.32
1994 Q3	6.69	5.01	6.35	6.02	4.77	4.97	4.34		4.29	4.11	3.97	5.04			5.21		4.71	4.06	5.09	5.97		5.37
1994 Q4	6.56	5.08	6.45	5.57	4.23	5.16	4.29		3.58	4.18	3.99	5.00			5.29		4.50	4.08	5.20	5.39		5.36

(*Continued*)

Table 4.1:   (Continued)

	Japan	UK	USA	Brazil	Rus.	Austr.	Belg.	Cypr.	Eston.	Finl.	Franc.	Germ.	Greec.	Irel.	Italy	Lux.	Malta	Neth.	Port.	Slova.	Slove.	Spain
1995 Q1	6.47	5.12	6.43	4.40	4.51	4.47	4.34	3.59	3.85	3.87	3.98	5.06			5.44	5.55	3.83	4.07	6.25	5.27	4.34	5.41
1995 Q2	6.51	5.12	6.43	4.79	5.02	4.73	4.38	4.43	3.76	4.22	3.97	5.03			5.43	5.71	4.32	4.08	5.42	5.44	4.38	5.38
1995 Q3	6.46	5.19	6.48	4.88	5.61	4.82	4.37	4.03	4.79	4.24	3.96	4.95			5.53	5.67	4.52	4.09	6.06	5.46	4.63	5.36
1995 Q4	6.40	5.18	6.58	4.91	5.41	4.81	4.32	2.47	3.95	4.50	3.94	4.87			5.60	5.37	4.79	4.08	4.62	4.53	4.53	5.37
1996 Q1	6.36	5.11	6.56	4.74	4.52	4.50	4.19	3.69	4.20	3.87	3.96	4.91			5.42	5.36	3.60	4.24	6.35	4.44	4.51	5.38
1996 Q2	6.38	5.30	6.62	5.09	4.66	4.74	4.22	3.99	4.09	4.13	3.94	4.94			5.42	5.76	4.17	4.29	5.26	4.93	4.50	5.43
1996 Q3	6.33	5.33	6.69	5.09	5.55	4.86	4.26	3.49	5.32	4.09	3.93	4.90			5.46	5.70	4.56	4.27	5.94	4.95	4.82	5.40
1996 Q4	6.38	5.33	6.70	4.97	5.50	4.83	4.39	2.26	4.27	4.40	3.90	4.94			5.34	5.00	4.39	4.28	4.50	4.22	4.69	5.45
1997 Q1	6.40	5.38	6.74	4.64	4.33	4.72	4.09	3.20	4.64	3.91	3.91	4.93		3.08	5.39	5.36	4.09	4.32	6.20	5.41	4.49	5.50
1997 Q2	6.35	5.52	6.77	5.02	4.40	4.92	4.41	3.43	4.49	4.24	3.93	4.98		3.43	5.40	5.54	4.07	4.36	5.27	5.18	4.76	5.54
1997 Q3	6.41	5.64	6.86	5.16	5.14	5.08	4.48	3.46	5.98	4.30	3.95	5.07		3.49	5.39	5.58	4.72	4.40	5.84	5.15	5.00	5.63
1997 Q4	6.35	5.54	6.84	5.29	4.99	5.13	4.56	2.41	4.66	4.63	4.00	5.14		3.70	5.43	5.06	4.82	4.40	4.70	4.45	4.86	5.67
1998 Q1	6.22	5.63	6.94	4.46	5.24	4.76	4.17	3.02	5.14	4.21	4.06	5.08		3.93	5.49	5.82	4.44	4.40	6.02	5.35	4.65	5.59
1998 Q2	6.17	5.61	6.89	4.97	5.62	4.99	4.48	3.94	4.61	4.42	4.10	5.07		4.18	5.46	6.26	4.93	4.42	5.25	5.08	4.75	5.64
1998 Q3	6.18	5.57	6.97	4.95	5.46	5.07	4.50	3.72	5.84	4.57	4.11	5.10		4.23	5.46	6.09	5.19	4.39	5.84	4.89	5.04	5.68
1998 Q4	6.08	5.59	6.99	5.01	4.72	5.16	4.53	2.78	4.34	4.56	4.09	5.10		3.89	5.42	4.86	4.06	4.38	4.72	4.36	5.00	5.67
1999 Q1	6.01	5.53	6.97	4.59	5.67	4.79	4.12	3.21	4.70	4.36	4.07	5.04		4.50	5.49	5.75	4.68	4.38	6.14	5.90	4.73	5.66
1999 Q2	5.96	5.38	6.97	5.06	6.39	5.02	4.43	3.83	4.31	4.55	4.08	5.05		4.63	5.48	6.25	4.85	4.39	5.35	5.63	4.88	5.73
1999 Q3	5.95	5.43	6.92	4.95	7.51	5.24	4.53	3.88	5.54	4.62	4.09	5.04		5.06	5.45	6.18	5.22	4.41	5.95	5.54	5.03	5.73
1999 Q4	5.94	5.47	6.92	5.10	7.60	4.74	4.50	2.71	4.22	4.48	4.10	5.12		5.02	5.46	5.42	4.88	4.40	4.66	4.58	5.06	5.68
2000 Q1	5.93	5.51	6.96	5.14	6.05	4.95	4.20	3.92	5.14	4.55	4.12	5.08	3.75	4.99	5.43	6.22	4.59	4.44	5.98	5.99	4.77	5.74
2000 Q2	5.82	5.34	6.96	5.42	6.47	5.17	4.48	4.69	4.77	4.70	4.13	5.17	4.13	5.24	5.43	6.37	5.12	4.47	5.03	5.83	4.80	5.73
2000 Q3	5.72	5.24	6.97	4.72	6.93	5.40	4.59	4.13	5.98	4.83	4.14	5.12	4.28	5.23	5.40	6.47	5.45	4.48	5.67	5.61	4.94	5.66
2000 Q4	5.73	5.26	6.96	4.72	6.93	4.91	4.49	3.03	4.88	4.72	4.18	5.12	4.10	4.99	5.42	5.50	4.93	4.45	4.47	4.31	4.80	5.77
2001 Q1	5.67	5.28	6.82	5.36	5.53	5.17	4.24	3.79	5.54	4.70	4.19	5.15	3.98	5.18	5.40	6.20	4.55	4.38	5.69	6.00	4.65	5.76
2001 Q2	5.58	5.32	6.78	5.37	5.79	5.26	4.45	4.40	5.11	4.69	4.20	5.19	4.26	5.21	5.29	5.92	4.68	4.37	4.87	5.61	4.65	5.75
2001 Q3	5.48	5.20	6.69	5.69	6.63	5.48	4.43	4.16	6.28	4.77	4.18	5.18	4.47	5.04	5.23	5.86	5.14	4.31	5.46	5.29	4.89	5.81
2001 Q4	5.42	5.07	6.65	4.16	6.40	4.89	4.30	2.96	4.90	4.57	4.13	5.09	4.41	4.60	5.17	5.14	4.23	4.28	4.54	4.23	4.74	5.76

(Continued)

Table 4.1: (Continued)

	Japan	UK	USA	Brazil	Rus.	Austr.	Belg.	Cypr.	Eston.	Finl.	Franc.	Germ.	Greec.	Irel.	Italy	Lux.	Malta	Neth.	Port.	Slova.	Slove.	Spain
2002 Q1	5.31	5.07	6.55	4.97	4.94	5.17	4.08	3.58	5.61	4.39	4.12	5.11	3.81	5.01	5.22	6.04	4.29	4.19	5.63	5.92	4.74	5.78
2002 Q2	5.39	4.98	6.50	4.91	5.32	5.36	4.23	4.08	5.37	4.53	4.07	5.08	4.17	4.94	5.21	6.01	4.49	4.17	4.91	5.38	4.73	5.76
2002 Q3	5.38	4.98	6.48	5.59	6.16	5.55	4.29	3.90	6.31	4.70	4.05	5.12	4.36	5.01	5.13	5.65	5.03	4.12	5.31	5.51	5.04	5.70
2002 Q4	5.40	4.99	6.38	4.22	6.06	5.01	4.28	3.02	4.94	4.50	4.02	5.04	4.28	5.04	5.26	4.96	4.94	4.11	4.44	4.44	4.84	5.70
2003 Q1	5.37	4.91	6.30	5.60	5.14	5.09	4.00	3.51	5.59	4.33	4.03	5.08	4.18	4.93	5.19	5.61	3.97	4.07	5.41	5.95	4.69	5.70
2003 Q2	5.31	4.84	6.25	5.25	5.34	5.27	4.17	4.06	5.22	4.37	4.00	5.07	4.61	5.14	5.10	6.02	4.43	3.98	4.86	5.64	4.81	5.68
2003 Q3	5.35	4.86	6.36	5.46	6.18	5.42	4.14	3.91	6.56	4.51	4.01	5.01	4.82	4.92	4.92	5.77	5.11	4.01	5.16	5.60	5.15	5.69
2003 Q4	5.44	4.85	6.41	4.55	6.07	5.03	4.27	2.63	4.99	4.34	4.01	5.08	4.72	5.20	5.13	5.38	4.79	4.00	4.45	4.08	4.92	5.67
2004 Q1	5.45	4.89	6.35	5.74	5.07	5.05	4.02	4.00	6.03	4.28	4.01	5.16	4.21	5.34	5.05	5.54	4.12	4.08	5.40	6.55	4.82	5.58
2004 Q2	5.39	4.77	6.36	5.53	5.60	5.38	4.25	4.25	5.36	4.30	4.01	5.17	4.64	5.11	4.95	5.63	4.57	4.02	4.90	5.70	4.86	5.56
2004 Q3	5.36	4.71	6.35	5.51	6.47	5.58	4.35	4.23	6.75	4.51	4.02	5.14	4.88	4.78	5.11	5.77	4.89	4.06	5.11	5.86	5.16	5.53
2004 Q4	5.33	4.69	6.39	4.38	6.47	5.10	4.27	3.38	5.06	4.40	4.04	5.20	4.79	4.94	5.02	5.23	4.56	4.05	4.26	4.52	4.96	5.53
2005 Q1	5.34	4.75	6.37	5.42	5.20	5.15	4.04	4.28	5.92	4.27	4.03	5.23	4.03	5.12	4.95	5.62	4.54	4.16	5.09	6.69	4.72	5.50
2005 Q2	5.37	4.64	6.38	5.38	5.67	5.32	4.18	4.45	5.82	4.28	4.02	5.17	4.41	5.37	5.00	5.87	4.72	4.16	4.70	6.10	4.99	5.50
2005 Q3	5.36	4.68	6.34	5.40	6.48	5.57	4.27	4.82	6.82	4.45	4.01	5.20	4.74	4.96	5.00	6.00	5.20	4.13	4.94	5.97	5.12	5.50
2005 Q4	5.34	4.68	6.40	4.22	6.41	5.17	4.32	2.98	5.17	4.27	4.05	5.23	4.62	5.14	4.76	5.39	4.68	4.16	4.14	4.64	4.79	5.47
2006 Q1	5.39	4.68	6.36	5.33	5.14	5.16	4.07	3.88	6.15	4.29	4.06	5.24	4.33	5.45	5.00	6.16	4.49	3.93	5.31	5.78	4.97	5.52
2006 Q2	5.39	4.65	6.39	5.35	5.49	5.41	4.25	4.08	5.97	4.34	4.08	5.34	4.81	5.23	4.85	6.42	4.90	3.93	4.66	5.78	5.28	5.50
2006 Q3	5.39	4.63	6.37	5.36	6.19	5.62	4.36	4.26	7.32	4.52	4.09	5.37	5.07	4.99	4.97	6.27	5.03	3.93	5.28	6.19	5.02	5.50
2006 Q4	5.47	4.68	6.40	4.23	6.14	5.18	4.36	3.63	5.67	4.38	4.13	5.40	4.99	5.03	5.08	5.87	4.51	3.92	4.27	4.63	5.32	5.46
2007 Q1	5.49	4.73	6.36	5.22	4.90	5.37	4.13	4.19	6.29	4.38	4.14	5.47	4.26	5.33	5.09	6.46	4.80	3.91	5.45	6.27	5.41	5.46
2007 Q2	5.44	4.74	6.34	5.17	5.42	5.59	4.34	4.95	5.82	4.56	4.15	5.49	4.72	5.12	5.13	6.73	5.07	3.91	4.78	6.54	5.77	5.42
2007 Q3	5.42	4.76	6.30	5.26	6.09	5.59	4.40	4.74	6.93	4.70	4.18	5.53	4.94	4.60	5.17	6.68	5.30	3.90	5.44	6.61	5.39	5.36
2007 Q4	5.37	4.84	6.27	4.30	6.37	5.14	4.36	3.45	5.34	4.49	4.19	5.47	4.74	4.96	4.96	6.02	4.57	3.94	4.49	4.98	5.25	5.33
2008 Q1	5.37	4.67	6.10	5.24	5.14	5.34	4.12	4.89	5.35	4.34	4.21	5.48	4.31	4.76	5.10	6.25	4.57	3.89	5.45	6.78	5.38	5.24
2008 Q2	5.35	4.59	6.06	5.27	5.66	5.31	4.24	5.27	5.39	4.39	4.16	5.39	4.72	4.49	4.91	6.49	4.78	3.87	4.76	6.28	5.51	5.16
2008 Q3	5.28	4.56	5.94	5.34	6.32	5.54	4.23	4.15	5.96	4.56	4.12	5.37	4.85	4.29	4.97	6.35	4.82	3.83	5.46	6.48	5.51	5.03
2008 Q4	5.14	4.38	5.88	4.23	5.61	4.81	4.01	3.49	4.41	4.12	4.05	5.20	4.63	4.22	4.86	5.60	4.52	3.75	4.30	4.74	4.86	4.88

(Continued)

Table 4.1: (Continued)

	Japan	UK	USA	Brazil	Rus.	Austr.	Belg.	Cypr.	Eston.	Finl.	Franc.	Germ.	Greec.	Irel.	Italy	Lux.	Malta	Neth.	Port.	Slova.	Slove.	Spain
2009 Q1	4.93	4.30	5.82	4.76	4.32	4.83	3.74	4.34	4.51	3.91	3.95	4.87	4.41	4.12	4.66	5.57	4.32	3.56	4.79	5.77	4.64	4.74
2009 Q2	4.97	4.26	5.67	5.04	4.67	4.99	3.88	4.68	4.46	3.81	3.89	4.88	4.19	4.27	4.64	5.50	4.53	3.43	4.37	5.20	4.64	4.64
2009 Q3	4.87	4.21	5.60	5.13	5.25	5.05	3.96	4.52	5.10	4.01	3.85	4.87	4.49	3.99	4.59	5.61	4.77	3.39	4.84	5.82	4.96	4.60
2009 Q4	4.91	4.28	5.60	4.14	5.30	4.90	3.95	2.68	4.27	3.79	3.83	4.94	3.45	3.99	4.68	5.18	4.76	3.38	4.07	4.35	4.64	4.56
2010 Q1	4.97	4.31	5.61	5.02	4.75	4.76	3.76	4.21	4.36	3.76	3.84	4.88	4.67	4.44	4.70	5.75	4.61	3.47	4.93	5.64	4.44	4.61
2010 Q2	4.96	4.34	5.64	4.96	5.20	5.05	3.99	4.58	4.76	3.98	3.86	5.05	4.59	4.52	4.68	5.92	4.51	3.47	4.25	5.37	4.58	4.55
2010 Q3	4.98	4.41	5.69	5.09	5.63	5.36	4.06	4.58	5.60	4.13	3.88	5.04	4.95	4.30	4.69	5.91	5.08	3.47	5.06	5.98	4.84	4.60
2010 Q4	4.96	4.39	5.75	4.08	5.92	5.01	4.03	2.88	4.68	3.92	3.89	5.07	4.00	4.07	4.74	5.38	4.52	3.48	4.24	4.62	4.49	4.71
2011 Q1	4.81	4.39	5.77	5.36	4.89	5.11	3.85	4.39	4.81	3.95	3.92	5.08	5.07	4.48	4.80	5.95	4.50	3.57	5.28	5.88	4.46	4.59
2011 Q2	4.72	4.53	5.78	4.96	5.33	5.32	4.00	4.64	5.15	3.96	3.92	5.08	4.94	4.70	4.85	6.03	4.68	3.53	4.67	5.92	4.59	4.71
2011 Q3	4.82	4.56	5.84	5.19	5.95	5.28	3.98	4.27	5.77	4.22	3.93	5.10	5.06	4.34	4.88	5.96	5.08	3.52	5.46	6.36	4.82	4.80
2011 Q4	4.82	4.53	5.95	4.12	6.27	5.09	3.96	2.94	4.95	3.93	3.94	5.07	3.97	4.63	4.86	5.49	4.37	3.50	4.46	5.00	4.38	4.78
2012 Q1	4.81	4.42	5.98	5.09	4.85	5.03	3.94	4.22	4.91	3.88	3.92	5.05	4.54	4.75	4.81	5.72	4.25	3.48		5.98	4.46	4.75
2012 Q2	4.82	4.54	6.03	4.82	5.27	5.29	3.90	4.57	5.05	3.91	3.92	5.07	4.56	4.94	4.87	5.86	4.56	3.49		6.14	4.64	4.80
2012 Q3	4.75	4.58	6.03	4.99	5.68	5.50	3.88	4.54	5.93	4.10	3.92	5.06	5.18	4.54	4.86	5.76	4.73	3.45		6.50	4.88	4.95
2012 Q4	4.73	4.52	6.15	3.99	5.87	5.12	3.87			3.88	3.90	4.98	4.04				4.33	3.47		5.03	4.42	5.19

for quarter 1 of 1981 to quarter 4 of 2012. The multipliers in these tables noticeably exceed a value of one for most countries in most years, providing support for a Keynesian model. Classical economists might respond by saying their model is for the long run and that quarterly data is temporally too short for testing their model. Unfortunately, using annual data (or data for even longer time periods) would result in too few observations for trustworthy estimation for most of the countries analyzed in this chapter. Furthermore, it should be remembered that I know of no major macroeconomic model which considers the possibility of a surplus of savings, which I continue to argue is the fundamental problem plaguing the world's current economy.

Figure 4.1 shows that $\partial GDP/\partial G$ exceeded a value of eight for Japan between 1966 and 1979. No other country examined produced a government spending multiplier of eight or higher. A multiplier of "eight" means that for every additional yen, the Japanese government spent, GDP increased by eight yen. This is good news. The Japanese government, beginning in the late 1950s, purposefully targeted improving Japan's income distribution as a major goal of government policy. This led to the ratio of the wage bill to profits increasing from 0.902 to 3.065 between 1952 and 1981 (Leightner, 1992). The average real personal income for Japan's urban workers and farmers nearly doubled between 1955 and 1959 (Ozawa, 1985). These changes led to Japan enjoying several waves of consumption-driven growth.

TV sets, which were used in only 16% of [Japanese] households in 1958, were used in as many as 91% by 1963. The popular consumer durables in the early 1950s were relatively low-income products such as radios, fluorescent lamps, bicycles, electric fans, and sewing machines. The later 1950s saw a growth in demand for monochrome TV sets, washing machines, and automatic rice cookers. The demand for more sophisticated high-income goods such as color TVs, refrigerators, air conditioners, and automobiles expanded phenomenally throughout the 1960s, but especially in the latter years of the decade.

Consumer demand for clothing similarly underwent a qualitative change: synthetic fiber or blended fiber products became increasingly popular as many of them had a permanent press feature. And tastes for fashion-oriented clothing, too, developed significantly. Many of these consumer goods are time saving in nature for housewives and created more leisure time. On average, the Japanese housewife spent 11 hours per day on household chores before the war but less than 8 hours at the end of the 1960s. Innovations in the consumer goods sector, therefore, in turn created new demands for leisure-related goods and services (Ozawa, 1985, pp. 233–234).

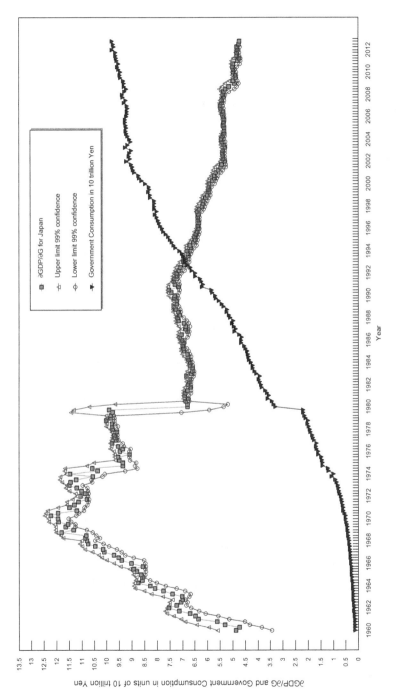

Figure 4.1: ∂(Nominal GDP)/∂(Nominal Government Consumption) for Japan: Seasonally Adjusted

A major theme of this book is that the world today is suffering from a surplus of savings. Many economic models assume that savings constrains investment, thus, if savings increases so will investment. Clearly that is not the case in today's world (Casselman, 2012; Chasan, 2013; Dvorak and Warnock, 2013a; Fidler, 2012; Gara, 2012; Hilsenrath and Simon, 2011; Monga, 2011; Sidel, 2013). For investment to occur, two things are necessary. First, there must be savings to fund the investment. Second, there must be a reasonable hope that what the investment produces can be sold; in other words, there must be sufficient consumption to provide a reason to invest.

Figure 4.1 shows that while the Japanese government was actively pursuing income equality, its government spending multiplier rose and stayed relatively high. This result fits with the simple Keynesian model discussed above. Remember the simplest Keynesian model has a multiplier of $[1/(1-MPC)]$. If income is re-distributed to the relatively poorer segments of society, then MPC rises causing the multiplier effect from government spending to rise also. The Japanese results shown in Figure 4.1 provide us with the hope that if governments around the world would actively pursue pro-equality policies, then the effectiveness of government spending will noticeably improve.

Unfortunately, the situation in Japan changed in the 1980s and the multiplier effect of government spending immediately fell from 9.92 in quarter 4 of 1979 to 6.79 in quarter 1 of 1980 for a 31.5% decline. Figure 4.1 shows that this precipitous fall in Japan's ∂GDP/∂G (the top line in 1980) corresponds to a 50% increase in government spending (the bottom line in 1980). Every time the government of one of the countries examined increased government consumption by an unusually large amount, the corresponding government spending multiplier fell. For examples, see Greece in quarter 4 of 2009 (Figure 4.8), France in the first quarters of 1977 and 1978 (Figure A2.5 in Appendix 2), and the Netherlands in the first quarter of 2006 (Figure A2.8 in Appendix 2). Governments that hope to stimulate their economies by unusually large increases in government spending will find that the effects of government spending on GDP decline noticeably.

After Japan's government spending multiplier fell 31.5% in the first quarter of 1980, it then rose 10.9% to 7.54 in quarter 3 of 1990; however, after 1990, the Japanese government multiplier has been steadily falling and at the end of 2012, it was 4.73. Thus, the Japanese multiplier fell 37%

between 1990 and the end of 2012 (see also Leightner and Inoue, 2009). Japan's economic problems became severe in 1990 and thereafter its ability to help the economy through government spending steadily declined. The UK was a harbinger of the Great Depression when it fell into crisis in the 1920s. Even if Japan is a harbinger of future worldwide economic woes, its policies of the 1950s and 1960s provide a path of escape — redistribute income to the poorer classes so that consumption will rise, providing a reason to invest, in expanding production, the savings that are currently sitting idle, funding speculative bubbles, or seeking a return from rent or deception.

Table 4.1 and Figures 4.2 and 4.3 show that, after 1990, the government multiplier followed a similar pattern for the UK and the USA. $\partial GDP/\partial G$ peaked in quarter 3 of 1997 for the UK at 5.64, fell to a low of 4.21 in quarter 3 of 2009, and then partially rebounded to 4.52 by quarter 4 of 2012. A close comparison of the top and bottom lines in Figure 4.2 reveals that this fall in $\partial GDP/\partial G$ began when government spending shifted to a steeper trajectory over time[2] and the rebound occurred when government spending leveled off. The net fall in $\partial GDP/\partial G$ for the UK between quarter 3 of 1997 and quarter 4 of 2012 was 19.87%. Likewise, Figure 4.3 shows that $\partial GDP/\partial G$ peaked in quarter 4 of 1998 for the USA at 6.99, fell to a low of 5.60 in quarter 3 of 2009, and then partially rebounded to 6.15 by quarter 4 of 2012. Again, this fall in $\partial GDP/\partial G$ corresponds to when government spending shifted to a steeper trajectory and the rebound occurred when government spending leveled off.[3] The net fall in $\partial GDP/\partial G$ for the USA between quarter 4 of 1998 and of 2012 was 11.96%. Using government spending to combat a recession is made more difficult by the government spending multiplier ($\partial GDP/\partial G$) falling when government spending is noticeably increased.

Figure 4.4 for Brazil shows that there are strong seasonal patterns in the Brazilian data which affect the $\partial GDP/\partial G$ estimates. Specifically, in the fourth quarter of every year since 2000, when government spending increases, $\partial GDP/\partial G$ falls. During the first three quarters of every year, when government spending is less, $\partial GDP/\partial G$ is higher. For example, in

---

[2]In other words, the slope of the bottom line increased.
[3]A similar rebound in $\partial GDP/\partial G$ after government spending leveled off can also be seen for Estonia and the Netherlands in graphs A2.3 and A2.8 respectively in Appendix 2.

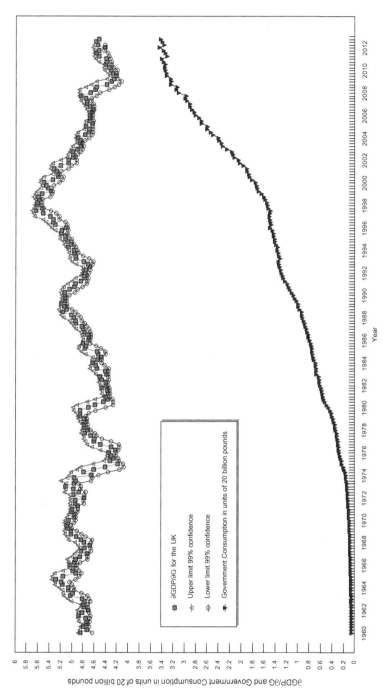

Figure 4.2: ∂(Nominal GDP)/∂(Nominal Government Consumption) for the UK: Seasonally Adjusted

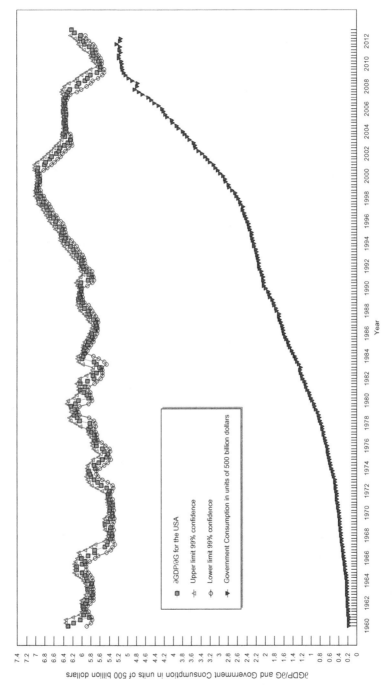

Figure 4.3: ∂(Nominal GDP)/∂(Nominal Government Consumption) for the USA: Seasonally Adjusted

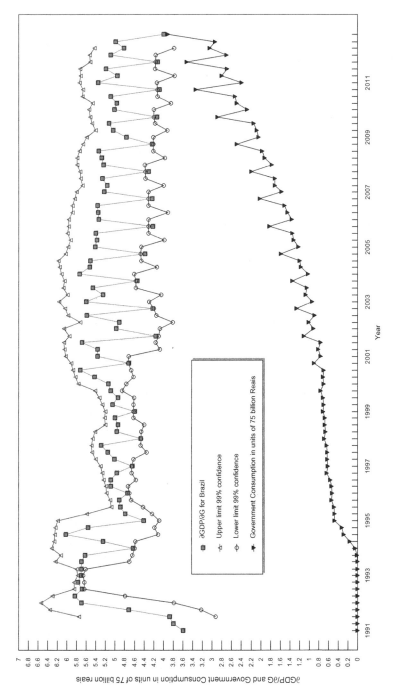

Figure 4.4: ∂(Nominal GDP)/∂(Nominal Government Consumption) for Brazil: Not Seasonally Adjusted

the fourth quarter of 2012, when government spending in Brazil was 33% higher than the third quarter of 2012, the government spending multiplier was 20% lower. A similar pattern is found in the results for Cyprus, Greece, Estonia, Luxembourg, Portugal, and Slovakia.[4] Also notice that ∂GDP/∂G for Brazil is on a downward trend. If we take the average value for ∂GDP/∂G of the marked quarter and the past three quarters (in order to eliminate seasonal variation), we find that ∂GDP/∂G for Brazil fell from an average of 5.75 in the first quarter of 1993 to an average of 4.60 in the fourth quarter of 2012 for a 20.04% decline.

The bottom line in Figure 4.5 shows an annual stair step pattern in the government spending data for the Russian Federation for 2000 to 2008. Furthermore, at the beginning of each year, when government spending steps up to a new higher level, ∂GDP/∂G falls. When government spending increases less rapidly for the rest of the year, ∂GDP/∂G rises. A similar pattern can be seen in the data and ∂GDP/∂G estimates for Austria from 1977 to 1995 and for Finland from 1974 to 1991.[5] By taking the average of any given quarter's ∂GDP/∂G with the ∂GDP/∂G for the past three quarters (in order to eliminate seasonal variations), we find that average ∂GDP/∂G for the Russian Federation fell from 6.91 in quarter 2 of 2000 to 5.42 in quarter 4 of 2012 for a 21.56% decline.

∂GDP/∂Gs for the countries using the euro tended to move together more after 1999, when the euro was established, than they did before 1999. The most noticeable common movement of ∂GDP/∂G occurs between 2007 and 2008 when ∂GDP/∂G fell for most countries and then only partially rebounded in 2010–2012. Prior to 2008, ∂GDP/∂G for the euro zone as a whole was not on a downward trend. Indeed, the average ∂GDP/∂G for the euro zone between the first quarters of 1990 and 2008 was 4.80 with a variance of only 0.035. However, the average ∂GDP/∂G for the euro zone fell from 5.02 in the first quarter of 2008 to 4.20 in the fourth quarter of 2009 for a 16.33% fall and then rebounded to only 4.38 by the fourth quarter of 2012 for a net fall of 12.73% between the first quarter of 2008 and fourth quarter of 2012.

---

[4] See Figures 4.6, 4.8, A2.3, A2.6, A2.9, and A2.10 respectively where the figures that start with "A2" are in Appendix 2.

[5] See Figures A2.1 and A2.4 respectively in Appendix 2.

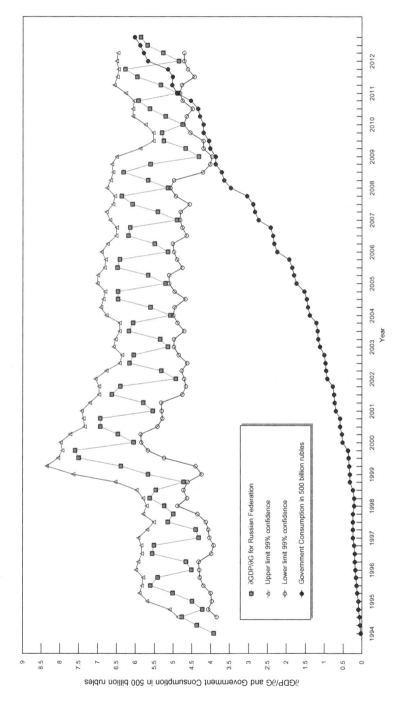

Figure 4.5: ∂(Nominal GDP)/∂(Nominal Government Consumption) for the Russian Federation: Not Seasonally Adjusted

Figure 4.6 shows a government consumption and ∂GDP/∂G pattern for Cyprus that is similar to Brazil's.[6] When government spending was increased in quarter 4 of 2011 in Cyprus, ∂GDP/∂G was 2.95; when government spending was decreased in quarter 1 of 2012 for Cyprus, ∂GDP/∂G was 4.22. The multiplier for the fall in government spending is 43% greater than the multiplier for increases in government spending in Cyprus. This means that the cut in government spending in Cyprus of 423 million euros in the first quarter of 2012 was correlated with a 1785 million euro fall in GDP (423 times 4.22). To undo that damage to GDP Cyprus would need to increase spending by 605 million euros (or 43% more than was cut). Furthermore, since 2008, ∂GDP/∂G for Cyprus has been on a downward trend — annual average ∂GDP/∂G[7] fell from 4.59 in the second quarter of 2008 to 4.07 in the third quarter of 2012 for a 10.7% decline.

The euro using countries that were selected for inclusion in the analysis of Chapters 4 and 5 were the countries hardest hit by the 2007–2008 crisis: Cyprus, Greece, Ireland, Italy, Portugal, and Spain, with one exception — Germany.[8] Germany was included in Chapters 4 and 5 because it presents some interesting results immediately after East and West Germany were united in the second half of 1990. Table 4.1 and Figure 4.7 show that while government consumption was very steadily increasing for a cumulative 52.5% increase between the second quarter of 1975 and the fourth quarter of 1990, Germany's government consumption multiplier increased by 19.9%. However, when Germany's government consumption dramatically increased by 30.3% between the fourth quarter of 1990 and the second quarter of 1991, Germany's ∂GDP/∂G fell by 7.8%. Even for Germany, relatively large increases in government spending are associated with much smaller multiplier effects.

---

[6]Cyprus' pattern differs from Brazil's pattern in that government consumption spiked in Brazil every fourth quarter whereas it spikes in Cyprus every first quarter.

[7]Where the annual average for a given quarter is the value for that quarter averaged with the values for the previous three quarters; i.e., the annual average is taken in the same way it was taken for Brazil and the Russian Federation.

[8]Graphs for all the other euro using countries are included in Appendix 2. Portugal's graph was also included in Appendix 2 because including it in Chapter 4 would not have added significantly to what was said about the other crisis countries.

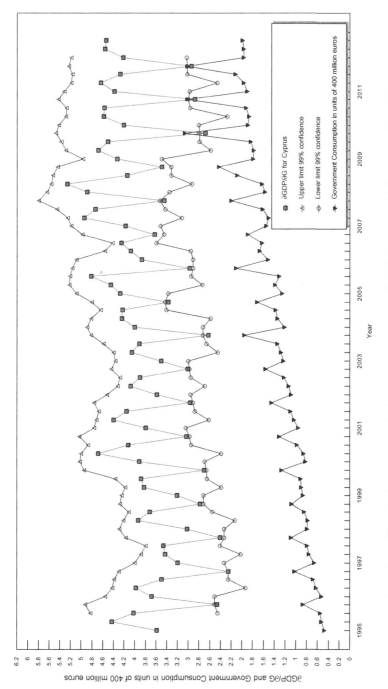

Figure 4.6: ∂(Nominal GDP)/∂(Nominal Government Consumption) for Cyprus: Not Seasonally Adjusted

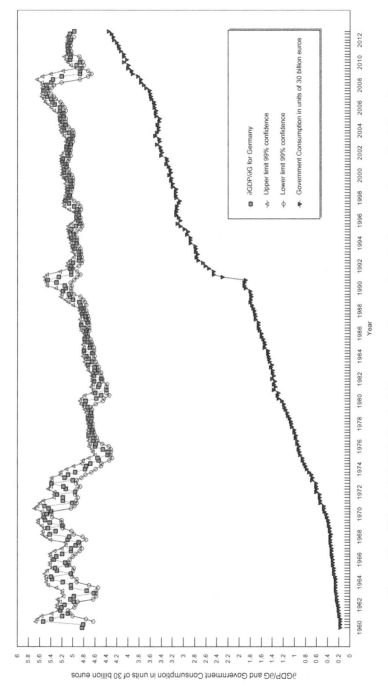

Figure 4.7: ∂(Nominal GDP)/∂(Nominal Government Consumption) for Germany: Seasonally Adjusted

Alternatively, it is possible to see the entire period between the second quarter of 1975 and the third quarter of 2007 as a time of steadily increasing ∂GDP/∂G for Germany with the period between the first quarter of 1989 and the second quarter of 1992 being an anomaly due to German reunification. This alternative view implies that the permanent shift upward in the government consumption line for Germany that occurred in early 1991(see bottom line in Figure 4.7) had no long-lasting effects.[9] In this alternative view, Germany's ∂GDP/∂G increased from 4.38 in the second quarter of 1975 to 5.53 in the third quarter of 2007 for a 26.3% increase. However, by the first quarter of 2009, Germany's ∂GDP/∂G had fallen to 4.87 for an 11.9% fall from its peak; it then partially rebounded to 4.98 in the fourth quarter of 2012. The net change in ∂GDP/∂G between the third quarter of 2007 and the fourth quarter of 2012 for Germany was a 9.9% decline.

Figure 4.8 shows that as Greek government consumption steadily rose between 2000 and 2007, ∂GDP/∂G for Greece was on an upward trend. However, when Greek government consumption increased by 53.3% between the first and fourth quarters of 2009, Greek ∂GDP/∂G fell by 21.7%. Yet again, relatively large increases in government consumption are associated with a declining effect on GDP. Between the fourth quarters of 2009 and 2012, annual average quarterly ∂GDP/∂G for Greece rose from 4.14 to 4.58 for a 10.6% increase. However, this is NOT good news because during this time period, government consumption was falling due to IMF imposed austerity (see the bottom line in Figure 4.8). When Greece decreased government spending in the third quarter of 2012, ∂GDP/∂G was 5.18; when Greece increased government spending in the fourth quarter of 2012, ∂GDP/∂G was only 4.04 for a 22% fall in the multiplier effect. This means that the Greek government's cutting spending by 561 million euros in the third quarter of 2012 was correlated with a 2906 million euro drop in GDP (561 times 5.18); to undo this damage in the fourth quarter of 2012 would require an increase in Greek government spending of 719 million euros (2906/4.04).

Figure 4.9 shows that a relatively steady upward trend in government consumption for Ireland between the first quarter of 1997 and the fourth

---

[9]This result contrasts sharply with what we will find for ∂GDP/∂X for Germany in Chapter 5 (see Figure 5.11).

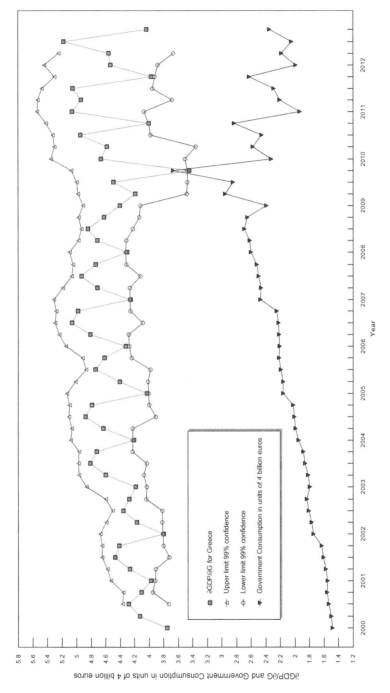

Figure 4.8: ∂(Nominal GDP)/∂(Nominal Government Consumption) for Greece: Not Seasonally Adjusted

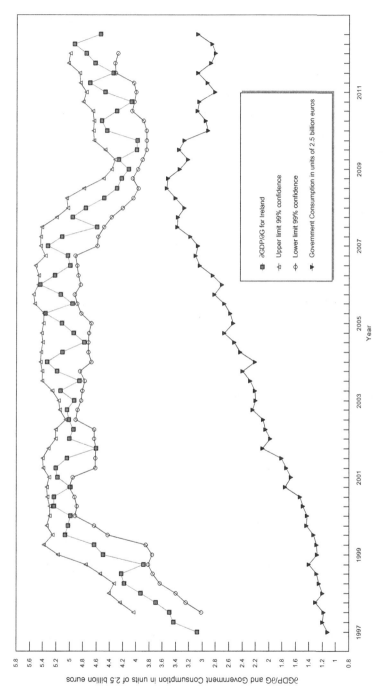

Figure 4.9: ∂(Nominal GDP)/∂(Nominal Government Consumption) for Ireland: Not Seasonally Adjusted

quarter of 2008 (the bottom line) was associated with an increasing trend in $\partial GDP/\partial G$ between the first quarter of 1997 and the second quarter of 2000, a relatively steady trend in $\partial GDP/\partial G$ between the second quarters of 2000 and 2007, and then a falling trend between the second quarter of 2007 and the fourth quarter of 2008 (top line). However, when Ireland started cutting government spending due to austerity measures in the fourth quarter of 2008, Irish $\partial GDP/\partial G$ rose implying that cuts in government spending cause GDP to fall more than increases in government spending cause GDP to rise.[10]

A comparison of the two lines in Figure 4.10 shows that $\partial GDP/\partial G$ for Italy rose between the fourth quarters of 1990 and 1995, which is when government spending in Italy increased at a much slower pace than immediately before 1990. A similar pattern can be seen for the United Kingdom between the third quarters of 1992 and 1997 (see Figure 4.2), and for the USA between the first quarters of 1991 and 1998 (see Figure 4.3). Furthermore, when Italian government spending began a steady decline in the fourth quarter of 2009, the $\partial GDP/\partial G$ multiplier began a steady increase. Cuts in government spending are correlated with larger decreases in GDP than increases in government spending are correlated with rising GDP.

A similar phenomenon can be seen for Spain in Figure 4.11. The last time Spain noticeably increased government spending was in the first quarter of 2011 when $\partial GDP/\partial G$ was 4.59. When Spain cut government spending in the fourth quarter of 2012, $\partial GDP/\partial G$ was 5.19 thus $\partial GDP/\partial G$ increased by 13.07% when Spain switched from increasing government spending to decreasing it. This means that if Spain wanted to undo the negative effects of cutting government spending in the fourth quarter of 2012, they would have to spend 13% more than they cut. In other words, cutting government spending by 2.88 billion in the fourth quarter of 2012 was correlated with Spain's GDP falling by 14.95 billion [(2.88 billion euros)(5.19)]; in order to undo that fall in GDP, Spain would have to increase government

---

[10]Using annual averages, Irish government consumption fell by 15.6% between the fourth quarter of 2008 and third quarter of 2012 while the $\partial GDP/\partial G$ multiplier rose by 6.14%. Thus, to undo the damage to GDP done by cutting government spending by 879 million euros between the fourth quarter of 2009 and the first quarter of 2010 would require Ireland to increase government spending by 933 million euros (or 6.14% more than was cut).

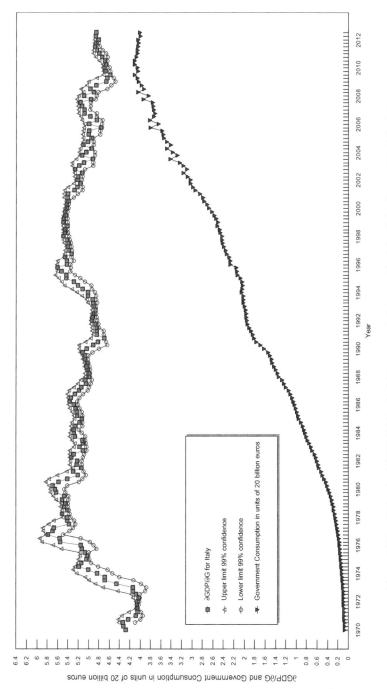

Figure 4.10: ∂(Nominal GDP)/∂(Nominal Government Consumption) for Italy: Seasonally Adjusted

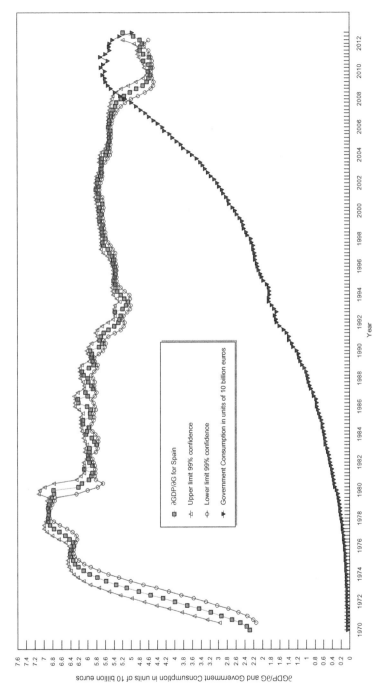

Figure 4.11: ∂(Nominal GDP)/∂(Nominal Government Consumption) for Spain: Seasonally Adjusted

spending by 3.26 billion euros [14.95 billion years/4.59]. The government spending of 3.26 is 13% more than 2.88. Moreover, as Spain repeatedly increased government spending between the fourth quarters of 1977 and 2009, $\partial GDP/\partial G$ for Spain fell from 6.90 to 4.56 for a 33.9% fall.

Cuts in government spending (austerity) are much stronger (have a larger effect on GDP) than increases in government spending. Governments that go into debt in order to help their economies (and to get re-elected) need to be aware that the pain needed to someday pay off that debt may be much greater than the benefit gained today. The effectiveness of government spending is falling. What the world needs is not a band-aid, i.e., more government spending. What the world needs is greater consumption which will provide a reason to invest the current surplus of savings in ways that expand production.

Chapter 5

TRADE POLICY

Most economists, including the author of this book, firmly believe that both traders gain from **naturally** occurring trade. These gains are illustrated in the Theory of Comparative Advantage which was developed by David Ricardo (1817). This theory can be applied to individuals, cities, states, provinces, nations, or continents. For example, assume that Dr. Frankenstein can dig up six corpses in a night or stitch together three monsters, whereas Igor can only dig up four corpses in a night or stitch together one monster. Note that Dr. Frankenstein is better at both digging up corpses and stitching together monsters. Does this mean that he should fire Igor? No, because Igor gives up less to dig up corpses than Dr. Frankenstein gives up. For every corpse that Dr. Frankenstein digs up, he forgoes stitching a half of a monster (3 stitched/6 dug up). For every corpse that Igor digs up, he forgoes stitching up a fourth of a monster (1 stitched/4 dug up). Therefore, Dr. Frankenstein and Igor can gain if they specialize and trade — Igor digging and Dr. Frankenstein stitching.

If we assume that it takes 20 corpses to make 15 monsters (due to damaged parts) then, by specializing, Dr. Frankenstein and Igor can produce 15 monsters in a five-day week. If Dr. Frankenstein worked alone, he could only produce nine monsters in a five-day period (digging two nights and stitching three nights). Even if Igor gets lucky and digs up four perfect bodies (so that each body could produce one monster), he could produce a maximum of four monsters in a week (digging one night, and stitching four nights). Working separately, they could produce a maximum of 13 monsters and this assumes that Igor finds four perfect corpses. By specializing and trading, they can produce two more monsters every week.

Similar examples of comparative advantage can be found in almost all international trade textbooks; however, these textbooks tend to use examples where the goods produced are "good" for humanity — like England and Portugal trading wine for cloth or Robinson Crusoe and Friday trading fish for coconuts. I have purposefully used an example where the item produced, monsters, is "bad" for humanity. I have done this to make the point that we need to evaluate the value of what we produce. Syria having a comparative advantage in producing chemical weapons and North Korea having a comparative advantage in producing nuclear weapons does not mean that their specializing and trading is good for humanity. When economists are dealing with trade issues, they tend to not judge what other people value — if Dr. Frankenstein values monsters, then that is his business and he should not be judged.[1] However, in the context of external costs (like pollution and monsters that kill people), other economists would advocate curtailing Dr. Frankenstein's activities.[2]

The issue of what is good for humanity is relevant when many countries, like China, have suppressed wage rates and the organization of labor in order to enhance their comparative advantage.[3] Because the rich can export what their factories produce (and thus do not require a large domestic market which would require a more equal distribution of income), they can pay their workers just enough to survive which increases company profits. For a while, export promotion growth strategies made it possible for increased growth and increased inequality to go hand in hand. However, Chapters 5

---

[1] Economists try to not judge the values of the traders; however, the traders' values are involved. For example, the USA produces and consumes hormone-treated beef, but the European Union regards such beef as harmful and will not permit imports of it from the USA.

[2] I would like to apologize to Mary Shelley for having referenced the much shallower movie version of her tale instead of her much deeper version that deals with issues such as can science and technology be pushed too far and the relationship between fathers and sons, creators, and monsters (Shelley, 1818).

[3] China is a relatively labor-abundant country and, thus, would naturally have a lower wage rate than a capital-abundant country like the USA. However, prior to 2008, Chinese authorities pushed the wage rate below its natural level by making non-government sponsored (controlled) labor unions illegal, by using the police/military to suppress strikes, by maintaining a household registration system that made all rural migrants illegal and, thus, powerless against urban employers who often refused to pay even what they initially promise to pay, etc.

and 6 of this book argue that the current global surplus of savings has ended those days. Growth based on export promotion is no longer a viable option — contrary to the hopes of the International Monetary Fund (IMF). Increased trade, via the suppression of wages rates and exchange rates, is one of the primary forces that has created the global surplus of savings (by making greater inequality possible) that is plaguing our world. Is the current situation really what is best for humanity? Trade in a world where income distribution has been increasingly less and less equal has resulted in the proliferation of toys for the rich while many of the poor barely survive. Is this what is really best for humanity as a whole?

It is very important for the reader to understand that I, like most economists, strongly believe in the gains from **naturally** occurring trade. However, I do not believe that those naturally occurring gains can be increased by adding market distortions like suppressed wage rates and exchange rates. From a long term, global point of view, these distortions hurt more than they help. Trade is good, but increasing trade by hurting labor is bad in a world awash in a surplus of savings.

Consider Figure 5.1 which is in most international trade textbooks. "P_1" is the price prior to trade in both countries because it is the price where the domestic quantity demanded equals the domestic quantity supplied. Note that the country labeled "exporter" has a lower price for this

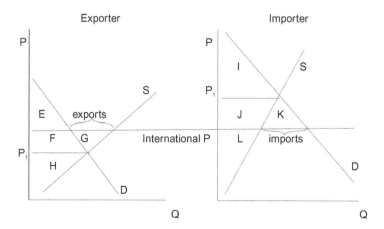

Figure 5.1:   Gains and Losses from Trade

good prior to trade than the "importer" has. When these countries begin to trade, the price in the exporting country will rise and the price in the importing country will fall. If there are no transportation costs (and no tariffs), then the price with trade will be the same in both countries. This price will occur where the domestic surplus generated in the exporting country equals the domestic shortage in the importing country — this surplus and shortage are labeled "exports" and "imports" on the appropriate graphs.

We usually think of the demand curve (labeled "D") as tracing out the quantities that buyers are willing and able to buy at different prices, holding everything else constant. However, we can also think of Demand as showing the maximum prices that people are willing and able to pay for different quantities. The difference between the maximum price people would be willing and able to pay and the price they actually do pay is "consumer surplus value." Prior to trade, consumer surplus value in the exporting country is areas "E + F" and in the importing country, it is area "I." After trade, consumer surplus value in the exporting country is area "E" and in the importing country, it is areas "I + J + K." Thus, the consumers in the exporting country lose area "F" and the consumers in the importing country gain areas "J + K" when these countries trade. Trade hurts the consumers in the exporting country and helps the consumers in the importing country.

For similar reasons, the supply curve traces out the minimum prices producers would accept for different quantities sold. Thus, the difference between the actual price they receive and the minimum price they would accept is "producer surplus value." Prior to trade, producer surplus value in the exporting country is area "H" and in the importing country, it is areas "J + L." After trade begins, producer surplus value in the exporting country is areas "F + G + H" and in the importing country, it is area "L." Thus, producers gain in the exporting country and lose in the importing country.

Note that if a dollar going to a consumer is worth the same as a dollar going to a producer, then both countries have a net gain from trade. In the exporting country, the consumers lose "F" but the producers gain "F + G," producing a net gain of "G" for the country. In the importing country, producers lose "J" but the consumers gain "J + K," for a net gain of "K" for the country. However, the assumption that a dollar going to a consumer is worth the same as a dollar going to a producer is often questionable — especially when the producers are very wealthy and the consumers are relatively poor, perhaps due to the suppression of wages in order to promote exports. If the billionaire currency speculator George Soros gets another dollar, he values that additional dollar less than Bob, the homeless beggar, would value it.

One of the most fundamental conclusions from western economics is that (if a dollar to a consumer is equal to a dollar to a producer), free trade benefits both traders. However, that conclusion does not imply that countries can increase both traders' gains by trying to increase trade beyond what would naturally occur by introducing market distortions like (1) devalued fixed exchange rates, (2) suppressed wages, (3) subsidized production, or (4) internal devaluations encouraged by the IMF.

Consider what happens if the exporter devalues its currency and the price is given in the importing country's currency. As Figure 5.2 shows, such a devaluation pivots the exporter's demand and supply curves downward.[4] The international price falls as a consequence in order to make the

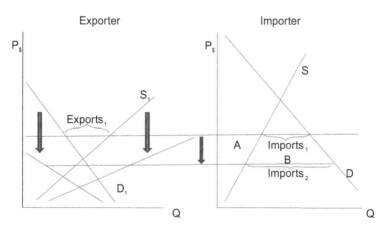

Figure 5.2: Exporter Devaluation — Price in the Importing Country's Currency [Also Importer Devaluation If All the Arrows are Reversed and "1"s and "2"s Switched.]

---

[4]The supply and demand lines pivot around the X-axis intercepts. This can easily be seen by graphing a simple numerical example where the price is given in US dollars and a country,

surplus exported equal to the shortage covered by imports. Figure 5.2 shows that, in the importing country, the consumers gain areas "A + B" and the producers lose area "A" for a net gain of "B." Figure 5.2 also shows that the effects of the exporter devaluing on the exporting country itself are ambiguous if the price is given in the importing currency — there are areas that both producers and consumers gain and lose. However, if we recreate the effects of this devaluation while measuring price in the exporting country's currency, then we get Figure 5.3 which shows that the consumers in the exporting country lose area "E" and the producers gain areas "E + F."[5] Both countries benefit when an exporter devalues and the price is given in each country's currency.

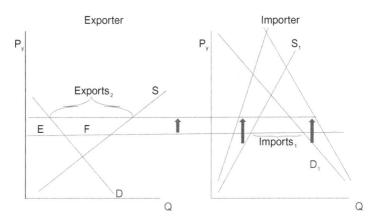

Figure 5.3: Exporter Devaluation — Price in the Exporting Country's Currency [Also Importer Devaluation If All the Arrows are Reversed and "1"s and "2"s Switched.]

like Thailand, devalues its currency, the baht. For example, graph the following example where going from 25 baht/$ to 50 baht/$ is a devaluation.

Price in baht	Qd	Qs	Price in $s (25 baht/$)	Qd	Qs	Price in $s (50 baht/$)	Qd	Qs
100 baht	80	50	4$	80	50	2$	80	50
150 baht	60	60	6$	60	60	3$	60	60
200 baht	40	70	8$	40	70	4$	40	70

[5]Again the supply and demand lines pivot around the X-axis intercepts for reasons parallel to those given in footnote 4.

Since, countries both export and import, it is necessary to consider the impact of currency devaluations by importing countries also. When an importing country devalues its currency, then both the exporter and importer lose. The graphs that show this are Figures 5.2 and 5.3 with all the arrows reversed. When an importing country devalues (Figure 5.2 with reversed arrows), the consumers in the importing country lose areas "A + B" and the producers in the importing country gain area "A" for a net loss of area "B." Additionally, when an importing country devalues (Figure 5.3 with reversed arrows), the producers in the exporting country lose areas "E + F" while the consumers gain only area "E" for a net loss of area "F." Thus, when a country that both exports and imports devalues its currency, it becomes difficult to discern if that country and if the rest of the world gain or lose even when the price is measured in the currency of each country. If the price is measured in only one country's currency, then the results are even more ambiguous. Furthermore, the above assumes a two country world. If there are three countries in the world, two exporters and one importer, and one of the exporters devalues its currency, the other exporting country will suffer a loss which may cause a net loss to the world even without considering the fact that the same country imports. In such a world, there can be a "devaluation" war (price war) between exporters as each exporter tries to devalue its currency more than other exporters.

Figures 5.4 and 5.5 show what happens when exporters and importers suppress wages. Some exporters, like China from 1984 through 2007,

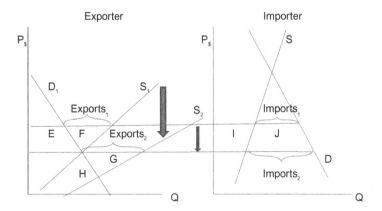

Figure 5.4:   Exporter Suppresses Wages

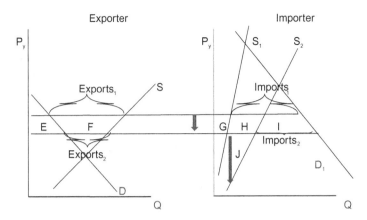

Figure 5.5:   Importer Suppresses Wages

suppressed wages in order to increase exports. China suppressed wages by making labor unions that were not controlled by the government illegal, by using the police and military to stop labor strikes, and by giving no legal protection to rural migrants which resulted in many migrants not being paid for their work.[6] IMF recommended suppression of wages policies in Europe for the purposes of "internal devaluations" include cutting the minimum wage in Greece, cutting public sector wages in Ireland, Latvia, Portugal, and Romania, and a reduction in employment protection and severance pay in Portugal (Blanchard *et al.*, 2013).[7] When a country suppresses

---

[6]If a rural migrant were to complain to the police for not being paid the wages he or she was promised, the police would ask for residence papers and when the migrant could not produce them, the migrant was (at best) sent back to his or her home town or, worse, was put into a detention center where the migrant was often beaten, raped, and/or forced to pay bribes. Due to some courageous reporters, the abuses at these detention centers have been revealed, and the Chinese government has shut them down. However, this has not stopped the practice of hiring, but not paying, rural migrants especially at construction sites. Furthermore, if you are an employer in a purely competitive industry and your competition hires rural migrants and does not pay them, then you will be forced to do the same (because if you do not, your average cost will exceed the price you get for your product).

[7]Several of these recommendations (for example, the cut in the minimum wage in Greece) were based on reducing differences between different European countries. This effort to push all European countries to the mean resulted in the IMF recommending an increase in the minimum wage in Romania. However, pushing all countries to the mean does not address the fundamental problem with the world's economy — insufficient consumption.

its wage rate, the supply curve for the goods it produces shifts vertically downward.[8] Figure 5.4 shows that the consumers in the exporting country gain area "E," while the producers lose areas "E + F" but gain areas "H + G." If "H + G" is greater than "E + F," then both the consumers and producers in the exporting country gain from the suppression of wages. Figure 5.4 also shows that when an exporter suppresses wage rates, the consumers in the importing country gain areas "I + J" and the producers in the importing country lose area "I," for a net gain in the importing country of area "J." Thus, as in the case of devaluation, it is possible that when an exporter suppresses wages that both the exporting and importing countries gain (if the value of a dollar going to a producer equals the value of a dollar going to a consumer). Keep in mind, however, that countries both export and import.

Figure 5.5 shows that when an importer suppresses wages, its citizens gain of "H + I + J." Therefore, just as some exporting countries have an incentive to suppress wages, so do some importing countries. However, when an importing country suppresses its wages, then the producers in the country exporting to it lose areas "E + F" and the consumers in that country gain only area "E." Consequentially, when an importing country suppresses its wages, the country that exports to it suffers a net loss of area "F" in Figure 5.5. Moreover, when an importer suppresses its wages, it is also possible that there is a net loss to the world. This possibility is increased in a world that suffers from insufficient consumption.[9]

The two key points developed in this chapter are (1) both traders benefit from free trade if the value of a dollar going to a consumer equals the value of a dollar going to a producer and if the items being traded are not "bad" things like nuclear weapons and chemical weapons and (2) countries trying to increase exports beyond what naturally would occur by devaluing their currencies, subsidizing their producers, and/or suppressing wages may

---

[8]This is because the marginal cost of production falls as the wage rate falls. Also Figures 5.4 and 5.5 assume that demand does not shift downward due to the suppression of wages. The dubiousness of such an assumption is increased in a world of insufficient consumption. If demand does shift downward, then Figures 5.2 and 5.3 can be used to analyze the effects of the suppression of wages.

[9]The effects of the suppression of wages on demand were not considered in Figures 5.4 and 5.5.

or may not be benefiting themselves and/or the world. In other words, free trade is helpful because it allows countries to specialize in producing what they produce at lower opportunity costs; however, artificially trying to increase trade may not be helpful. Furthermore, just because trade is good, it does not necessarily follow that trade deficits and trade surpluses are good (Leightner, 2010b).[10]

Finally, and very importantly, if what is limiting global economic growth is insufficient demand (as this book argues) and if a fall in wages reduces demand further (which is reasonable for normal goods), then nations suppressing their wage rates will reduce global demand making the fundamental problem in the world worse. In other words, nations implementing internal devaluations in order to suppress wages and export more produce a net loss for the world. Although the countries that cause their own wages to fall the most might individually gain, the world as a whole will lose.

What is the true motivation behind governments attempt to increase their exports by devaluing their currencies, subsidizing their exporters, and/or suppressing wages? Are they taking these actions for the good of their entire countries? Since all of these policies hurt consumers and help producers, I wonder if these actions are taken for the good of the rich (in contrast to the good of the nation) who are the government leaders and/or who collaborate with the government to the detriment of labor and consumers. In a world with a global surplus of savings and insufficient consumption, such policies will increase savings and decrease consumption and, thus, could backfire (Stockhammer, 2008).

In the 1950s through the 1970s, many developing nations (especially ones in Latin America) embraced a development strategy that focused on "import substitution." The key idea behind this strategy is that developing nations should not continue to export basic commodities and import industrial goods. Instead, developing nations should industrialize. This strategy

---

[10]Countries with trade deficits are trading either goods from the past or the future for more goods in the present. Countries with trade surpluses are trading goods in the present for more goods in the future or to pay off past trade deficits. Due to the time dimension involved in trade deficits and surpluses, the likelihood of mistakes increases. Possible mistakes include countries, like China, not foreseeing the financial crisis of 2007–2008 that greatly diminished her exports upon which she was dependent.

lost favor in the 1980s partially because of the success of an "export promotion" strategy used by Japan, South Korea, and Taiwan. However, the "import substitution" and "export promotion" strategies were not as mutually exclusive as their names imply because both strategies encouraged industrialization — the goods that Japan, South Korea, and Taiwan exported were industrial goods, not basic commodities.

When China entered the world of international trade in the 1980s, it embraced an export promotion strategy. By the 1990s, China was using an export promotion strategy in its most extreme form — China was suppressing labor power, wages, and its exchange rate so that it could increase exports. When the USA and Europe went into crisis in 2008, China suffered due to declining demand for its exports. In response, China has announced a shift from "export promotion growth" to "domestic consumption-driven growth." Although China needs to solve some serious problems — like broken health care and pension systems and problems with corruption — to fully implement a "consumption-driven growth model," China has the right idea. What the world needs is more consumption to provide a reason to invest the glut of savings that currently plagues the world's economy.

Perversely, instead of embracing a consumption-driven growth model, crisis European countries are attempting to lower their wage rates and decrease the power of labor so that they can export more. Without the ability to devalue their exchange rates or print more money (because they have adopted the euro), crisis European countries are attempting to force an "internal devaluation." "Internal devaluation" is a euphemism for hurting labor in order to export more. Holding world demand constant, a "successful" internal devaluation by Spain implies that Portugal (or other countries that compete with Spain's exports) will be able to export less. This is called a "zero sum" game because what one country gains, another loses. However, if you consider that Cyprus, Ireland, Italy, Greece, Portugal, and Spain driving down their wage rates will cause a reduction in world demand, then an "internal devaluation" strategy is a "negative sum game" — the exports one country gains will cause an even larger drop in exports by other countries because total world demand has fallen.

This is the opposite of what the theory of comparative advantage predicts. The theory of comparative advantage assumes that there is no surplus of savings, and, thus, total demand does not constrain production. Under the theory of comparative advantage, all nations making the goods for which they sacrifice less than other countries sacrifice (or for which they have lower opportunity costs) leads to all nations enjoying increasing incomes and increasing consumption. However (assuming profits are primarily saved and wages primarily consumed) increased trade based on internal devaluations results in profits increasing while wages fall, resulting in an enlarged global surplus of savings and falling world demand for goods. The falling world demand for goods can change trade into a negative sum game.

In this chapter, I use Reiterative Truncated Projected Least Squares (RTPLS) to estimate ∂GDP/∂Exports — the multiplier effect that would occur if exports were increased one unit. This chapter's estimates do not capture the fact that, in a world where many countries are attempting "internal devaluations," it is increasingly difficult to increase exports. Nor do the results of this chapter capture the fact that governments may be unable to increase exports because exports depend heavily on what is happening in the corresponding importing country. China discovered in 2008 that no matter how much it suppressed its wage rates and exchange rates, China's exports would fall when two of its major customers, the USA and Europe, suffered from financial crises. Thus, this chapter's estimates show what happens to GDP if a country does successfully increase its exports; it does not deal with whether or not a country can successfully increase its exports. Table 5.1 lists the 1981 to 2012 RTPLS estimates of ∂GDP/∂Exports and Figures 5.6–5.15 and Figures A3.1–A3.12 (in Appendix 3) graphically depict these results.

First, some general observations will be made about this chapter's empirical results and then the results for specific countries will be examined. The ∂GDP/∂Exports results reported in Table 5.1 are noticeably different from the ∂GDP/∂G results reported in Table 4.1. In contrast, a simple Keynesian macroeconomic model would predict that ∂GDP/∂Exports would equal ∂GDP/∂G.[11] One possible explanation for the difference found

---

[11] The generic multiplier equation for the Keynesian model is $\partial \text{GDP} = \partial(Q_{AD\,initial})(1/(1-$ slope of $Q_{AD}))$. Since $Q_{AD} = C + I + G + X - M$, an equal increase in G and X would increase $Q_{AD\,initial}$ the same amount, and, thus, should have the same multiplier effect. If, however, the forces that change exports (X) also affect imports (M), then an equal increase in G and X would not have an equal effect on $Q_{AD\,initial}$. This explanation, however, leads to the conclusion that governments that just focus on export promotion, without considering the simultaneous effects on imports, are making a mistake.

Table 5.1: ∂GDP/∂Exports

	Japan	UK	USA	Brazil	Rus. F	Austr.	Belg.	Cypr	Eston.	Finl.	Franc	Germ.	Greec	Irel	Italy	Lux.	Malta	Neth.	Port.	Slova.	Slove.	Spain
1981 Q1	7.11	3.76	9.11			2.14	0.92			2.56	3.96	0.90			4.49			1.04	3.41			5.81
1981 Q2	6.78	3.69	9.13			2.24	0.97			2.52	3.86	0.91			4.18			1.00	3.17			5.08
1981 Q3	6.51	3.53	9.62			2.11	1.01			2.72	3.80	0.90			4.05			0.97	3.50			4.94
1981 Q4	6.71	3.55	9.60			2.41	1.04			2.66	4.02	0.90			4.23			1.01	3.43			5.03
1982 Q1	6.67	3.69	9.94			2.07	1.00			2.62	4.01	0.92			4.12			1.04	3.67			4.98
1982 Q2	6.84	3.66	10.08			2.33	0.96			2.85	4.15	0.94			4.27			1.02	3.71			5.41
1982 Q3	6.87	3.72	10.75			2.26	0.95			3.31	4.16	0.96			4.51			1.07	3.23			5.04
1982 Q4	7.07	3.68	11.47			2.55	0.94			2.82	4.05	0.99			4.48			1.04	3.31			4.87
1983 Q1	7.21	3.71	11.50			2.23	0.91			2.85	4.14	1.07			4.42			1.09	3.22			4.91
1983 Q2	7.29	3.69	11.79			2.41	0.96			2.98	4.06	1.09			4.54			1.09	3.10			4.48
1983 Q3	7.15	3.64	11.93			2.25	0.99			3.16	3.95	1.13			4.58			1.08	2.96			4.51
1983 Q4	7.01	3.65	11.93			2.61	0.96			2.85	3.89	1.16			4.58			1.05	2.87			4.45
1984 Q1	6.79	3.53	12.08			2.09	0.86			2.79	3.85	1.17			4.32			1.03	2.57			4.08
1984 Q2	6.75	3.52	12.04			2.40	0.92			2.95	3.78	1.11			4.62			1.02	2.67			4.05
1984 Q3	6.62	3.40	12.13			2.18	1.00			3.03	3.76	1.15			4.40			1.02	2.70			4.03
1984 Q4	6.45	3.32	12.20			2.44	0.94			2.92	3.74	1.13			4.30			1.02	2.59			4.43
1985 Q1	6.56	3.23	12.60			1.92	0.86			3.03	3.75	1.09			4.30			0.99	2.57			4.34
1985 Q2	6.56	3.26	12.89			2.14	0.99			2.91	3.80	1.12			4.42			1.03	2.72			4.22
1985 Q3	7.07	3.51	13.50			2.24	1.05			3.14	4.00	1.18			4.35			1.02	2.79			4.30
1985 Q4	7.58	3.59	13.32			2.48	1.04			3.36	4.06	1.24			4.46			1.09	2.84			4.23
1986 Q1	8.32	3.71	13.18			2.20	1.02			3.32	4.24	1.24			4.71			1.18	3.77			4.92
1986 Q2	8.55	3.84	13.22			2.39	1.11			3.77	4.43	1.34			4.98			1.22	3.57			4.90
1986 Q3	9.30	3.93	13.19			2.43	1.14			3.36	4.52	1.40			5.02			1.30	3.64			5.15
1986 Q4	9.09	3.79	12.76			2.72	1.10			3.30	4.63	1.46			5.16			1.31	3.72			4.84
1987 Q1	9.22	3.73	12.90			2.34	1.17			3.50	4.72	1.42			5.29			1.26	3.71			5.05
1987 Q2	9.67	3.85	12.44			2.53	1.11			3.52	4.70	1.48			5.47			1.31	3.66			5.04
1987 Q3	9.66	3.82	12.10			2.45	1.12			3.46	4.59	1.50			4.90			1.31	3.60			5.02
1987 Q4	9.97	4.00	11.78			2.70	1.14			3.84	4.60	1.52			5.00			1.30	3.65			5.36

(Continued)

Table 5.1:   (Continued)

	Japan	UK	USA	Brazil	Rus. F	Austr.	Belg.	Cypr	Eston.	Finl.	Franc	Germ.	Greec	Irel	Italy	Lux.	Malta	Neth.	Port.	Slova.	Slove.	Spain
1988 Q1	10.37	4.24	11.18			2.38	1.12			3.90	4.63	1.53			5.72			1.33	3.68			5.19
1988 Q2	10.25	4.18	10.91			2.55	1.08			3.83	4.54	1.54			5.15			1.28	3.58			5.29
1988 Q3	9.70	4.19	10.77			2.48	1.07			3.87	4.42	1.55			5.21			1.23	3.43			5.25
1988 Q4	9.87	4.39	10.70			2.67	1.11			3.65	4.40	1.58			5.08			1.24	3.43			5.38
1989 Q1	9.84	4.22	10.52			2.22	1.03			3.71	4.24	1.54			5.35			1.25	3.42			5.30
1989 Q2	9.38	4.17	10.25			2.39	1.02			4.14	4.19	1.51			4.85			1.21	3.23			5.36
1989 Q3	9.40	4.11	10.36			2.40	1.07			4.12	4.29	1.54			4.99			1.24	3.36			5.73
1989 Q4	9.67	4.01	10.33			2.62	1.08			3.79	4.26	1.60			4.99			1.25	3.32			5.77
1990 Q1	9.22	3.98	10.12			2.24	1.08			4.15	4.28	1.65			5.28			1.23	3.20			5.95
1990 Q2	9.28	4.04	10.12			2.42	1.09			3.92	4.39	1.72			4.96			1.26	3.30			5.78
1990 Q3	9.80	4.15	10.04			2.40	1.11			4.38	4.46	1.64			5.15			1.24	3.54			5.82
1990 Q4	9.81	4.11	9.80			2.50	1.12			4.00	4.35	1.61			4.73			1.26	3.60			5.96
1991 Q1	9.87	4.31	9.76	1.42		2.35	1.10			4.44	4.41	2.29			5.28			1.24	3.63			5.75
1991 Q2	10.08	4.17	9.61	5.42		2.53	1.12			4.56	4.33	2.45			5.31			1.25	3.80			5.75
1991 Q3	9.88	4.11	9.57	9.42		2.53	1.17			4.13	4.24	2.38			5.52			1.25	3.94			6.10
1991 Q4	9.95	4.20	9.44	10.71		2.59	1.18			3.86	4.30	2.49			5.28			1.29	3.98			5.94
1992 Q1	10.05	4.19	9.44	8.68		2.39	1.20			3.78	4.30	2.56			5.39		0.97	1.29	3.95			5.80
1992 Q2	10.05	4.14	9.60	9.49		2.63	1.16			3.59	4.27	2.70			5.29		1.07	1.30	4.21			5.78
1992 Q3	10.08	4.29	9.54	9.36		2.67	1.24			3.59	4.33	2.69			5.28		0.95	1.33	4.18			5.59
1992 Q4	10.08	4.00	9.68	8.69		2.81	1.14			3.21	4.48	2.84			4.88		1.01	1.36	4.41			5.82
1993 Q1	10.35	3.80	9.73	9.43		2.54	1.25		1.08	2.99	4.40	2.88			4.62		1.06	1.40	4.40	0.59		5.45
1993 Q2	10.90	3.91	9.71	9.99		2.87	1.26		1.07	2.94	4.55	2.95			4.50		0.98	1.37	4.38	0.63		5.41
1993 Q3	11.01	3.85	9.85	9.55		2.74	1.24		0.94	2.94	4.49	3.00			4.44		0.91	1.35	4.19	0.64		5.30
1993 Q4	11.19	3.78	9.74	9.41		2.93	1.25		0.92	2.71	4.43	2.97			4.28		0.94	1.30	4.21	0.60		4.93
1994 Q1	11.02	3.74	9.76	8.53	2.70	2.53	1.22		0.97	2.81	4.46	2.97			4.18		1.03	1.32	4.08	0.78		4.62
1994 Q2	10.85	3.74	9.59	8.66	3.03	2.83	1.23		1.09	2.64	4.33	2.86			4.24		0.96	1.32	4.07	0.75		4.70
1994 Q3	11.12	3.65	9.31	10.49	3.44	2.77	1.22		0.99	2.71	4.29	2.92			4.17		0.89	1.32	3.87	0.81		4.70
1994 Q4	11.00	3.59	9.20	12.21	2.98	2.85	1.19		1.11	2.53	4.15	2.93			4.07		0.99	1.33	3.92	0.75		4.38

(Continued)

Table 5.1: *(Continued)*

	Japan	UK	USA	Brazil	Rus. F	Austr.	Belg.	Cypr.	Eston.	Finl.	Franc.	Germ.	Greec	Irel	Italy	Lux.	Malta	Neth.	Port.	Slova.	Slove.	Spain
1995 Q1	11.01	3.42	9.02	15.09	2.37	2.32	1.17	1.86	1.18	2.47	4.13	2.84			3.95	0.42	1.07	1.26	3.34	0.85	0.74	4.33
1995 Q2	11.38	3.53	8.88	13.67	2.64	2.80	1.26	1.46	1.27	2.45	4.09	2.88			3.72	0.45	1.03	1.26	3.45	1.01	0.94	4.39
1995 Q3	10.83	3.47	8.65	12.64	3.90	2.67	1.31	1.18	1.18	2.76	4.16	2.89			3.83	0.46	0.91	1.31	3.35	0.97	0.97	4.33
1995 Q4	10.59	3.38	8.67	14.07	3.82	2.85	1.32	1.38	1.18	2.60	4.11	2.85			3.84	0.52	1.03	1.31	3.53	0.90	1.00	4.28
1996 Q1	10.34	3.37	8.69	15.66	3.59	2.37	1.23	1.76	1.36	2.51	4.11	2.77			4.00	0.43	1.11	1.28	3.31	1.10	0.91	4.24
1996 Q2	10.41	3.36	8.77	14.44	3.53	2.80	1.26	1.44	1.46	2.41	4.13	2.82			4.01	0.49	1.02	1.33	3.40	1.10	1.05	4.21
1996 Q3	10.26	3.37	8.87	14.44	3.96	2.67	1.29	1.21	1.41	2.66	4.10	2.80			4.06	0.47	1.09	1.30	3.47	1.14	1.10	4.08
1996 Q4	9.89	3.34	8.57	16.45	3.52	2.61	1.27	1.41	1.34	2.52	3.97	2.70			4.02	0.47	1.11	1.29	3.73	1.07	1.15	3.94
1997 Q1	9.43	3.43	8.56	16.84	3.81	2.28	1.19	1.79	1.34	2.50	3.83	2.63		0.84	4.02	0.44	1.09	1.27	3.55	1.09	1.05	3.88
1997 Q2	9.15	3.44	8.38	13.87	3.87	2.46	1.20	1.42	1.29	2.39	3.70	2.57		0.86	3.97	0.43	1.08	1.25	3.40	1.08	1.17	3.75
1997 Q3	9.45	3.42	8.35	13.49	4.22	2.34	1.17	1.16	1.22	2.42	3.63	2.48		0.84	3.85	0.41	1.01	1.22	3.35	1.20	1.14	3.60
1997 Q4	8.94	3.52	8.50	15.05	3.70	2.35	1.23	1.47	1.14	2.44	3.58	2.46		0.91	3.87	0.48	1.26	1.24	3.45	1.08	1.17	3.59
1998 Q1	9.02	3.63	8.64	14.74	4.16	2.10	1.18	1.79	1.23	2.26	3.56	2.46		0.82	3.85	0.41	1.18	1.27	3.33	1.10	1.08	3.57
1998 Q2	8.98	3.68	8.89	13.76	4.26	2.34	1.19	1.51	1.19	2.42	3.59	2.41		0.85	3.87	0.41	1.06	1.27	3.30	1.16	1.23	3.58
1998 Q3	8.93	3.79	9.16	13.79	3.23	2.27	1.20	1.28	1.19	2.56	3.61	2.46		0.84	3.97	0.44	1.00	1.29	3.26	1.15	1.24	3.71
1998 Q4	9.82	3.79	9.05	15.58	2.09	2.35	1.26	1.61	1.22	2.59	3.68	2.51		0.83	4.17	0.45	1.11	1.30	3.71	1.07	1.34	3.76
1999 Q1	9.98	3.92	9.26	11.39	2.27	2.10	1.22	1.96	1.40	2.54	3.72	2.56		0.87	4.23	0.46	1.13	1.32	3.70	1.16	1.33	3.73
1999 Q2	9.79	3.82	9.25	11.18	2.29	2.34	1.23	1.51	1.35	2.51	3.68	2.41		0.83	4.21	0.48	1.07	1.29	3.69	1.18	1.47	3.73
1999 Q3	9.62	3.72	9.15	9.96	2.56	2.25	1.21	1.20	1.22	2.46	3.55	2.38		0.87	4.07	0.46	0.98	1.29	3.54	1.15	1.40	3.63
1999 Q4	9.55	3.71	9.08	10.21	2.05	2.20	1.21	1.53	1.21	2.32	3.51	2.34		0.85	3.97	0.44	1.03	1.26	3.63	1.00	1.43	3.57
2000 Q1	9.35	3.75	8.97	10.61	2.02	1.91	1.10	1.81	1.14	2.27	3.43	2.26	1.32	0.85	3.81	0.43	1.13	1.22	3.45	0.99	1.28	3.49
2000 Q2	9.19	3.60	8.89	10.00	2.11	2.13	1.10	1.43	1.13	2.23	3.33	2.20	1.32	0.82	3.81	0.43	1.04	1.20	3.52	1.05	1.32	3.38
2000 Q3	9.00	3.57	8.71	9.24	2.38	2.08	1.09	1.16	1.05	2.18	3.27	2.14	1.25	0.81	3.62	0.43	0.99	1.18	3.33	1.05	1.29	3.35
2000 Q4	8.88	3.41	8.87	10.38	2.43	1.99	1.04	1.49	1.04	2.10	3.19	2.00	1.38	0.79	3.59	0.45	1.02	1.14	3.35	0.97	1.29	3.26
2001 Q1	9.19	3.44	9.02	9.41	2.39	1.78	1.04	1.79	1.02	2.21	3.23	2.08	1.41	0.79	3.65	0.43	1.15	1.20	3.41	0.92	1.23	3.32
2001 Q2	9.45	3.56	9.49	8.15	2.50	2.02	1.10	1.39	1.12	2.32	3.35	2.07	1.50	0.81	3.61	0.43	1.16	1.23	3.49	1.02	1.32	3.41
2001 Q3	9.61	3.74	10.07	7.28	2.90	2.02	1.12	1.18	1.25	2.44	3.36	2.09	1.49	0.84	3.74	0.44	1.15	1.26	3.50	1.05	1.32	3.44
2001 Q4	9.66	3.82	10.52	8.32	2.99	1.99	1.17	1.57	1.26	2.26	3.49	2.07	1.82	0.85	3.83	0.51	1.22	1.30	3.65	1.06	1.40	3.57

(Continued)

Table 5.1: (*Continued*)

	Japan	UK	USA	Brazil	Rus. F	Austr.	Belg.	Cypr	Eston.	Finl.	Franc	Germ.	Greec	Irel	Italy	Lux.	Malta	Neth.	Port.	Slova.	Slove.	Spain
2002 Q1	9.12	3.79	10.51	9.87	2.95	1.76	1.08	2.06	1.34	2.37	3.47	2.08	2.19	0.82	3.89	0.45	1.28	1.32	3.64	1.05	1.33	3.58
2002 Q2	8.74	3.67	10.27	9.69	2.70	2.01	1.12	1.52	1.30	2.36	3.42	2.03	1.84	0.84	3.90	0.48	1.11	1.31	3.57	1.06	1.36	3.56
2002 Q3	8.96	3.74	10.22	5.74	2.84	2.01	1.14	1.32	1.31	2.42	3.46	2.03	1.64	0.92	3.93	0.48	1.05	1.32	3.48	1.08	1.37	3.61
2002 Q4	8.44	3.92	10.37	5.59	2.77	1.96	1.18	1.72	1.33	2.31	3.53	2.00	2.41	0.99	3.92	0.53	1.16	1.32	3.63	1.07	1.42	3.61
2003 Q1	8.46	3.72	10.49	6.36	2.63	1.79	1.12	2.51	1.45	2.40	3.61	2.04	2.54	1.01	4.00	0.50	1.30	1.32	3.52	1.01	1.38	3.66
2003 Q2	8.53	3.86	10.62	6.92	2.79	2.09	1.17	1.92	1.37	2.43	3.72	2.06	2.28	1.02	4.13	0.52	1.19	1.37	3.64	1.04	1.46	3.73
2003 Q3	8.29	3.89	10.55	6.59	3.00	2.02	1.20	1.36	1.33	2.58	3.72	2.04	1.97	1.00	4.11	0.50	1.07	1.36	3.49	1.04	1.46	3.77
2003 Q4	8.14	3.89	10.15	6.81	2.89	1.92	1.22	1.65	1.31	2.50	3.68	2.02	2.75	1.04	4.04	0.53	1.25	1.35	3.65	1.02	1.47	3.78
2004 Q1	7.83	3.97	9.94	6.74	2.96	1.75	1.14	2.04	1.39	2.34	3.70	1.97	2.49	1.02	4.04	0.46	1.27	1.35	3.55	1.06	1.36	3.77
2004 Q2	7.52	3.95	9.82	5.92	2.85	1.88	1.15	1.73	1.27	2.48	3.68	1.88	2.27	1.01	3.96	0.47	1.18	1.30	3.47	0.99	1.38	3.78
2004 Q3	7.39	3.87	9.84	5.57	2.95	1.89	1.15	1.46	1.27	2.47	3.68	1.91	1.86	1.02	3.91	0.47	1.14	1.26	3.46	1.15	1.37	3.83
2004 Q4	7.30	3.78	9.67	6.30	2.88	1.82	1.17	1.91	1.28	2.35	3.64	1.88	2.63	1.06	3.95	0.49	1.31	1.23	3.62	1.11	1.37	3.79
2005 Q1	7.40	3.89	9.58	6.53	2.92	1.67	1.08	2.09	1.28	2.27	3.69	1.85	2.44	1.09	3.94	0.48	1.34	1.27	3.66	1.09	1.27	3.92
2005 Q2	7.13	3.71	9.42	6.58	2.76	1.81	1.12	1.71	1.25	2.38	3.69	1.81	2.18	1.07	3.87	0.49	1.24	1.23	3.61	1.07	1.33	3.78
2005 Q3	6.84	3.65	9.52	6.28	2.90	1.81	1.13	1.44	1.21	2.31	3.62	1.77	1.90	1.04	3.80	0.47	1.20	1.22	3.40	1.10	1.28	3.84
2005 Q4	6.42	3.52	9.35	7.07	2.81	1.75	1.15	1.94	1.19	2.25	3.58	1.74	2.72	1.07	3.77	0.48	1.25	1.22	3.64	1.04	1.28	3.82
2006 Q1	6.32	3.24	9.12	7.30	2.80	1.61	1.05	2.01	1.35	2.14	3.53	1.70	2.63	1.13	3.68	0.44	1.10	1.19	3.25	0.98	1.17	3.76
2006 Q2	6.23	3.11	8.97	7.36	2.79	1.72	1.09	1.71	1.27	2.07	3.52	1.67	2.37	1.09	3.62	0.45	1.04	1.19	3.24	1.00	1.26	3.76
2006 Q3	6.00	3.64	8.92	6.23	3.07	1.75	1.10	1.41	1.31	2.17	3.59	1.65	1.99	1.11	3.60	0.45	1.01	1.20	3.04	1.00	1.26	3.79
2006 Q4	5.97	3.73	8.66	7.11	3.15	1.65	1.14	2.20	1.37	2.10	3.57	1.57	2.93	1.11	3.46	0.48	1.00	1.19	3.28	0.98	1.23	3.70
2007 Q1	5.80	3.73	8.56	7.40	3.21	1.53	1.06	2.13	1.45	2.14	3.60	1.63	2.85	1.14	3.46	0.45	1.10	1.18	3.06	0.94	1.13	3.65
2007 Q2	5.58	3.69	8.47	7.53	3.19	1.66	1.09	1.84	1.39	2.07	3.57	1.62	2.52	1.09	3.46	0.46	1.08	1.19	3.11	0.98	1.22	3.70
2007 Q3	5.49	3.68	8.20	7.17	3.43	1.68	1.08	1.37	1.44	2.07	3.58	1.61	2.10	1.07	3.46	0.44	1.05	1.19	2.95	1.05	1.23	3.59
2007 Q4	5.46	3.66	7.94	7.85	3.24	1.59	1.11	2.18	1.46	2.16	3.59	1.59	2.64	1.09	3.44	0.46	1.10	1.16	3.19	0.98	1.23	3.74
2008 Q1	5.45	3.54	7.70	8.80	3.05	1.47	1.01	2.23	1.38	2.02	3.49	1.58	2.82	1.10	3.36	0.43	1.05	1.14	2.92	0.96	1.16	3.70
2008 Q2	5.38	3.29	7.36	7.85	3.12	1.63	1.02	1.99	1.39	1.96	3.53	1.57	2.48	1.04	3.45	0.43	1.07	1.13	3.00	1.00	1.23	3.66
2008 Q3	5.13	3.23	7.30	6.93	3.19	1.65	1.02	1.57	1.31	2.08	3.53	1.57	2.05	1.06	3.49	0.42	1.02	1.13	2.88	1.11	1.28	3.61
2008 Q4	6.58	3.29	8.07	6.35	3.59	1.70	1.18	2.04	1.38	2.21	3.79	1.64	3.02	0.99	3.71	0.48	1.10	1.22	3.44	1.12	1.33	3.96

(*Continued*)

Table 5.1: (*Continued*)

	Japan	UK	USA	Brazil	Rus. F	Austr.	Belg.	Cypr	Eston.	Finl.	Franc	Germ.	Greec	Irel	Italy	Lux.	Malta	Neth.	Port.	Slova.	Slove.	Spain
2009 Q1	8.91	3.44	8.96	8.46	3.76	1.75	1.19	2.27	1.57	2.58	4.11	1.77	3.26	0.98	4.23	0.48	1.27	1.30	3.65	1.24	1.40	4.30
2009 Q2	8.11	3.50	8.93	8.52	3.70	1.99	1.25	2.19	1.53	2.63	4.16	1.82	3.22	0.94	4.28	0.49	1.17	1.31	3.61	1.23	1.47	4.19
2009 Q3	7.39	3.48	8.58	9.05	3.61	1.95	1.23	1.93	1.40	2.78	4.12	1.79	2.56	0.97	4.18	0.47	1.10	1.27	3.31	1.28	1.47	4.04
2009 Q4	7.04	3.37	8.13	10.45	3.52	1.93	1.25	2.23	1.44	2.38	4.08	1.75	3.76	0.93	4.12	0.48	1.22	1.23	3.57	1.12	1.39	4.00
2010 Q1	6.68	3.38	7.99	10.13	3.28	1.72	1.13	2.35	1.39	2.69	3.92	1.72	3.20	0.91	3.99	0.47	1.11	1.17	3.37	1.12	1.28	3.85
2010 Q2	6.39	3.24	7.80	9.07	3.40	1.78	1.13	2.15	1.25	2.41	3.79	1.63	2.72	0.86	3.81	0.47	0.98	1.13	3.24	1.08	1.31	3.63
2010 Q3	6.53	3.27	7.69	8.70	3.63	1.79	1.11	2.02	1.16	2.41	3.74	1.61	2.25	0.85	3.69	0.46	0.96	1.11	2.99	1.15	1.28	3.57
2010 Q4	6.49	3.14	7.42	9.10	3.46	1.75	1.14	1.93	1.12	2.18	3.69	1.59	2.62	0.80	3.58	0.48	1.03	1.08	3.19	0.98	1.23	3.50
2011 Q1	6.35	3.07	7.16	9.56	3.30	1.58	1.02	2.42	1.10	2.28	3.62	1.56	2.58	0.82	3.50	0.45	1.00	1.07	2.93	0.93	1.12	3.36
2011 Q2	6.70	3.06	7.04	8.59	3.24	1.72	1.06	2.07	1.06	2.43	3.60	1.56	2.28	0.84	3.48	0.46	0.94	1.07	2.80	0.96	1.19	3.29
2011 Q3	6.40	3.09	6.98	7.85	3.53	1.71	1.07	1.93	1.00	2.41	3.58	1.54	1.92	0.83	3.42	0.46	1.00	1.06	2.63	1.05	1.20	3.21
2011 Q4	6.70	3.02	7.10	7.95	3.24	1.68	1.13	1.93	1.09	2.39	3.53	1.54	2.36	0.81	3.39	0.49	0.96	1.05	2.82	0.94	1.15	3.20
2012 Q1	6.61	3.06	7.05	8.98	3.12	1.59	1.07	2.36	1.05	2.40	3.51	1.54	2.10	0.80	3.35	0.47	0.97	1.02		0.89	1.10	3.19
2012 Q2	6.56	3.14	7.00	7.79	3.32	1.73	1.07	1.93	1.06	2.45	3.53	1.50	2.01	0.81	3.30	0.49	0.90	1.01		0.90	1.13	3.12
2012 Q3	6.90	3.15	7.07	7.42	3.65	1.69	1.07	1.82	1.03	2.45	3.49	1.49	1.71	0.81	3.28	0.47	0.96	1.01		0.98	1.15	2.99
2012 Q4	7.01	3.20	7.12	7.88	3.60	1.68	1.09			2.45	3.51	1.51	2.11				1.01	1.00		0.89	1.10	2.99

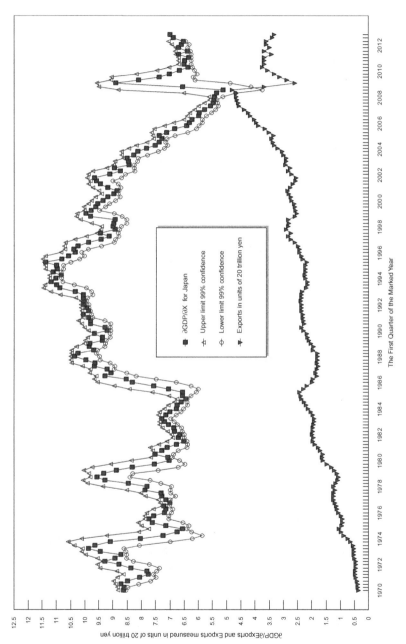

Figure 5.6:   ∂GDP/∂Exports for Japan: Seasonally Adjusted

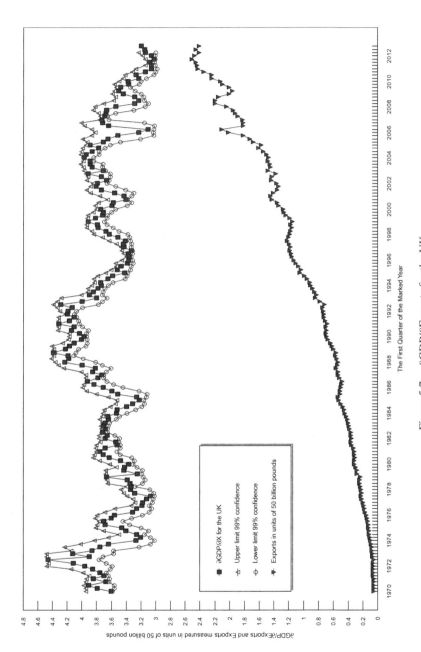

Figure 5.7: $\partial GDP/\partial$Exports for the UK

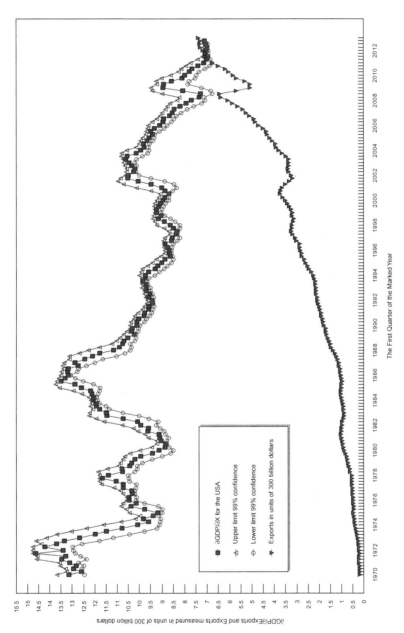

Figure 5.8: $\partial GDP/\partial$Exports for the USA

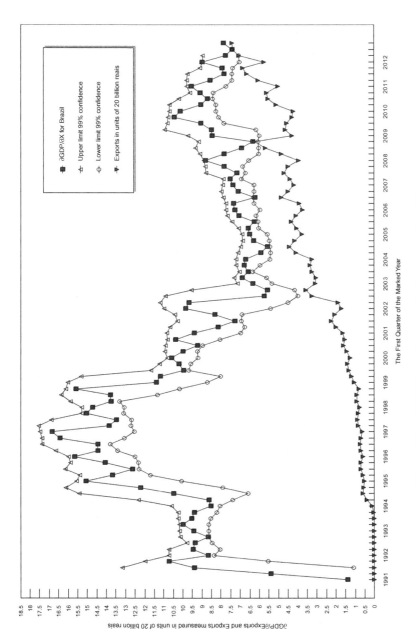

Figure 5.9: ∂GDP/∂Exports for Brazil: Not Seasonally Adjusted

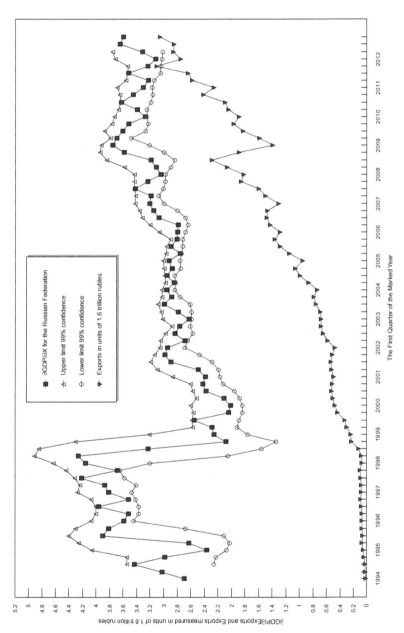

Figure 5.10: $\partial GDP/\partial Exports$ for the Russian Federation

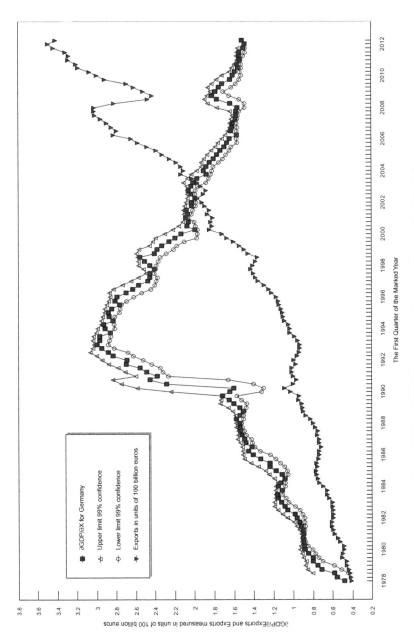

Figure 5.11: ∂GDP/∂Exports for Germany: Seasonally Adjusted

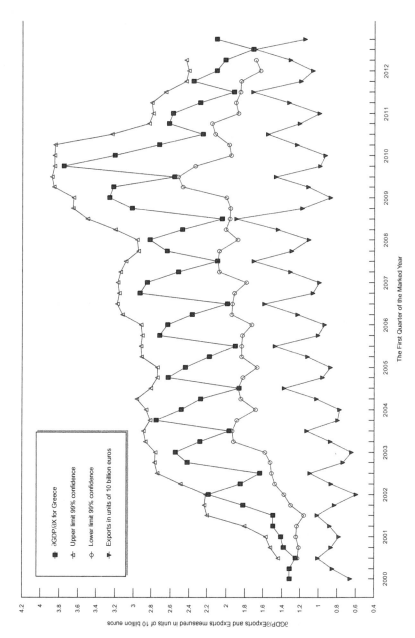

Figure 5.12: $\partial GDP/\partial Exports$ for Greece: Not Seasonally Adjusted

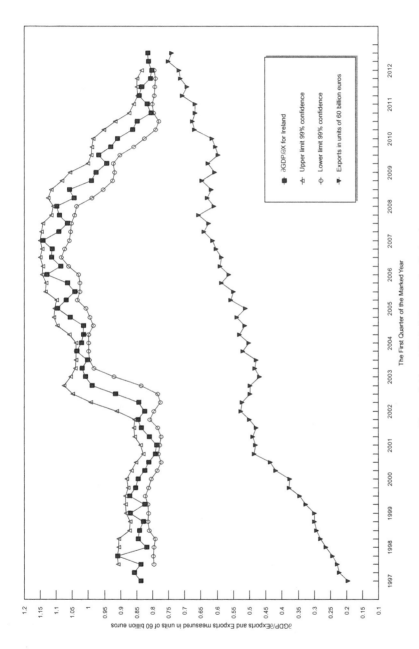

Figure 5.13: ∂GDP/∂Exports for Ireland

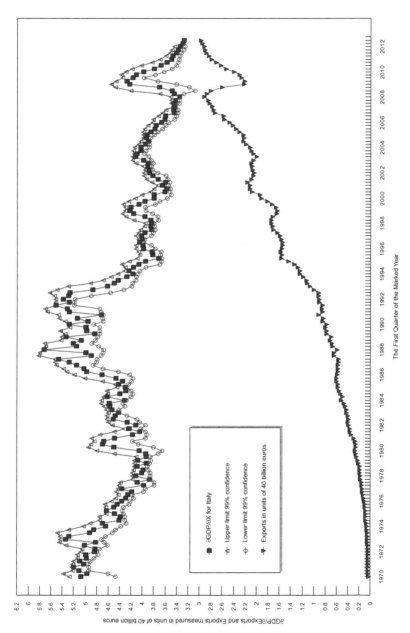

Figure 5.14: ∂GDP/∂Exports for Italy

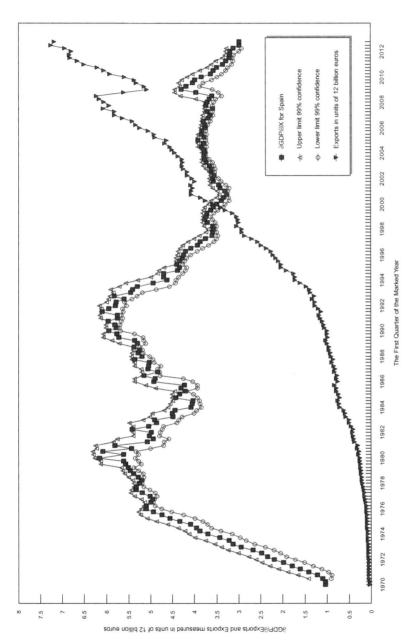

Figure 5.15: ∂GDP/∂Exports for Spain: Seasonally Adjusted

in this book between the export and government spending multipliers is that the forces that increase exports also affect imports, whereas an increase in government spending would not affect imports in the same way. Trade agreements that increase exports also would increase imports. Furthermore, many countries, like China, import many of the inputs needed to produce its exports. Therefore as their exports increase, so will their imports. When countries suppress their exchange rates or their wage rates, exports increase and imports decrease, *ceteris paribus*. However, this last effect should make the $\partial GDP/\partial Exports$ multiplier larger than the $\partial GDP/\partial G$ multiplier.

A comparison of Tables 5.1 and 4.1 reveals that $\partial GDP/\partial Exports$ was less than $\partial GDP/\partial G$ for all quarters after 1981 for the United Kingdom, the Russian Federation, Austria, Belgium, Cyprus, Estonia, Germany, Ireland, Luxembourg, Malta, the Netherlands, Portugal, Slovakia, and Slovenia. Furthermore, $\partial GDP/\partial G$ exceeded $\partial GDP/\partial Exports$ for all quarters in Finland except between the first quarters of 1991 and 1992, for all quarters in Italy except between the first quarter of 1988 and the fourth quarter of 1992, and for all quarters in Spain except between the first quarter of 1990 and the third quarter of 1993.[12] For the vast majority of the countries studied, the government spending multiplier ($\partial GDP/\partial G$) exceeded the export multiplier ($\partial GDP/\partial Exports$) for almost all quarters between the first quarter of 1981 and the fourth quarter of 2012. Therefore, government spending tends to have a more powerful effect on GDP than exports do. One possible explanation for this result is that the strategies often used to promote exports — the suppression of exchange rates and of wages — tend to reduce the marginal propensity to consume which reduces the multiplier effect.

Another common pattern in the $\partial GDP/\partial Exports$ results is that increases in exports tend to increase GDP less than decreases in exports cause GDP to fall. This is seen in Figures 5.6–5.15 and Figures A3.1–A3.12

---

[12]The exceptions to this statement are as follows: $\partial GDP/\partial Exports$ was greater than $\partial GDP/\partial G$ for the USA for all quarters between the first quarter of 1981 and the fourth quarter of 2012 and for Brazil for all quarters between the second quarter of 1991 and the fourth quarter of 2012. The Japanese, the French, and Greek results involved periods when $\partial GDP/\partial Exports$ was greater and periods in which it was less than $\partial GDP/\partial G$.

(in Appendix 3) by a symmetrical relationship between the top line and bottom line.[13] This is bad news for countries hoping to drive their economies off increased exporting. Countries do not have total control over their exports because their exports depend upon the conditions within the importing country which are beyond the control of the exporter. The fact that GDP is damaged more when exports fall than it is helped when exports increase should scare countries whose economies are dependent on exporting. A plausible reason for this phenomenon is that the strategies that promote exports — the suppression of wages and exchange rates — also hurt the domestic market. Thus, when exports fall, there is insufficient domestic market to cushion the fall creating a strong negative effect on GDP. In contrast, when exports initially increase, production for the domestic market decreases, resulting in a smaller positive effect on GDP.

Recall that Japan had the highest $\partial GDP/\partial G$ for all countries studied between 1966 and 1979 (see Figure 4.1). The explanation offered for this phenomenon was that Japan's pro-equality policies during that time period increased real income for Japan's farmers and workers and, thus, drove up Japan's marginal propensity to consume which increased the multiplier effect. In contrast, Figure 5.6 shows that Japan did not enjoy an unusually high $\partial GDP/\partial Exports$ during the 1970 to 1980 time period. This difference between the $\partial GDP/\partial G$ and $\partial GDP/\partial Exports$ results could be due to an increase in real income in Japan causing the multiplier effect of government spending to increase while simultaneously decreasing Japan's international competitiveness in selling exports.

Figure 5.6 shows that $\partial GDP/\partial Exports$ for Japan hit a peak of 11.38 in the second quarter of 1995 and then fell to 5.13 in the third quarter of 2008 for a 55% decline in effectiveness. However, in the fourth quarter of 2012, $\partial GDP/\partial Exports$ for Japan had risen again to 7.01; the net fall in $\partial GDP/\partial Exports$ between 1995 and 2012 is 38%. When Japan's quarterly exports fell by 45.9% between the third quarter of 2008 and the first quarter of 2009, Japan's $\partial GDP/\partial Exports$ multiplier increased by 73.9%.

---

[13]The exceptions to this statement are the Russian Federation (Figure 5.10), Ireland (Figure 5.13), and Luxembourg (Figure A3.7 in Appendix 3). This type of result was much more common in the $\partial GDP/\partial Export$ results than it was in the $\partial GDP/\partial$(Money Supply) and $\partial GDP/\partial G$ results.

This implies that decreases in Japan's exports cause 73.9% more damage to GDP than increases in exports cause GDP to rise.

Figure 5.7 shows that ∂GDP/∂Exports for the United Kingdom was much more stable than it was for Japan. However, even for the United Kingdom, ∂GDP/∂Exports fell from a peak of 4.39 in the fourth quarter of 1988 to 3.20 in the fourth quarter of 2012 for a 27% fall in effectiveness. Furthermore, when the UK's quarterly exports fell by 10.7% between the third quarter of 2008 and the second quarter of 2009, the UK's ∂GDP/∂Exports multiplier increased by 8.4%.

Figure 5.8 shows that ∂GDP/∂Exports for the USA hit a local peak of 13.5 in the third quarter of 1985 and then fell to 7.12 in the fourth quarter of 2012 for a 47% decline. When US quarterly exports fell 21.2% between the third quarter of 2008 and the first quarter of 2009, US ∂GDP/∂Exports increased 22.7%. This means that decreases in US exports caused US GDP to fall 22.7% more than increases in exports caused GDP to rise.

Figures 5.9 and 5.10 depict Brazil's and the Russian Federation's ∂GDP/∂Exports, respectively. The financial crisis that began in Thailand in 1997 led to currency devaluations and IMF loans to Thailand, Indonesia, South Korea, Brazil, and the Russian Federation. While Brazil was steadily devaluing its currency, the real, between the third quarter of 1994 and the fourth quarter of 1998, Brazilian exports were steadily rising but the ∂GDP/∂Exports multiplier was noticeably fluctuating. In the first quarter of 1999, Brazil began a series of devaluations that would take the Brazilian real from 1.1958 real/dollar to 3.6686 real/dollar in the fourth quarter of 2002 (i.e., during this time, the real lost 67% of its former value). This devaluation corresponded to Brazil's exports increasing at a faster rate and a 64% decline in Brazil's ∂GDP/∂Exports multiplier from 15.58 to 5.58. After the fourth quarter of 2002, Brazil's exports kept rising in spite of the Brazilian real appreciating in value. During this time period, both Brazil's exports and ∂GDP/∂Exports were on an upward trend. However, after factoring out this trend, Figure 5.9 also shows that after 2001, every time Brazil's exports increased, ∂GDP/∂Exports decreased and every time Brazil's exports decreased, ∂GDP/∂Exports rose. This means that the positive effects of increases in Brazil's exports are smaller than the negative effects of decreases in its exports. The net fall in Brazil's ∂GDP/∂Exports between the first quarter of 1997 (immediately before the Thai financial crisis) and the fourth quarter of 2012 is 53%.

Figure 5.10 shows that as the Russian Federation devalued the ruble from 6.15 rubles/dollar in the second quarter of 1998 to 28.46 rubles/dollar in the first quarter of 2000 (i.e., the ruble lost 78% of its value during this time), Russian exports increased by a factor of 5.68 but $\partial GDP/\partial Exports$ declined from 4.26 to 2.02 for a 53% decline in the multiplier effect. However, as the Russian ruble appreciated between the fourth quarter of 2002 and the second quarter of 2008, Russian exports continued to climb. Unlike most of the other countries, the Russian results do not show a pattern where increases in exports correspond to smaller multiplier effects than decreases.

For most Euro countries, $\partial GDP/\partial Exports$ had a local peak sometime in 2009 and then fell noticeably thereafter. From this peak to the fourth quarter of 2012, Austria's $\partial GDP/\partial Exports$ fell by 16%, Belgium's by 13%, Estonia's by 34%, Finland's by 12%, France's by 16%, Germany's by 17%, Greece's by 44%, Italy's by 23%, Malta's by 20%, Netherland's by 24%, Portugal's by 23%, Slovakia's by 30%, Slovenia's by 25%, and Spain's by 30%.

Furthermore, most of the above declines in the export multipliers between 2009 and 2012 were dwarfed by their net declines over longer time frames. By the fourth quarter of 2012, Austria's $\partial GDP/\partial Exports$ fell by 43% (from 1993 Q4), Belgium's by 17% (from 1995 Q4), Cyprus' by 27% (from 2003 Q1), Finland's by 46% (from 1991 Q2), France's by 26% (from 1987 Q1), Germany's by 50% (from 1993 Q3), Ireland's by 29% (from 2007 Q1), Italy's by 43% (from 1988 Q1), Malta's by 25% (from 2005 Q1), the Netherland's by 29% (from 1993 Q1), Portugal's by 36% (from 1992 Q4), and Spain's by 51% (from 1991 Q3). Therefore, even if the Euro countries can increase their exports by internal devaluations, the multiplier effects from such increases have been noticeably falling since at least the mid-1990s for the majority of these countries.

Figure 5.11 shows that between the first quarter of 1978 and the third quarter of 1993, both German exports and the multiplier effect from those exports ($\partial GDP/\partial Exports$) were on an upward trend. After the third quarter of 1993, German exports continued to increase while the multiplier effect fell noticeably. However, increases in exports above the trend were correlated with a falling multiplier effect and decreases in exports below the trend with a rising multiplier effect since 1978. The largest increase in Germany's ∂GDP/∂Exports occurred in the first quarter of 1991 during the time period in which Germany was adjusting to its reunification. Recall that Figure 4.7 showed that government spending in Germany permanently increased around the time of the reunification; in contrast, Figure 5.11 shows that German exports did not permanently increase around the time of the reunification. Figure 4.7 also showed that the effects of the German reunification on ∂GDP/∂G appear to have been short lived; however, Figure 5.11 shows that the effects of German reunification on ∂GDP/∂Exports persisted for several years.

Greece's most important export is food, which constitutes approximately 19% of Greece's total exports. Therefore, the seasonal patterns seen in Figure 5.12 for Greece's exports (bottom line) make sense: Greek exports increase in the second and third quarters and are the lowest in the first and fourth quarters. Even though Greek exports have not changed much between 2000 and 2012 (bottom line), the multiplier effect from exports (∂GDP/∂Exports) fell from a high of 3.76 to 2.11 between the fourth quarters of 2009 and 2012 for a 44% decline.

Figure 5.13 shows that between the first quarter of 1997 and the second quarter of 2002 and between the fourth quarter of 2008 and the third quarter of 2012, Ireland's ∂GDP/∂Exports did not even exceed one.[14] This implies that a one euro increase in Ireland's exports did not increase Ireland's GDP by even one euro. Figure A3.7 (in Appendix 3) shows that Luxembourg's ∂GDP/∂Exports never exceeded a value of one between 1995 and 2012. Furthermore, many of the Euro countries had surprisingly low export multipliers — the maximum ∂GDP/∂Exports for Belgium was 1.32 (1995 Q4), for Estonia was 1.57 (2009 Q1), for Ireland was 1.14 (2007 Q1), for Luxembourg was 0.53 (2002 Q4), for Malta was 1.34 (2005 Q1), for the Netherlands was 1.40 (1993 Q1), for Slovakia was 1.28 (2009 Q3), and for Slovenia was 1.47 (2009 Q3). An export promotion growth

---

[14]Figure A3.2 shows a similar result for Belgium between the first quarter of 1982 and the second quarter of 1985. Furthermore, ∂GDP/∂Exports see-sawed around the value of one for many years for Malta, the Netherlands, and Slovakia (Figures A3.8, A3.9, A3.11 in Appendix 3 respectively).

strategy is not reasonable for countries with such low $\partial GDP/\partial Exports$ multipliers.

A close comparison of Figures 4.10 and 5.14 (or of Tables 4.1 and 5.1) reveals that Italy was one of the few countries in which $\partial GDP/\partial Exports$ sometimes exceeded $\partial GDP/\partial G$; however, after the fourth quarter of 1992, $\partial GDP/\partial Exports$ always was less than $\partial GDP/\partial G$ for Italy. A similar result can be found by comparing Figures 5.15 and 4.11 for Spain — $\partial GDP/\partial Exports$ was always less than $\partial GDP/\partial G$ after the third quarter of 1993. $\partial GDP/\partial Exports$ was less than $\partial GDP/\partial G$ for all quarters after 1981 for the United Kingdom, the Russian Federation, Austria, Belgium, Cyprus, Estonia, Germany, Ireland, Luxembourg, Malta, the Netherlands, Portugal, Slovakia, and Slovenia.

This chapter's empirical results imply that an export promotion growth strategy is probably not a good idea for several reasons. First, the government spending multiplier exceeds the export multiplier for most countries in most years. Second, countries have much less control over their exports than they do over their government spending — exports depend upon the internal conditions of the importing country which the exporting country cannot control. Third, the multiplier effect for decreases in exports noticeably exceeds the multiplier effect for increases in exports for the vast majority of the countries studied. This implies that when exports fall, perhaps due to recessions in the importing countries, the exporter's GDP falls more than its GDP rises when exports increase. In other words, the damage done by a fall in exports, which is often beyond the control of the exporter, is greater than the good done by exports increasing. Finally, the multiplier effect from increases in exports has been noticeably falling over time.

The estimates in this chapter demonstrate what happens to GDP if a country successfully increases its exports; it does not deal with whether or not a country can successfully increase its exports. In a world where many countries are attempting "internal devaluations," it is increasingly difficult to increase exports. Chapter 6 will examine the effectiveness of one of the primary ways that countries attempt to increase their exports — the suppression of their exchange rates.

Chapter 6

CURRENCY POLICY

Ben Bernanke (2005) discussed how a "global saving glut" was the core cause of the US trade deficit. However, Bernanke did not expand his analysis to the core cause of the world's problem, as I am doing in this book. Nor was Bernanke the first one to identify global savings gluts. Mummery and Hobson (1889, see also Leightner, 2000) developed a theory of underconsumption, which the classical school of economics ridiculed by saying, "In opposition to these palpable absurdities it was triumphantly established by political economists that consumption never needs encouragement" (Mill, 1967, p. 263). The Great Depression and Great Recession have proved that the classical school's "dismissal by ridicule" is inappropriate.

Most international finance textbooks contain a graph of the supply and demand for a currency; however, these graphs do not explicitly show exports and imports. Building upon the standard graph, I develop a slightly more complex graph which is much more useful in analyzing trade deficits, trade surpluses, and current government policies. I use this graph to explain how some countries try to drive economic growth by accumulating foreign reserves in order to increase exports. I provide estimates that show that the effectiveness of this policy, if actually used or if it had been used, was either declining or already totally ineffective by the mid-1980s in Japan, the USA, the UK, Austria, Belgium, Estonia, Finland, France, Germany, Italy, the Netherlands, Portugal, and Spain. Furthermore, I find that it was not effective for Brazil or Russia during the time period for which I have data. In none of the countries that I examine do I find evidence that this strategy has worked since the mid-1980s.

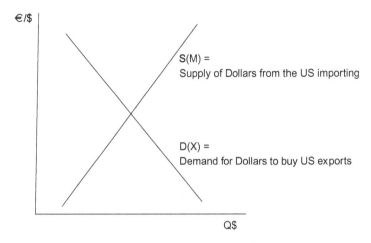

Figure 6.1:   S(M) and D(X)[1]

Consider Figure 6.1 which depicts the supply and demand for dollars from the US importing and exporting. Note that, like typical supply and demand diagrams, this diagram has quantity on the x-axis and price on the y-axis. Also notice that the price of a US dollar is the exchange rate calculated by placing the other currency on top. In Figure 6.1, this price is expressed as the number of euros it takes to purchase a dollar. Similarly, it could have been expressed as the number of British pounds it takes to purchase a dollar or the number of Japanese yen it takes to purchase a dollar, etc.

If the only demands and supplies for a currency are from exports and imports, then the equilibrium exchange rate would be where S(M) crosses D(X) and the dollar amount of exports would equal the dollar amount of imports. In this case, there would never be a trade deficit (M > X) or a trade surplus (X > M) if the exchange rate is allowed to float freely.

Clearly, there are trade deficits and trade surpluses, and they can be traced to the many demands and supplies for a currency other than for

---

[1]It is important to not confuse this diagram with its mirror-image twin. This diagram looks at the supply and demand for the US dollar *from the perspective of the USA*. This diagram's mirror-image twin looks at the supply and demand for dollars *from the perspective of Europe* which results a supply of dollars based on the US purchases of European exports and the demand for dollars based on Europe's imports of goods from the USA.

purchasing exports or selling imports on the international market. The demand for the US dollar for non-trade purposes (Dnt) would include (but is not limited to) foreign governments and citizens purchasing US dollars in order to hold them as foreign reserves or for speculative purposes, US expatriates living abroad exchanging foreign currencies for US dollars in order to remit part of their pay back to the USA, and foreign citizens exchanging foreign currencies for US dollars in order to travel to the USA or in order to purchase US stocks, bonds, and/or property.[2] The supply of US dollars from non-trade activities (Snt) would include (but is not limited to) the US government and US citizens paying dollars in order to purchase foreign currencies to be held as foreign reserves or for speculative purposes, US government foreign aid, foreign expatriates living in the USA exchanging dollars for their home currencies in order to remit part of their pay home, and US citizens exchanging dollars for foreign currencies in order to travel abroad or in order to purchase foreign stocks, bonds, and/or property.

To Figure 6.1, we could add two more lines — one of which shows the total supply of the US dollar as S(M) + Snt and another one that shows the total demand for the US dollar as D(X) + Dnt; however that produces a four line graph which can be confusing. Alternatively, we could draw just two lines — one for demand total and another for supply total, but such a graph does not show what happens to exports and imports, and thus does not show what happens to Gross Domestic Product. For examples of the above two standard approaches, see Appleyard and Field (2014, pp. 487–488).

In contrast to the above standard approaches, I define "net" non-trade demand for the US dollar as Dnt − Snt. I then define "total" demand for the US dollar as the demand for the US dollar to purchase US exports, D(X), plus net non-trade demand for the US dollar, Dnt − Snt. This makes it possible for me to show everything necessary with only three lines as shown in Figure 6.2.[3]

---

[2]Including property purchased by foreigners for foreign direct investment.

[3]An equally legitimate approach would have been to define "net" non-trade supply for the US dollar as Snt − Dnt and then define "supply total" as the supply of dollars from importing, S(M), plus net non-trade supply of dollars. Also notice that D(X) + Dnt − Snt will always be flatter than D(X) because the sum of two individual demand curves is always flatter than the original demand curves. Finally, realize that it is possible that the demand total line will cross the D(X) line. However, to avoid confusion, I will not draw it that way.

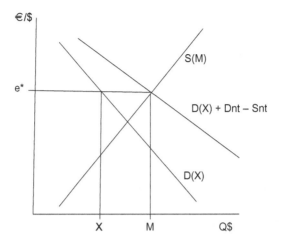

Figure 6.2:   S(M), D(X), and D(total)

Figure 6.2 shows the US's trade deficit (M > X) on the x-axis. The cause of the US trade deficit is the non-trade demand for the US dollar exceeds the non-trade supply of US dollars, Dnt > Snt. If Dnt = Snt, then D(X) + Dnt − Snt = D(X) and Figure 6.2 would look identical to Figure 6.1 in which there would never be trade deficits or trade surpluses (assuming a flexible exchange rate). In other words, when the US imports more than it exports (M > X), the money to finance that trade deficit must come from somewhere and it comes from Dnt − Snt. When other countries ship their goods and services to the USA and then just accumulate the dollars they are paid (i.e., do not use the dollars to purchase other things), then Dnt increases while Snt stays the same and the US trade deficit widens.[4]

The accumulation of foreign reserves is a type of savings. Thus, Ben Bernanke's claim that a global glut of savings is the cause of the US trade deficit makes sense. When other nations accumulate US dollars Dnt increases, shifting out the demand total for the US dollar making the

---

[4]Of course, the other components of Dnt and Snt also help fund the US's trade deficit. For example, when foreigners demand more dollars (and thus pay more of their currencies) to travel to the US or to purchase US stocks, bonds, and property than US citizens supply dollars to travel abroad and purchase foreign stocks, bonds and property, then the "extra" foreign currency (Dnt − Snt) can be used to purchase goods and services from those foreign countries.

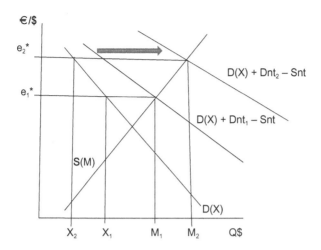

Figure 6.3:   An Increase in the Global Glut of Savings

US trade deficit bigger (see Figure 6.3). Since the US dollar is the dominant currency in the world, much of the world's accumulation of foreign reserves is via the accumulation of US dollars.

Recall from Chapter 1 that world holdings of foreign reserves increased relatively steadily from 5.55 trillion in 1976 to 37.87 trillion in 2001. In 2001, the world dramatically increased its accumulation of foreign reserves. By 2011, foreign reserves were 195.41 trillion, although they fell in 2012 to 184.92 trillion dollars. In the 35 years between 1976 and 2011, world holdings of foreign reserves grew 34-fold.

Figure 6.3 shows that as the world accumulates more and more US dollars, the US dollar exchange rate increases and the US trade deficit widens. Now, consider the case of China which began a massive accumulation of US dollars in 2001 and now has the world's largest holding of foreign reserves (see Figure 1.2). Figure 6.4 shows the international supply and demand for China's currency, the Renminbi (RMB).

Note that Demand total, $D(X) + Dnt - Snt$, is beneath $D(X)$ in Figure 6.4. This is because $Snt > Dnt$ for China which implies that China would have a trade surplus even if it had a floating exchange rate.[5] $Q_d - Q_s$

---

[5]According to http://www.xe.com/news/home.htm [accessed on 30 September 2013], China's exports minus imports (Goods + Services) were US$231.9 billion and China's

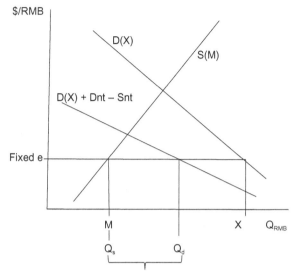

Figure 6.4:   China's Currency — the Renminbi (RMB)

is the shortage of renminbi. If China did nothing about this shortage, then the exchange rate would automatically increase, eliminating the shortage. However, if China wants to maintain the fixed exchange rate, then all China has to do is print more renminbi and use it to purchase US dollars (or other foreign currencies). When China does this its holdings of foreign currencies, as expressed in renminbi, increases by $Q_d - Q_s$. This is how China has accumulated 3.66 trillion dollars of foreign reserves by September 2013.

There are several possible reasons for countries like China to maintain fixed exchange rates below equilibrium. These reasons include (1) wanting to accumulate foreign reserves that can be used in the case of an emergency like an earthquake, tsunami, nuclear power plant melt down, typhoon, or speculative attack on the currency, (2) wanting to attract more foreign investment by reducing exchange rate risk, and (3) wanting to drive the economy

increase in foreign reserves ($Q_s - Q_d$) was US$ 96.6 billion in 2012. These numbers imply that Dnt − Snt was US$−135.3 billion in 2012 (231.9 − 96.6; however, this figure includes at least US$79.8 billion of errors and omissions). Because exports minus imports is bigger than the accumulation of foreign reserves, D(X) must be above D(X) + Dnt − Snt (i.e., Dnt − Snt is negative). However, according to the same website, Dnt − Snt must have been positive for the first quarter of 2013.

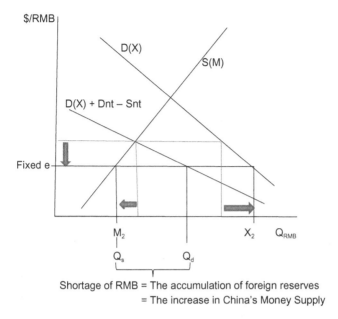

Figure 6.5: Using a Fixed Exchange Rate to Increase China's Exports

off increased exports. Figure 6.5 illustrates the third reason — by fixing the exchange rate lower, exports increase and imports decrease both of which would cause aggregate demand to increase and consequentially growth to occur.[6] However, notice that foreign reserves must be accumulated forever in order to perpetuate export-driven growth in this manner. If China ever stopped accumulating foreign reserves (assuming none of the lines shift in Figure 6.5), then the exchange rate would rise and exports would fall. Furthermore, notice that when China prints more renminbi and exchanges them for dollars, China's money supply increases by $Q_d - Q_s$.

---

[6]This diagram shows China accumulating foreign reserves in order to increase exports. It is possible to argue the opposite direction of causation — exports increased (due to some force other than the exchange rate changing) which shifted the D(X) and D(X) + Dnt − Snt lines up and China had to accumulate foreign reserves in order to keep its exchange rate fixed. However, even under this "alternative direction of causation view," once the initial shift in D(X) and D(X) + Dnt − Snt occurred, foreign reserves were accumulated in order to keep the exchange rate lower than it would naturally be, so that exports would be greater than they would be at an equilibrium exchange rate.

Thus, when a country like China tries to implement export-driven growth by lowering its exchange rate and accumulating foreign currency, it loses control over its money supply. China can attempt to regain control of its money supply by restricting the flow of money (capital) into and out of China and by forcing its banks to purchase government bonds. By forcing banks to buy government bonds, the Chinese government can withdraw from the market the extra currency they printed to keep the exchange rate fixed below equilibrium. This attempt to regain control of the money supply via capital controls is called "sterilization," and its effectiveness is controversial. Sterilization is more difficult the larger the economy and the more connected it is to the rest of the world.

The above analysis forms the core of what international economists call the "tri-lemma." According to the tri-lemma, countries would like to have fixed exchange rates, free capital, and control over the money supply. In reality, a country can only have two of the three. Hong Kong maintains a fixed exchange rate and free capital but gives up control over its money supply. The USA keeps free capital and control of its money supply but gives up the fixed exchange rate. China maintains a fixed exchange rate and control over its money supply but gives up free capital.

One set of economic models proposes that currency crises occur when nations are forced to (or attempt to) shift from one part of the tri-lemma to another (Flood and Garber, 1984; Krugman, 1979). For example, as depicted in Figure 6.6, Thailand between November 1984 and December 1996 had an exchange rate fixed below equilibrium which resulted in Thailand's 4 billion dollars of foreign reserves of November 1984 expanding to 36 billion dollars of foreign reserves as of December 1997.

As discussed in Chapter 2, Thailand had some problems in late 1996 to early 1997 that gave the currency speculator, George Soros, the ammunition he needed to lead a speculative attack against Thailand's currency, the baht. These events included the Bangkok Bank of Commerce case which involved a political scandal, a major bank official stealing two suitcases full of money from the bank and fleeing to Canada, and a failed cover-up by Thailand's central bank. In the spring of 1997, Somprasong Land Company defaulted on a 3 million dollar interest payment on some European debentures. On March 3, 1997, the Thai government suspended trade of all financial company stocks and bonds on the stock exchange of Thailand,

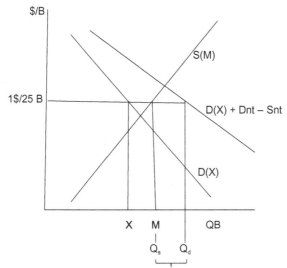

Figure 6.6:   The Thai Baht, November 1984–December 1996

increased reserve requirements for all financial institutions, and shut down 10 weak finance and securities companies.

In response to these events, George Soros took out forward contracts to exchange Thai baht for US dollars at a rate of 26 baht per dollar in January 1998.[7] Since Thailand had successfully maintained a fixed exchange rate at 25 baht per dollar for 13 years, financial institutions were quite willing to give forward contracts at the rate George Soros requested. Forward contracts, like the ones Soros took out, are normal and legal business transactions that are taken out every business day by companies and people who want "insurance" against the risk of exchange rate fluctuations. As soon as Soros had his forward contracts, he advertised Thailand's problems and advised everyone to sell baht before it fell in value. As a result, Thailand's Dnt fell and Snt rose dramatically, causing Thailand's Dtotal line to plummet as depicted in Figure 6.7.

---

[7]The actual amounts involved in this speculative attack are not in the public record. Thus, the numbers in this example are fictional; however, they illustrate how someone can perform a speculative attack.

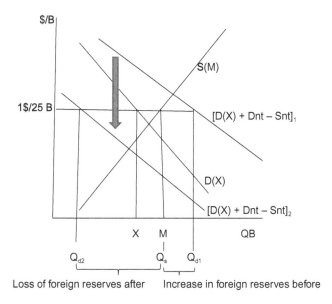

Figure 6.7:   Results of Soros' Speculative Attack against the Thai Baht

During Soros' speculative attack, Thailand's fixed exchange rate of 25 baht per dollar was above the equilibrium exchange rate producing a surplus of Thai baht. If the Thai government did not buy up this surplus baht, then the value of the baht would automatically fall. Not wanting that to happen, Thailand bought up the surplus baht paying for it with its foreign reserves (US dollars). Thus, Thailand's holdings of foreign reserves (as measured in baht) fell by $Q_s - Q_{d2}$ in Figure 6.7. Between January 1997 and July 2, 1997, Thailand spent at least US$32 billion defending the 25 baht per US dollar fixed exchange rate. At the end of June 1997, Thailand had only 4 billion dollars of foreign reserves left — not enough to even defend the baht for an additional month. Thus, on July 2, 1997, Thailand stopped buying up the surplus baht and allowed the baht's value to fall.

The baht immediately fell by 40% and then kept falling until it hit 54 baht per dollar in January 1998. In January 1998, George Soros took 1 billion dollars to the spot exchange market and bought 54 billion baht with it. He then used his forward contracts to exchange the 54 billion baht for 2 billion dollars. Thus, Soros was able to double his money by causing the collapse of Thailand's fixed exchange rate (Leightner, 1999, 2007b). Prior to

1997, most experts agreed that Thailand had sufficient foreign reserves for any emergency. In the wake of Thailand's currency crisis, many countries have dramatically increased their holdings of foreign reserves because they are now unsure of what amount of foreign reserves is sufficient to handle a possible speculative attack.

Even China has been concerned about possible speculative attacks. In 2009, one of the leaders of China's Institute for Reform and Development (CIRD) told the author of this book that George Soros had been denied a visa to visit China. Soros then contacted CIRD and asked for their help with getting a visa. CIRD contacted the government of China and asked why Soros had been denied a visa. CIRD was told that Soros was a known currency speculator and, thus, was an undesirable person — "China does not want him in China." CIRD then told the Chinese government that if they allow Soros into China, CIRD would ask him to never have a speculative attack against the Chinese renminbi and would ask him how a country could best defend itself against a speculative attack. The Chinese government said that if CIRD really thought they could get such information from Soros, they would give him the visa. When Soros came to China, CIRD's leadership could not get a commitment from Soros to never attack the renminbi; however, for approximately two hours, Soros did explain to CIRD's leadership how a country can best defend against a speculative attack.

China's foreign reserves were 172 billion in 2000 but grew to 3,663 billion dollars by September 2013 for a 20.3-fold increase in 13 years. World holdings of foreign reserves increased from 37.87 trillion in 2001 to 195.41 trillion in 2011 for a 4-fold increase in 10 years. Although I do not know the exact percentage, it is safe to assume that at least half of total world foreign reserves are held in US dollars since the US dollar is the world's dominant reserve currency.

The USA has gained tremendously by having the world's reserve currency. The world accumulated at least 79 trillion [(195.41 trillion − 37.87 trillion)/2] US dollars between 2001 and 2011. This means that the USA has received 79 trillion dollars of goods and services in exchange for printed paper. If this printed paper is never traded in, then the USA has gotten 79 trillion dollars of goods and services for just the cost of printing the dollar bills. Remember, countries that try to drive their economies by accumulating foreign reserves in order to drive down their exchange rates and increase their exports cannot stop accumulating dollars because doing so would increase their exchange rates and decrease exports. Such an export-driven growth strategy requires the perpetual accumulation of more and more foreign reserves to the perpetual benefit of the country issuing the reserve currency. The US manufacturers can legitimately argue that such an arrangement reduces the amount of goods and services the USA produces and, thus, US employment; however, would we rather get goods and services by the sweat of our brows or by printing more currency?

The benefits to the USA from its issuing the world's dominant reserve currency go significantly beyond just getting goods and services in exchange for printed paper as Lindsey (2006), using China as an example, explains.

> The Chinese clearly undervalue their exchange rate. This means American consumers are able to buy goods at an artificially low price, making them winners. In order to maintain this arrangement, the People's Bank of China must buy excess dollars, and has accumulated nearly $1 trillion of reserves [this is now over $3.66 trillion]. Since it has no domestic use for them, it turns around and lends them back to America in our Treasury, corporate and housing loan markets. This means that both Treasury borrowing costs and mortgage interest rates are lower than they otherwise would be. American homeowners and taxpayers are winners as a result.

By other countries accumulating US dollars in their foreign reserves, US consumers get lower prices, US tax payers pay lower taxes, and US home buyers pay lower mortgage interest rates. In return, China (and other accumulating countries) gain stable exchange rates that can encourage more foreign investment, foreign reserves that can be used to stave off a speculative attack, and an economy where the rich owners of export businesses (who often have family connections with the politicians) can get richer and richer at the expense of domestic consumers (remember Chapter 5). The big losers in this system are the US producers and the consumers in the foreign-reserve-accumulating countries.

Many countries were willing to play this game until the USA and European crisis began in 2008. When the USA and Europe went into crisis, their purchases of foreign exports dropped noticeably. Countries like China were significantly hurt when their companies had produced goods that the USA and Europe no longer wanted to purchase. In the wake of the 2008 crisis, China and Russia have been especially vocal about moving the international financial system away from a dominant US dollar (Batson, 2009).

Furthermore, after the crisis that began in 2008, China announced that it will shift its economy from an export-driven one to a domestic consumption-driven one (see Chapter 7). If China were to successfully switch to a domestic consumption-driven growth model, then it would no longer need the 3.66 trillion dollars of foreign reserves it has accumulated by September of 2013 nor would it need to maintain a fixed exchange rate below equilibrium. China could exchange its dollar, euro, and yen foreign reserves for Chinese renminbi on the international market, driving up the value of the renminbi and causing the value of the US dollar, the European euro, and the Japanese yen to plummet. If China did this, the world might switch from using the US dollar as the dominant reserve currency to using the renminbi. China could then enjoy the benefits of having the world's dominant reserve currency (other countries would then ship their goods and services to China in exchange for accumulating Chinese renminbi). At an economic conference on Hainan Island October 31, 2009, the author of this book heard three different Chinese scholars in three different papers call for "the Chinese renminbi to move from the periphery to the center where it belongs within the next 10 years."

This desire to replace the US dollar as the world's reserve currency is not unique to China. Europe wanted the euro to replace the dollar when it was established in 1999. In the early 1990s, Japan argued that Asian debtor countries should hold foreign reserves in the currency that they most owed — which was the Japanese yen for most of them. However, for the Chinese renminbi to become a dominant reserve currency, China will have to free up its capital market and abandon its fixed exchange rate. It is significant that China has been making almost continuous small incremental moves to free up its capital market and loosen its fixed exchange rate since 2008. These moves include China removing its minimum corporate lending interest rate in July 2013 and doubling the ban that the renminbi trades in April 2012 (China doubled this ban again in March of 2014). Leightner (2010d) used Reiterative Truncated Projected Least Squares (RTPLS) to estimate that if China sold 10% of its foreign reserves, the value of the US dollar would fall by 4.5%. Since such a sale would hurt the value of the remainder of China's US dollar reserves, China either has the incentive to support the value of the US dollar or to try and sell all of its dollar reserves simultaneously.

In essence, when countries have shipped their goods and services to the USA in exchange for printed US dollars, they have exchanged current goods and services for a claim on future US production (they are saving). However, an export-driven growth model through the accumulation of foreign reserves requires that those foreign reserves never be cashed in for US goods and services. In this situation, the USA is like the person who gets loan after loan from a bank that never asks to be repaid. However, if China can establish a domestic consumption-driven growth model, it would no longer need to keep giving loans to the USA, and it could call in its existing loans. Since WWII, the USA has gained tremendously from having the world's dominant reserve currency, but now the USA is in a very vulnerable position because China holds enough US dollar reserves (approximately 2 trillion of its 3.66 trillion total) to cause the value of the US dollar to plummet and to spook the rest of the world into dumping its holdings of US dollars.

The likelihood of such a scenario increases if the return to accumulating additional foreign reserves is less than its cost (Xin and Fion, 2013). I estimate the change in exports for a one unit change in foreign reserves (∂exports/∂reserves, see Table 6.1) and the change in exports minus imports for a one unit change in foreign reserves (∂(exports $-$ imports)/∂reserves, see Table 6.2) for Japan, the UK, the USA, Brazil, Russia, and for as many of the euro using countries as possible. Unfortunately, quarterly data on exports and imports is not available for China. The only quarterly data on foreign reserves I could find are from the OECD and are measured in Standard Drawing Rights (SDRs) which is a restricted currency created by the International Monetary Fund (IMF). Exports and imports are measured in the national currencies of Japan, the UK, the USA, Brazil, and Russia and are measured in euros for the euro using countries. The exchange rate between national currencies and SDRs was calculated from the IMF website (see the six right-hand side columns of Tables 6.1 and 6.2). Unfortunately, this website only provides SDR exchange rates for 1995 through the present. If the national currency per SDR exchange rate exceeds the value for ∂(exports as measured in the national currency)/∂(reserves as measured in SDRs), then accumulating a dollar of foreign reserves

Table 6.1: ∂Exports/∂(Foreign Reserves)

	Japan	UK	USA	Brazil	Rus. F	Austr.	Belg.	Eston.	Finl.	Franc.	Germ.	Italy	Neth.	Port.	Spain	Euro	Yen	Pound	Dollar	Reais	Ruble
1981 Q1	1470	1.08	24.33			1.60	1.45		1.51	1.12	2.51	0.92	1.74	0.20	0.43						
1981 Q2	1429	1.27	24.11			1.66	1.48		1.73	1.29	2.48	1.00	2.11	0.24	0.50						
1981 Q3	1480	1.49	23.68			1.85	1.48		1.71	1.55	2.62	0.97	2.33	0.21	0.49						
1981 Q4	1455	1.55	23.74			1.44	1.79		2.02	1.54	2.89	0.94	2.18	0.27	0.53						
1982 Q1	1490	1.55	22.73			1.54	2.01		1.78	1.72	2.96	1.24	2.14	0.32	0.61						
1982 Q2	1523	1.73	21.96			1.45	2.73		2.26	2.11	2.87	1.27	2.24	0.31	0.61						
1982 Q3	1586	1.66	20.92			1.67	2.13		2.12	2.41	2.87	1.14	2.14	0.34	0.67						
1982 Q4	1647	1.87	18.92			1.40	2.80		2.07	2.11	2.69	1.32	1.92	0.44	0.84						
1983 Q1	1538	2.02	18.63			1.45	2.25		2.45	2.15	2.38	1.34	1.74	0.40	1.02						
1983 Q2	1472	2.00	18.79			1.55	2.12		2.80	2.05	2.67	1.07	1.83	0.56	1.21						
1983 Q3	1515	2.05	19.31			1.76	2.09		3.44	1.89	2.69	1.05	1.95	0.56	1.06						
1983 Q4	1574	2.12	19.05			1.64	2.62		2.69	2.00	2.76	1.06	2.02	0.75	1.02						
1984 Q1	1645	2.20	18.77			1.67	2.99		1.98	2.05	2.65	1.21	2.05	0.92	1.03						
1984 Q2	1639	2.53	18.88			1.70	3.15		1.19	1.98	2.68	1.10	2.18	0.89	0.91						
1984 Q3	1630	2.72	18.70			2.07	2.42		1.22	1.90	2.89	1.12	2.23	0.72	0.76						
1984 Q4	1610	2.73	18.18			1.83	2.96		1.32	1.99	2.98	1.10	2.34	0.95	0.69						
1985 Q1	1626	2.87	17.93			2.31	3.09		1.02	2.00	3.27	1.27	2.62	0.81	0.74						
1985 Q2	1617	2.73	17.64			2.25	2.69		1.09	1.87	3.14	1.18	2.53	0.81	0.85						
1985 Q3	1607	2.59	17.10			2.17	2.63		1.04	1.97	3.11	1.30	2.33	0.64	0.79						
1985 Q4	1627	2.30	15.74			1.91	3.05		1.01	1.80	3.06	1.70	2.30	0.70	0.96						
1986 Q1	1468	2.17	15.75			1.91	2.93		1.13	1.81	3.11	1.75	2.15	0.75	0.83						
1986 Q2	1236	2.08	15.63			1.79	2.59		1.38	1.44	3.22	1.39	2.15	0.85	0.90						
1986 Q3	966	1.72	15.65			1.96	2.66		2.31	1.52	3.02	1.48	1.96	0.64	0.73						
1986 Q4	988	1.85	15.98			1.62	2.92		2.61	1.60	2.89	1.43	1.95	0.83	0.82						
1987 Q1	743	1.73	16.54			1.62	2.37		1.22	1.64	2.58	1.21	1.94	0.88	0.80						
1987 Q2	606	1.29	18.30			1.62	2.28		0.98	1.64	2.54	1.32	1.77	0.85	0.65						
1987 Q3	599	1.33	18.81			1.79	2.05		0.89	1.76	2.49	1.55	1.77	0.58	0.50						
1987 Q4	584	1.02	20.58			1.62	2.21		0.82	1.86	2.28	1.26	1.78	0.63	0.49						

(Continued)

Table 6.1: (*Continued*)

	Japan	UK	USA	Brazil	Rus. F	Austr.	Belg.	Eston.	Finl.	Franc.	Germ.	Italy	Neth.	Port.	Spain	Euro	Yen	Pound	Dollar	Reais	Ruble
1988 Q1	542	0.98	22.25			1.56	2.21		0.72	1.94	2.39	1.15	1.77	0.53	0.47						
1988 Q2	502	0.98	23.09			1.60	2.47		0.67	1.99	2.58	1.33	1.86	0.57	0.43						
1988 Q3	518	0.96	20.02			1.74	2.42		0.81	2.15	2.87	1.24	1.95	0.58	0.44						
1988 Q4	503	0.93	21.01			1.75	2.54		0.97	2.51	3.00	1.15	1.92	0.57	0.42						
1989 Q1	494	1.01	20.03			1.94	2.42		0.85	2.56	3.17	1.00	1.91	0.56	0.43						
1989 Q2	554	1.10	16.52			1.89	2.71		0.81	2.56	3.08	1.02	1.98	0.51	0.39						
1989 Q3	606	1.17	14.99			1.97	2.41		0.86	2.56	3.07	0.89	1.97	0.39	0.36						
1989 Q4	636	1.35	14.17			1.62	2.63		1.25	2.79	3.02	0.94	2.00	0.38	0.38						
1990 Q1	753	1.40	14.13			1.87	2.45		0.70	2.71	3.02	0.83	1.98	0.36	0.38						
1990 Q2	785	1.44	14.31			1.77	2.42		0.75	2.45	2.97	0.74	1.98	0.33	0.39						
1990 Q3	773	1.43	14.59			1.85	2.40		0.62	2.31	3.25	0.72	2.10	0.31	0.37						
1990 Q4	774	1.47	14.50			1.83	2.61		0.69	2.11	3.28	0.86	2.16	0.32	0.37						
1991 Q1	798	1.30	14.87			1.79	2.69		0.62	2.04	3.35	0.79	2.23	0.33	0.36						
1991 Q2	800	1.30	15.46			1.81	2.86		0.66	2.29	3.28	0.87	2.27	0.29	0.33						
1991 Q3	861	1.31	16.21			1.77	2.51		0.91	2.29	3.30	0.85	2.26	0.24	0.30						
1991 Q4	881	1.31	16.46			1.77	2.67		0.84	2.60	3.37	1.09	2.24	0.24	0.32						
1992 Q1	848	1.33	16.71	0.32		1.71	2.63		0.86	2.44	3.32	1.19	2.29	0.22	0.32						
1992 Q2	902	1.33	16.79	0.25		1.57	2.33		0.97	2.50	3.24	1.52	2.24	0.19	0.30						
1992 Q3	902	1.39	17.14	0.25		1.38	2.41		1.22	2.87	1.86	1.89	1.86	0.22	0.42						
1992 Q4	847	1.55	17.81	0.22		1.39	2.52		1.43	2.79	2.22	1.94	1.73	0.24	0.46						
1993 Q1	834	1.68	17.36	0.24		1.40	2.23	0.39	1.80	2.64	2.84	2.01	1.47	0.27	0.51						
1993 Q2	642	1.64	17.69	0.22		1.32	2.37	0.58	1.35	2.42	2.92	2.18	1.63	0.29	0.56						
1993 Q3	580	1.66	17.36	0.22		1.46	2.55	0.65	1.93	2.69	2.39	2.07	1.32	0.30	0.60						
1993 Q4	558	1.72	17.82	0.20	-16.20	1.19	2.90	0.73	1.69	3.34	2.57	2.29	1.40	0.32	0.64						
1994 Q1	561	1.74	17.63	0.22	-21.94	1.22	2.53	0.70	1.20	3.25	2.61	2.08	1.42	0.35	0.70						
1994 Q2	533	1.73	18.71	0.39	-11.46	1.07	2.60	0.90	1.07	3.29	2.64	2.06	1.42	0.41	0.71						
1994 Q3	507	1.79	19.30	0.55	-18.51	1.14	2.45	0.86	0.99	3.45	2.64	2.20	1.42	0.40	0.73						
1994 Q4	485	1.83	20.17	0.57	-11.95	1.21	2.94	0.99	1.07	3.45	2.90	2.34	1.47	0.41	0.80						

(*Continued*)

Table 6.1: *(Continued)*

	Japan	UK	USA	Brazil	Rus. F	Austr.	Belg.	Eston.	Finl.	Franc.	Germ.	Italy	Neth.	Port.	Spain	Euro	Yen	Pound	Dollar	Reais	Ruble
1995 Q1	454	1.99	18.75	0.68	−4.75	1.21	2.97	0.91	1.08	3.63	3.00	3.00	1.62	0.54	1.08		144	0.94	1.49	1.28	
1995 Q2	406	1.94	18.45	0.79	1.71	0.98	2.57	1.01	1.24	3.67	3.00	2.49	1.71	0.53	1.13		132	0.98	1.57	1.41	
1995 Q3	363	1.95	18.96	0.57	−0.08	1.02	2.39	1.04	1.12	3.49	2.88	2.75	1.65	0.55	1.10		142	0.96	1.52	1.42	
1995 Q4	362	2.02	19.16	0.52	1.16	1.14	2.49	1.09	1.30	3.51	2.82	2.59	1.73	0.54	1.10		151	0.96	1.49	1.44	
1996 Q1	331	2.17	19.39	0.42	0.67	1.07	2.30	0.95	1.40	3.53	2.80	2.48	1.88	0.50	0.92		155	0.96	1.47	1.43	
1996 Q2	318	2.20	19.55	0.44	2.28	1.01	2.40	1.08	2.00	3.51	2.78	1.80	1.89	0.55	0.78		156	0.95	1.45	1.44	
1996 Q3	315	2.29	21.51	0.47	3.86	1.03	2.16	1.17	1.71	3.53	2.81	1.81	2.13	0.53	0.77		158	0.93	1.45	1.47	
1996 Q4	327	2.20	22.44	0.44	6.32	1.02	2.49	1.19	1.94	3.65	2.95	1.93	2.28	0.52	0.74		163	0.88	1.44	1.49	
1997 Q1	332	2.38	24.56	0.39	2.95	1.14	2.48	1.17	1.07	3.47	2.99	1.99	2.20	0.53	0.70		169	0.85	1.39	1.46	
1997 Q2	339	2.42	25.09	0.50	2.15	1.14	2.69	1.54	1.33	3.60	3.05	2.11	2.41	0.59	0.70		165	0.85	1.38	1.47	
1997 Q3	318	2.43	25.38	0.48	3.23	1.19	2.60	1.48	1.28	3.64	3.24	1.69	2.57	0.64	0.69		161	0.84	1.36	1.48	
1997 Q4	341	2.57	24.04	0.54	6.21	1.29	2.78	1.49	1.72	3.51	3.23	1.66	2.71	0.60	0.69		171	0.82	1.37	1.51	8.14
1998 Q1	323	2.69	23.95	0.38	2.35	1.32	2.35	1.51	2.02	3.34	3.21	1.73	2.82	0.60	0.69		172	0.82	1.35	1.52	8.25
1998 Q2	349	2.60	22.99	0.41	3.41	1.27	2.39	1.44	1.66	2.90	3.18	1.97	2.91	0.63	0.72		182	0.81	1.34	1.54	10.41
1998 Q3	350	2.49	21.97	0.67	13.75	1.32	2.14	1.50	1.73	2.74	3.16	2.34	2.92	0.62	0.70		187	0.81	1.34	1.57	22.36
1998 Q4	321	2.62	21.37	0.65	43.49	1.22	2.61	1.45	1.55	2.60	3.46	2.89	3.24	0.62	0.91	1.19	168	0.84	1.40	1.67	
1999 Q1	293	2.72	22.58	1.07	52.99			1.29								1.23	161	0.85	1.38	2.37	
1999 Q2	265	2.79	23.32	0.93	55.88			1.51								1.28	163	0.84	1.35	2.31	
1999 Q3	252	2.98	24.02	1.01	80.25			1.61								1.30	154	0.85	1.36	2.52	
1999 Q4	238	2.67	24.97	1.24	89.60			1.52								1.33	144	0.85	1.38	2.64	
2000 Q1	228	2.98	25.29	1.02	72.68			1.85								1.37	145	0.84	1.35	2.40	
2000 Q2	208	2.96	26.88	1.60	51.47			1.94								1.42	141	0.87	1.33	2.39	
2000 Q3	203	2.78	27.47	1.53	43.14			2.08								1.45	141	0.89	1.31	2.37	
2000 Q4	200	2.47	26.86	1.37	38.00			1.94								1.48	141	0.89	1.29	2.48	
2001 Q1	188	2.72	27.23	1.34	32.84			2.23								1.40	152	0.89	1.29	2.60	
2001 Q2	178	2.59	25.93	1.46	28.84			2.29								1.44	155	0.89	1.26	2.87	
2001 Q3	163	2.57	23.33	1.56	27.77			2.00								1.43	155	0.88	1.27	3.22	
2001 Q4	155	2.54	22.91	1.59	27.19			1.93								1.42	157	0.88	1.27	3.23	

(Continued)

Table 6.1:   (Continued)

	Japan	UK	USA	Brazil	Rus. F	Austr.	Belg.	Eston.	Finl.	Franc.	Germ.	Italy	Neth.	Port.	Spain	Euro	Yen	Pound	Dollar	Reais	Ruble
2002 Q1	163	2.62	23.38	1.29	24.25			1.60								1.43	165	0.88	1.25	2.97	
2002 Q2	164	2.69	22.92	1.33	27.22			1.95								1.39	162	0.87	1.28	3.17	
2002 Q3	154	2.59	22.71	2.37	29.30			1.84								1.35	158	0.86	1.32	4.09	
2002 Q4	166	2.58	22.19	2.70	29.81			1.84								1.33	163	0.85	1.33	4.88	
2003 Q1	156	3.40	22.12	2.13	25.66			1.52								1.28	163	0.85	1.37	4.77	
2003 Q2	145	3.24	22.03	1.89	22.87			1.80								1.23	165	0.86	1.40	4.17	43.3
2003 Q3	138	3.07	22.19	1.88	26.78			1.76								1.24	164	0.87	1.39	4.08	42.4
2003 Q4	131	3.20	23.50	2.15	23.40			1.66								1.21	157	0.85	1.44	4.19	43.0
2004 Q1	112	3.10	24.30	1.99	19.87			1.66								1.19	159	0.81	1.49	4.30	42.5
2004 Q2	116	3.26	25.37	2.53	22.20			1.81								1.21	160	0.81	1.46	4.43	42.2
2004 Q3	116	3.28	25.69	2.77	23.69			1.68								1.20	161	0.81	1.47	4.36	42.8
2004 Q4	122	3.21	26.31	2.56	20.47			1.55								1.17	160	0.81	1.51	4.22	43.1
2005 Q1	118	3.13	28.90	1.95	16.07			1.37								1.16	159	0.81	1.52	4.06	42.4
2005 Q2	118	3.24	29.53	2.08	17.10			1.75								1.18	160	0.80	1.49	3.70	41.9
2005 Q3	123	3.28	31.73	2.31	18.04			1.86								1.20	163	0.82	1.46	3.44	41.7
2005 Q4	129	3.46	35.16	2.28	16.83			1.69								1.21	168	0.82	1.43	3.23	41.2
2006 Q1	132	3.86	36.60	1.91	14.17			1.54								1.20	168	0.82	1.44	3.16	40.5
2006 Q2	136	3.89	36.90	1.95	13.27			1.69								1.17	168	0.81	1.47	3.17	40.1
2006 Q3	138	3.36	38.19	2.04	12.93			1.52								1.16	172	0.79	1.48	3.22	39.7
2006 Q4	141	3.43	40.32	1.66	11.43			1.32								1.16	175	0.78	1.49	3.21	39.6
2007 Q1	144	3.25	40.87	1.21	9.05			1.23								1.14	179	0.77	1.50	3.16	39.5
2007 Q2	150	3.45	42.20	0.95	8.77			1.43								1.12	183	0.76	1.52	3.02	39.2
2007 Q3	150	3.55	42.88	0.94	9.19			1.18								1.12	181	0.76	1.53	2.93	39.1
2007 Q4	150	3.22	44.05	0.83	9.72			1.32								1.09	178	0.77	1.57	2.81	38.8
2008 Q1	150	3.38	43.70	0.70	9.28			1.14								1.07	168	0.81	1.60	2.77	38.8
2008 Q2	152	3.76	45.61	0.82	9.42			1.16								1.04	170	0.83	1.63	2.70	38.4
2008 Q3	149	4.10	46.37	0.89	10.23			1.25								1.06	171	0.84	1.59	2.64	38.6
2008 Q4	108	3.80	38.40	1.02	10.89			1.05								1.14	144	0.96	1.51	3.41	41.1

(Continued)

Table 6.1: *(Continued)*

	Japan	UK	USA	Brazil	Rus. F	Austr.	Belg.	Eston.	Finl.	Franc.	Germ.	Italy	Neth.	Port.	Spain	Euro	Yen	Pound	Dollar	Reais	Ruble
2009 Q1	74	3.83	35.15	0.71	8.60			0.83								1.15	139	1.04	1.49	3.45	51.2
2009 Q2	86	3.45	33.48	0.74	9.52			0.87								1.12	148	0.98	1.52	3.15	48.9
2009 Q3	93	2.83	21.80	0.68	11.36			0.97								1.09	146	0.95	1.56	2.92	49.0
2009 Q4	98	3.02	23.47	0.59	11.41			0.89								1.08	143	0.97	1.59	2.76	46.9
2010 Q1	103	2.86	23.90	0.55	10.48			0.90								1.12	140	0.99	1.54	2.78	46.1
2010 Q2	105	2.76	24.63	0.62	10.81			1.11								1.17	137	1.00	1.49	2.66	45.0
2010 Q3	103	2.64	24.68	0.65	11.01			1.48								1.17	130	0.98	1.52	2.65	46.4
2010 Q4	103	2.70	25.59	0.62	13.03			1.95								1.14	128	0.98	1.56	2.64	47.8
2011 Q1	104	2.61	25.89	0.52	11.95											1.14	129	0.98	1.56	2.61	45.7
2011 Q2	96	2.50	25.32	0.60	13.28											1.11	130	0.98	1.60	2.55	44.7
2011 Q3	96	2.48	25.05	0.61	13.58											1.13	124	0.99	1.59	2.59	46.3
2011 Q4	82	2.48	24.62	0.62	16.38											1.16	121	0.99	1.56	2.80	48.7
2012 Q1	86	2.37	25.02	0.51	14.26											1.18	122	0.98	1.54	2.72	46.4
2012 Q2	86	2.22	24.74	0.59	14.44											1.19	123	0.97	1.53	2.99	47.4
2012 Q3	82	2.20	24.69	0.62	14.38											1.21	119	0.96	1.52	3.08	48.5
2012 Q4	80	2.13	25.00	0.63	15.08											1.18	125	0.96	1.54	3.16	47.7

Table 6.2:   ∂(Exports − Imports)/∂(Foreign Reserves)

	Japan	UK	USA	Brazil	Rus. F	Austr.	Belg.	Eston.	Finl.	Franc.	Germ.	Italy	Neth.	Port.	Spain	Euro	Yen	Pound	Dollar	Reais	Ruble
1981 Q1	64	0.198	5.76			−0.011	0.180		0.300	−0.021	0.561	−0.091	0.233	0.270	−0.05						
1981 Q2	62	0.187	5.70			−0.061	0.183		0.167	−0.018	0.595	−0.048	0.242	0.238	−0.00						
1981 Q3	125	0.124	5.89			0.080	0.159		0.076	−0.024	0.629	−0.013	0.293	0.231	−0.01						
1981 Q4	94	0.153	5.61			−0.078	0.206		0.195	−0.088	0.745	−0.020	0.391	0.222	0.00						
1982 Q1	83	0.153	5.41			0.115	−0.051		0.333	−0.077	0.746	−0.045	0.413	0.211	−0.01						
1982 Q2	93	0.132	5.65			0.022	0.299		0.276	−0.166	0.754	0.014	0.357	0.203	−0.05						
1982 Q3	93	0.157	4.61			0.192	0.388		−0.036	−0.258	0.736	−0.063	0.275	0.114	−0.01						
1982 Q4	85	0.219	4.28			0.057	0.303		0.003	−0.137	0.713	−0.013	0.251	0.306	0.00						
1983 Q1	174	0.152	4.34			0.165	0.128		0.214	−0.093	0.650	0.089	0.280	0.186	−0.08						
1983 Q2	206	0.105	3.68			0.063	0.441		0.171	−0.010	0.687	0.040	0.289	0.263	0.08						
1983 Q3	242	0.151	3.08			0.216	0.327		0.050	0.053	0.656	0.035	0.244	0.241	0.07						
1983 Q4	219	0.118	2.80			−0.104	0.292		0.185	0.068	0.662	0.036	0.249	0.274	0.02						
1984 Q1	281	0.138	1.98			0.170	0.268		0.385	0.034	0.650	0.044	0.275	0.346	0.13						
1984 Q2	313	0.052	1.67			−0.118	0.525		0.132	0.059	0.645	0.000	0.310	0.310	0.18						
1984 Q3	299	0.058	1.66			0.173	0.311		0.112	0.078	0.714	−0.011	0.373	0.244	0.08						
1984 Q4	362	0.025	1.49			−0.073	0.224		0.227	0.038	0.778	−0.007	0.349	0.246	0.07						
1985 Q1	351	0.041	1.95			0.217	0.411		0.105	0.008	0.790	−0.036	0.304	0.258	0.04						
1985 Q2	406	0.229	1.23			−0.061	0.343		0.095	0.042	0.799	−0.013	0.325	0.272	0.11						
1985 Q3	431	0.208	1.12			0.072	0.363		0.121	0.006	0.809	0.025	0.295	0.195	0.11						
1985 Q4	487	0.169	0.59			−0.037	0.245		−0.003	0.027	0.811	0.033	0.359	0.176	0.15						
1986 Q1	450	0.095	0.78			0.139	0.394		−0.008	0.063	0.865	0.075	0.311	0.215	0.12						
1986 Q2	480	0.021	0.71			0.054	0.463		0.213	0.030	0.923	0.094	0.380	0.193	0.12						
1986 Q3	413	−0.028	0.47			0.136	0.492		0.140	0.044	0.914	0.157	0.281	0.137	0.08						
1986 Q4	397	−0.016	0.61			−0.018	0.369		0.481	0.056	0.879	0.136	0.172	0.140	0.13						
1987 Q1	289	0.062	0.43			0.135	0.291		0.055	−0.025	0.772	0.067	0.216	0.061	0.05						
1987 Q2	196	0.001	0.29			0.003	0.390		0.064	−0.023	0.759	0.020	0.251	−0.039	0.04						
1987 Q3	172	−0.007	0.34			0.136	0.377		0.068	0.003	0.708	0.078	0.187	−0.048	0.01						
1987 Q4	165	−0.040	0.36			−0.088	0.220		0.018	−0.007	0.668	0.051	0.185	−0.046	0.00						

(Continued)

Table 6.2: *(Continued)*

	Japan	UK	USA	Brazil	Rus. F	Austr.	Belg.	Eston.	Finl.	Franc.	Germ.	Italy	Neth.	Port.	Spain	Euro	Yen	Pound	Dollar	Reais	Ruble
1988 Q1	138	-0.061	1.03			0.126	0.307		0.027	0.007	0.715	0.002	0.234	-0.070	0.01						
1988 Q2	110	-0.076	1.58			0.013	0.321		-0.009	0.008	0.749	0.061	0.210	-0.120	-0.01						
1988 Q3	116	-0.096	1.53			0.072	0.351		-0.077	-0.013	0.808	0.007	0.249	-0.121	-0.02						
1988 Q4	136	-0.131	1.34			-0.021	0.337		0.084	-0.002	0.884	0.033	0.274	-0.119	-0.04						
1989 Q1	99	-0.127	1.42			0.148	0.273		0.020	0.003	0.922	-0.043	0.211	-0.049	-0.04						
1989 Q2	96	-0.135	1.39			-0.003	0.295		-0.056	-0.048	0.863	0.012	0.208	-0.103	-0.05						
1989 Q3	92	-0.143	1.51			0.132	0.345		-0.109	-0.032	0.865	0.017	0.214	-0.060	-0.08						
1989 Q4	83	-0.088	1.29			-0.061	0.234		-0.086	-0.063	0.806	0.034	0.245	-0.049	-0.09						
1990 Q1	91	-0.113	1.15			0.080	0.166		-0.027	-0.006	0.854	-0.023	0.215	-0.077	-0.10						
1990 Q2	95	-0.101	1.51			0.054	0.302		-0.033	-0.034	0.798	0.028	0.238	-0.062	-0.06						
1990 Q3	86	-0.047	1.42			0.103	0.294		-0.014	-0.084	0.944	0.015	0.329	-0.071	-0.06						
1990 Q4	45	-0.024	1.32			0.024	0.252		-0.045	-0.087	0.905	0.026	0.304	-0.069	-0.05						
1991 Q1	117	-0.013	1.90			0.112	0.191		-0.049	-0.076	0.552	0.018	0.312	-0.108	-0.05						
1991 Q2	139	0.020	2.36			-0.110	0.330		-0.027	-0.048	0.467	0.015	0.293	-0.086	-0.04						
1991 Q3	156	0.018	2.48			0.058	0.289		0.057	-0.018	0.512	-0.026	0.291	-0.075	-0.06						
1991 Q4	178	0.012	2.45			0.049	0.300		0.026	0.034	0.542	0.043	0.296	-0.060	-0.06						
1992 Q1	193	0.021	2.51	1.115		0.126	0.211		0.005	0.070	0.512	0.001	0.292	-0.064	-0.05						
1992 Q2	203	-0.002	2.29	0.870		-0.008	0.233		0.042	0.119	0.477	0.008	0.303	-0.069	-0.05						
1992 Q3	212	-0.038	2.20	0.882		0.035	0.337		0.159	0.130	0.312	-0.015	0.236	-0.077	-0.03						
1992 Q4	219	-0.022	2.12	0.761		-0.069	0.362		0.161	0.088	0.321	0.071	0.196	-0.082	-0.08						
1993 Q1	221	0.012	1.90	0.833		0.149	0.208	0.677	0.200	0.174	0.496	0.230	0.212	-0.098	-0.02						
1993 Q2	166	-0.010	1.77	0.758		-0.028	0.291	0.539	0.270	0.149	0.487	0.308	0.280	-0.086	-0.01						
1993 Q3	157	0.012	1.64	0.698		0.083	0.407	0.478	0.414	0.212	0.388	0.285	0.225	-0.086	-0.01						
1993 Q4	144	0.031	1.55	0.565	-8.51	-0.023	0.461	0.254	0.372	0.258	0.448	0.423	0.263	-0.067	0.01						
1994 Q1	154	0.033	1.38	0.402	-12.15	0.094	0.264	0.194	0.293	0.193	0.454	0.358	0.266	-0.100	0.02						
1994 Q2	131	0.012	1.23	0.206	-6.79	-0.061	0.332	0.278	0.235	0.208	0.464	0.316	0.246	-0.109	0.01						
1994 Q3	111	0.045	1.13	0.710	-11.37	0.013	0.409	0.274	0.225	0.239	0.418	0.298	0.231	-0.102	-0.00						
1994 Q4	104	0.042	1.05	0.576	-11.83	-0.094	0.378	0.140	0.143	0.257	0.448	0.293	0.225	-0.118	0.00						

(Continued)

Table 6.2: (Continued)

	Japan	UK	USA	Brazil	Rus. F	Austr.	Belg.	Eston.	Finl.	Franc.	Germ.	Italy	Neth.	Port.	Spain	Euro	Yen	Pound	Dollar	Reais	Ruble
1995 Q1	90	0.144	0.89	0.444	−9.09	0.080	0.427	0.175	0.249	0.282	0.501	0.450	0.240	−0.071	0.00		144	0.94	1.49	1.28	
1995 Q2	78	0.018	0.79	0.436	−3.96	−0.063	0.341	0.162	0.332	0.290	0.495	0.369	0.250	−0.099	0.04		132	0.98	1.57	1.41	
1995 Q3	56	0.006	1.38	0.346	−5.27	−0.001	0.287	0.309	0.254	0.233	0.475	0.402	0.247	0.013	0.01		142	0.96	1.52	1.42	
1995 Q4	41	0.059	1.46	0.317	−4.05	−0.089	0.294	0.073	0.300	0.248	0.481	0.380	0.224	−0.071	0.03		151	0.96	1.49	1.44	
1996 Q1	30	0.018	1.16	0.290	−2.84	0.042	0.238	0.075	0.258	0.290	0.481	0.404	0.267	−0.056	0.02		155	0.96	1.47	1.43	
1996 Q2	12	0.044	1.08	0.257	−3.22	−0.086	0.298	0.096	0.521	0.264	0.470	0.358	0.249	−0.075	0.04		156	0.95	1.45	1.44	
1996 Q3	12	0.066	0.81	0.205	−3.15	−0.042	0.231	0.098	0.389	0.317	0.497	0.364	0.302	−0.026	0.03		158	0.93	1.45	1.47	
1996 Q4	17	0.080	1.29	0.142	−1.13	−0.053	0.289	−0.095	0.397	0.347	0.508	0.347	0.267	−0.127	0.04		163	0.88	1.44	1.49	
1997 Q1	18	0.099	1.00	0.175	−2.56	0.029	0.269	0.053	0.208	0.410	0.472	0.349	0.284	−0.105	0.05		169	0.85	1.39	1.46	
1997 Q2	38	0.072	1.46	0.207	−2.35	−0.040	0.280	0.063	0.291	0.506	0.515	0.329	0.297	−0.107	0.03		165	0.85	1.38	1.47	
1997 Q3	34	0.109	1.22	0.158	−2.61	−0.003	0.352	0.013	0.317	0.466	0.557	0.244	0.337	−0.061	0.03		161	0.84	1.36	1.48	
1997 Q4	54	0.032	0.78	0.180	−3.39	−0.005	0.283	−0.141	0.365	0.441	0.565	0.224	0.351	−0.151	0.02		171	0.82	1.37	1.51	
1998 Q1	53	0.038	0.44	0.157	−5.51	0.069	0.245	−0.062	0.472	0.398	0.516	0.211	0.270	−0.149	0.01		172	0.82	1.35	1.52	8.14
1998 Q2	67	−0.060	−0.08	0.180	−5.24	0.009	0.286	0.009	0.392	0.331	0.528	0.274	0.336	−0.152	0.02		182	0.81	1.34	1.54	8.25
1998 Q3	65	−0.045	−0.29	0.220	−1.47	0.033	0.225	0.001	0.412	0.322	0.521	0.306	0.329	−0.057	0.00		187	0.81	1.34	1.57	10.41
1998 Q4	67	−0.066	−0.33	0.201	16.84	0.004	0.293	−0.024	0.368	0.273	0.574	0.285	0.382	−0.192	−0.03		168	0.84	1.40	1.67	22.36
1999 Q1	57	−0.163	−0.97	0.424	14.50			0.037								1.19	161	0.85	1.38	2.37	
1999 Q2	45	−0.108	−1.71	0.320	18.11			0.120								1.23	163	0.84	1.35	2.31	
1999 Q3	39	−0.099	−2.31	0.288	30.30			0.217								1.28	154	0.85	1.36	2.52	
1999 Q4	38	−0.119	−2.72	0.280	42.35			−0.005								1.30	144	0.85	1.38	2.64	
2000 Q1	39	−0.161	−3.74	0.320	36.36			0.127								1.33	145	0.84	1.35	2.40	
2000 Q2	34	−0.143	−4.00	0.451	25.19			0.136								1.37	141	0.87	1.33	2.39	
2000 Q3	29	−0.189	−4.61	0.332	19.25			0.235								1.42	141	0.89	1.31	2.37	
2000 Q4	22	−0.129	−4.80	0.126	14.92			−0.067								1.45	141	0.89	1.29	2.48	
2001 Q1	14	−0.129	−4.63	0.219	14.82			0.107								1.48	152	0.89	1.29	2.60	
2001 Q2	9	−0.201	−3.94	0.261	9.75			0.181								1.40	155	0.89	1.26	2.87	
2001 Q3	9	−0.213	−3.76	0.317	8.51			0.156								1.44	155	0.88	1.27	3.22	
2001 Q4	15	−0.208	−3.64	0.334	6.13			0.044								1.43	157	0.88	1.27	3.23	

(Continued)

Table 6.2: (*Continued*)

	Japan	UK	USA	Brazil	Rus. F	Austr.	Belg.	Eston.	Finl.	Franc.	Germ.	Italy	Neth.	Port.	Spain	Euro	Yen	Pound	Dollar	Reais	Ruble
2002 Q1	21	−0.254	−3.99	0.363	7.01			−0.035								1.43	165	0.88	1.25	2.97	
2002 Q2	23	−0.229	−4.57	0.362	8.06			−0.028								1.39	162	0.87	1.28	3.17	
2002 Q3	18	−0.204	−4.78	0.865	8.85			0.005								1.35	158	0.86	1.32	4.09	
2002 Q4	22	−0.273	−5.45	0.927	8.09			−0.090								1.33	163	0.85	1.33	4.88	
2003 Q1	17	−0.230	−5.83	0.674	9.66			−0.104								1.28	163	0.85	1.37	4.77	
2003 Q2	22	−0.233	−5.82	0.731	6.99			−0.012								1.23	165	0.86	1.40	4.17	43.3
2003 Q3	22	−0.236	−5.65	0.754	7.63			−0.022								1.24	164	0.87	1.39	4.08	42.4
2003 Q4	23	−0.291	−5.90	0.806	6.65			−0.083								1.21	157	0.85	1.44	4.19	43.0
2004 Q1	20	−0.286	−6.56	0.753	7.00			0.003								1.19	159	0.81	1.49	4.30	42.5
2004 Q2	19	−0.343	−7.73	1.010	7.74			−0.167								1.21	160	0.81	1.46	4.43	42.2
2004 Q3	17	−0.316	−8.27	1.070	8.17			0.053								1.20	161	0.81	1.47	4.36	42.8
2004 Q4	17	−0.295	−9.11	0.872	7.19			−0.106								1.17	160	0.81	1.51	4.22	43.1
2005 Q1	15	−0.340	−9.61	0.711	6.43			−0.029								1.16	159	0.81	1.52	4.06	42.4
2005 Q2	13	−0.281	−9.83	0.765	7.04			−0.041								1.18	160	0.80	1.49	3.70	41.9
2005 Q3	11	−0.330	−11.36	0.905	6.88			−0.027								1.20	163	0.82	1.46	3.44	41.7
2005 Q4	13	−0.283	−13.44	0.859	6.03			−0.106								1.21	168	0.82	1.43	3.23	41.2
2006 Q1	10	−0.307	−13.19	0.646	6.63			−0.143								1.20	168	0.82	1.44	3.16	40.5
2006 Q2	10	−0.246	−13.10	0.630	5.46			−0.144								1.17	168	0.81	1.47	3.17	40.1
2006 Q3	11	−0.323	−13.93	0.720	4.74			−0.113								1.16	172	0.79	1.48	3.22	39.7
2006 Q4	13	−0.311	−12.20	0.536	3.01			−0.180								1.16	175	0.78	1.49	3.21	39.6
2007 Q1	15	−0.316	−12.36	0.312	2.91			−0.214								1.14	179	0.77	1.50	3.16	39.5
2007 Q2	15	−0.260	−12.57	0.262	2.45			−0.184								1.12	183	0.76	1.52	3.02	39.2
2007 Q3	17	−0.323	−11.75	0.223	2.23			−0.102								1.12	181	0.76	1.53	2.93	39.1
2007 Q4	12	−0.312	−11.46	0.171	2.72			−0.118								1.09	178	0.77	1.57	2.81	38.8
2008 Q1	10	−0.325	−12.05	0.076	3.49			−0.056								1.07	168	0.81	1.60	2.77	38.8
2008 Q2	7	−0.286	−12.07	0.121	3.00			−0.012								1.04	170	0.83	1.63	2.70	38.4
2008 Q3	−1	−0.285	−12.43	0.127	3.04			−0.013								1.06	171	0.84	1.59	2.64	38.6
2008 Q4	−7	−0.145	−8.32	0.121	1.82			−0.002								1.14	144	0.96	1.51	3.41	41.1

(*Continued*)

Table 6.2: (*Continued*)

	Japan	UK	USA	Brazil	Rus. F	Austr.	Belg.	Eston.	Finl.	Franc.	Germ.	Italy	Neth.	Port.	Spain	Euro	Yen	Pound	Dollar	Reais	Ruble
2009 Q1	−6	−0.205	−4.39	0.068	1.88			0.070								1.15	139	1.04	1.49	3.45	51.2
2009 Q2	5	−0.194	−3.19	0.151	2.37			0.151								1.12	148	0.98	1.52	3.15	48.9
2009 Q3	5	−0.092	−2.77	0.083	3.22			0.186								1.09	146	0.95	1.56	2.92	49.0
2009 Q4	8	−0.104	−3.29	0.035	3.12			0.118								1.08	143	0.97	1.59	2.76	46.9
2010 Q1	10	−0.180	−3.87	−0.009	4.31			0.084								1.12	140	0.99	1.54	2.78	46.1
2010 Q2	10	−0.153	−4.23	0.040	3.26			0.129								1.17	137	1.00	1.49	2.66	45.0
2010 Q3	9	−0.197	−4.29	0.002	1.88			0.255								1.14	130	0.98	1.52	2.65	46.4
2010 Q4	7	−0.165	−3.91	0.030	2.91			0.252								1.14	128	0.98	1.56	2.64	47.8
2011 Q1	1	−0.070	−4.42	0.002	4.00											1.11	129	0.98	1.56	2.61	45.7
2011 Q2	−9	−0.117	−4.39	0.035	3.76											1.13	130	0.98	1.60	2.55	44.7
2011 Q3	−5	−0.146	−4.03	0.040	3.07											1.16	124	0.99	1.59	2.59	46.3
2011 Q4	−9	−0.100	−4.45	0.013	4.53											1.18	121	0.99	1.56	2.80	48.7
2012 Q1	−9	−0.137	−4.66	−0.022	4.93											1.18	122	0.98	1.54	2.72	46.4
2012 Q2	−10	−0.179	−4.17	−0.008	3.78											1.19	123	0.97	1.53	2.99	47.4
2012 Q3	−13	−0.131	−3.55	0.017	2.30											1.21	119	0.96	1.52	3.08	48.5
2012 Q4	−15	−0.156	−3.74	−0.041	3.19											1.18	125	0.96	1.54	3.16	47.7

(which would never be used under an export-driven growth strategy) does not even produce a dollar of exports.

The estimated value for ∂exports/∂reserves for Japan after the first quarter of 2003 (see Table 6.1, Column 2) is always less than the yen/SDR exchange rate (see Table 6.1, Column 17) implying that, after 2003, Japan did not even get a yen worth of exports for every yen of foreign currency it accumulated. Figure 6.8, which plots the ∂exports/∂reserves estimates for Japan, shows that Japan's ∂exports/∂reserves has been falling since the fourth quarter of 1985 with a relatively small rebound between the first quarter of 1989 and the third quarter of 1992. These dates are significant. September 22, 1985 is when France, West Germany, Japan, the USA, and the UK signed the Plaza Accord which was an agreement to bring down the value of the US dollar relative to the Japanese Yen and German Mark. The Louvre Accord, which was signed on February 22, 1987 between these same countries plus Canada, stated that the US dollar had fallen far enough and that these countries would now focus on stabilizing international exchange rates. The second quarter of 1987 is when Japan's ∂exports/∂reserves stopped its rapid fall. However, the value of the US dollar relative to the yen continued to fall until the fourth quarter of 1988. The first quarter of 1989 is when Japan's ∂exports/∂reserves began its brief rebound. However, between the fourth quarters of 1985 and 2012, Japan's ∂exports/∂reserves fell by 95%.

In contrast to Japan, Table 6.1 reveals that ∂exports/∂reserves for the USA (Column 4) was always noticeably greater than the US dollar/SDR exchange rate (Column 20) after 1995. However, this fact does not make accumulating foreign reserves an appropriate policy tool for the USA because the US dollar is the dominant reserve currency in the world and the dominant reserve currency must be free floating. In other words, when countries systematically accumulate foreign reserves, they are in essence fixing their exchange rates below equilibrium. If the USA tried to fix its exchange rate, it would be placing more importance on to whatever the US dollar was fixed than on the US dollar itself, undercutting (at least theoretically) what it means to be the dominant reserve currency. Under the Bretton Woods system, which lasted from 1945 to August 15, 1971, gold was the ultimate reserve currency because the US dollar was fixed to gold and other currencies were fixed to the dollar. Since August 15, 1971, the

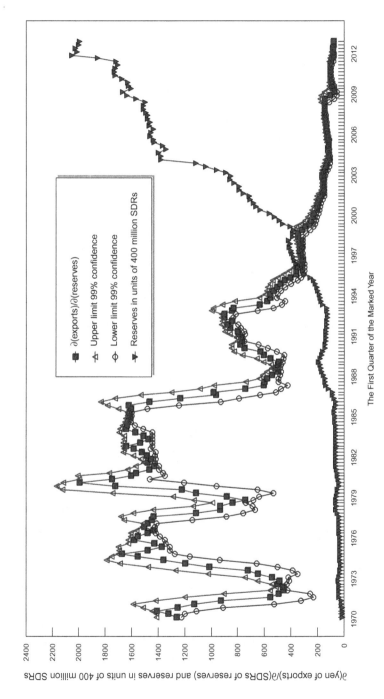

Figure 6.8: ∂(Exports)/∂(Reserves) for Japan: Exports Measured in Yen, Reserves Measured in SDRs

US dollar has been the dominant reserve currency and has been one of the most flexible currencies in the world.[8]

Figure 6.9 shows that US holdings for foreign reserves have changed over time. However, in the fourth quarter of 1989, the USA had 57.5 billion SDRs of foreign reserves and in the second quarter of 2009, the USA had 54.5 billion SDRs of foreign reserves. Thus, during this time period, the USA was not systematically changing its holdings of foreign reserves[9]; instead, the USA was both buying and selling dollars in order to stabilize exchange rates as promised in the Louvre Accord. Note that Figure 6.9 shows that when US holdings of foreign reserves increased, ∂exports/∂reserves fell and when US holdings of foreign reserves fell, ∂exports/∂reserves rose (the direction of change in the two lines in Figure 6.9 are mirror images of each other). This means that the positive effects of accumulating foreign reserves on exports is less than the negative effects on exports of using foreign reserves. A similar phenomenon is shown in Figure 6.10 for the British pound.

Above, I argued theoretically that those countries that accumulate foreign reserves in order to suppress their exchange rates so that they can export more need to perpetually increase foreign reserves. If they ever stop accumulating foreign reserves, their exports will fall. For the US dollar and British pound, I find an empirical result that is even stronger than the theoretical argument that I offered above — I find that using foreign reserves decreased exports more than increasing foreign reserves increased exports.

Table 6.1 and Figure 6.10 show that the UK's ∂exports/∂reserves fell during the time of the Plaza Accord (September 22, 1985–February 22, 1987) and for a year after it and then rose from the fourth quarter of 1988 until the third quarter of 2008. Table 6.1 (Columns 3 and 19) and Figure 6.10 also show that the UK's ∂exports/∂reserves exceeded the pound per SDR

---

[8]I did not say that the US dollar has been perfectly flexible because a country with a perfectly flexible exchange rate would never change its holdings of foreign reserves.

[9]Furthermore, the relatively large increase in US holdings of foreign reserves that occurred in the third quarter of 2009 corresponds to the IMF creating new SDRs and allocating them in order to help the world overcome the financial crisis that began in 2007–2008. Thus, this increase should not be interpreted as an effort by the US government to devalue its currency in order to increase exports.

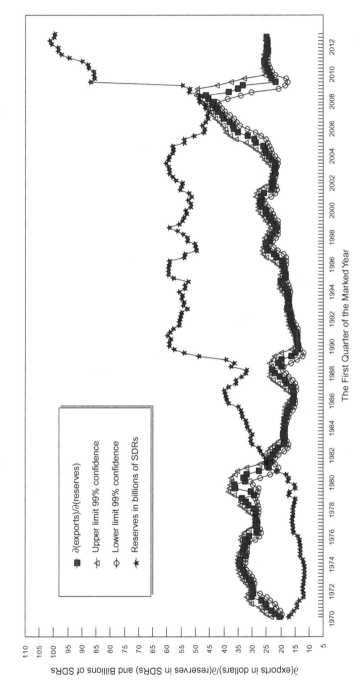

Figure 6.9: $\partial(Exports)/\partial(Reserves)$ for the USA: Exports Measured in Dollars, Reserves Measured in SDRs

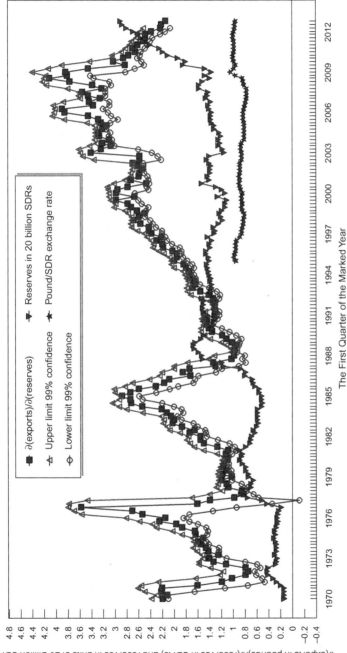

Figure 6.10: ∂(Exports)/∂(Reserves) for the UK: Exports Measured in Pounds, Reserves Measured in SDRs

exchange rate after 1995, implying that the UK accumulating an additional pound of foreign reserves would have increased the UK's exports by more than a pound. The opposite is true for Brazil (Figure 6.11) and the Russian Federation (Figure 6.12). For both Brazil and the Russian Federation, ∂exports/∂reserves were noticeably lower than the SDR exchange rate for all quarters after the fourth quarter of 1994 for Brazil and after the first quarter of 2003 for the Russian Federation.

Of the 17 countries using the euro, I had the data necessary to estimate ∂exports/∂reserves for the 10 countries shown in Figure 6.13. The national currencies for these countries were translated into euros prior to the analysis, and the analysis was conducted for as many quarters as possible up to when they switched to using solely euros. In the fourth quarter of 1998, 1.19 euros exchanged for one SDR. Table 6.1 and Figure 6.12 show that Austria, Belgium, Estonia, Finland, France, Germany, Italy, and the Netherlands had ∂exports/∂reserves that exceeded the euro per SDR exchange rate in the fourth quarter of 1998. Portugal and Spain did not. Thus, Portugal and Spain did not even get an additional euro of exports for every euro of foreign reserves they accumulated in the fourth quarter of 1998.

However, both exports and imports affect GDP. Thus, a true comparison of the benefits and costs of an export-driven growth model via accumulating foreign reserves requires estimating ∂(exports − imports)/∂reserves and comparing that relationship to the national currency per SDR exchange rate. Table 6.2 and Figure 6.14 show that none of the euro using countries (for which data was available) had ∂(exports − imports)/∂reserves that exceeded the euro per SDR exchange rate of 1.19 in the fourth quarter of 1998 or for any quarter prior to that date.

In 2012, there was major concern that Greece would exit the euro and devalue its currency in order to drive its economy off increased exports. Perhaps that strategy might help if Greece allowed its currency to fall to its equilibrium level.[10] However, the results shown in Figure 6.14 imply that Greece would not be able to further increase its GDP by driving its exchange rate below equilibrium via the accumulation of foreign reserves. Indeed, I found no countries for which the change in exports minus imports

---

[10]Perhaps, it would not help; remember from Chapter 5 that Greece's ∂GDP/∂exports has been falling since the fourth quarter of 2009.

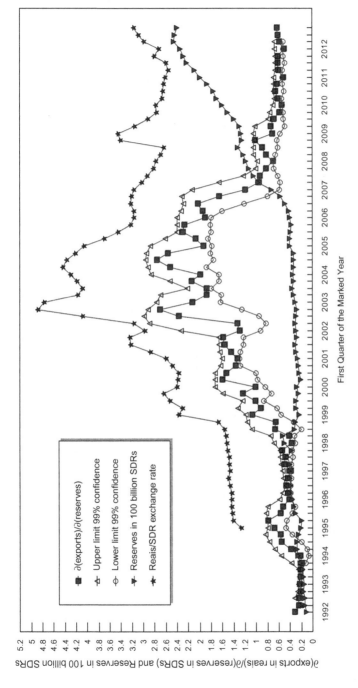

Figure 6.11: ∂(Exports)/∂(Reserves) for Brazil: Exports Measured in Reais, Reserves Measured in SDRs

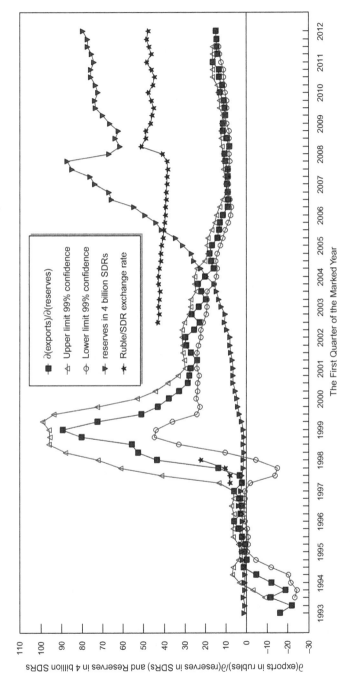

Figure 6.12: ∂(Exports)/∂(Reserves) for Russia: Exports Measured in Rubles, Reserves Measured in SDRs

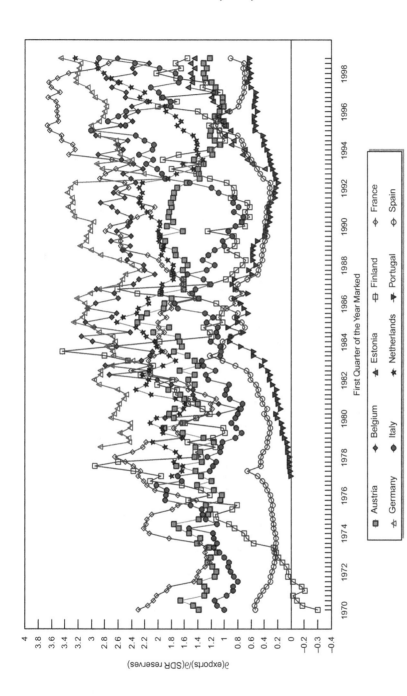

Figure 6.13: $\partial(\text{Exports})/\partial(\text{Reserves})$ for Europe: Exports Measured in Euros, Reserves Measured in SDRs

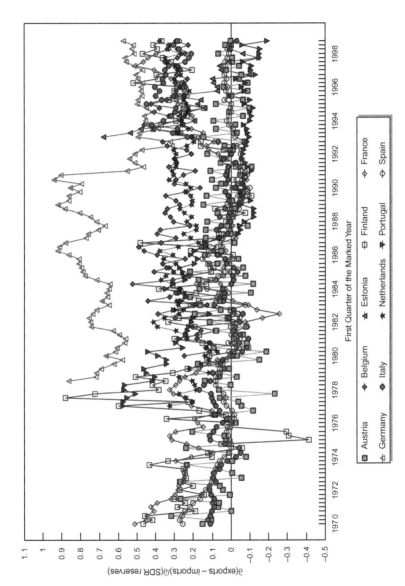

Figure 6.14: ∂(Exports $-$ Imports)/∂(Reserves) for Europe: Exports $-$ Imports Measured in Euros, Reserves Measured in SDRs

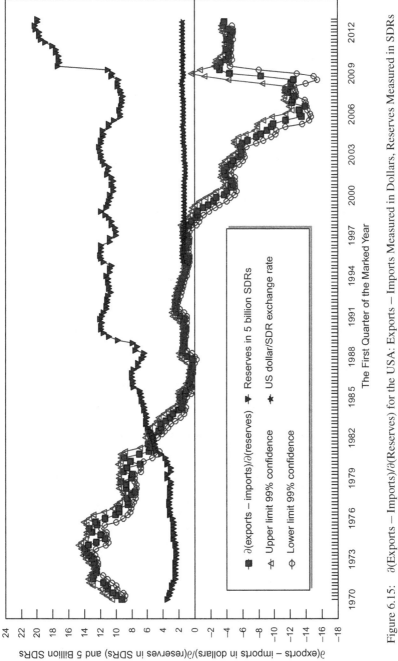

Figure 6.15: $\partial(\text{Exports} - \text{Imports})/\partial(\text{Reserves})$ for the USA: Exports $-$ Imports Measured in Dollars, Reserves Measured in SDRs

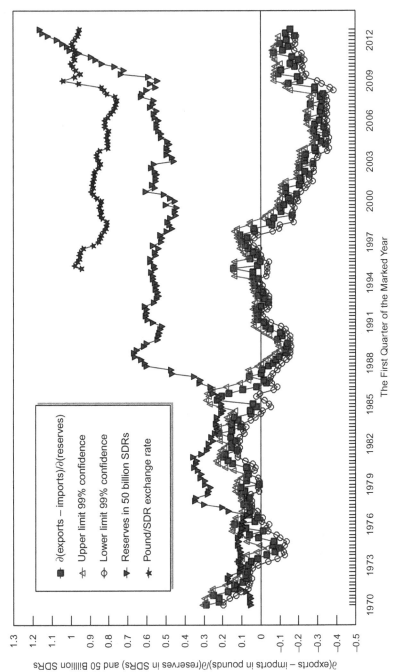

Figure 6.16: ∂(Exports − Imports)/∂(Reserves) for the UK: Exports − Imports Measured in Pounds, Reserves Measured in SDRs

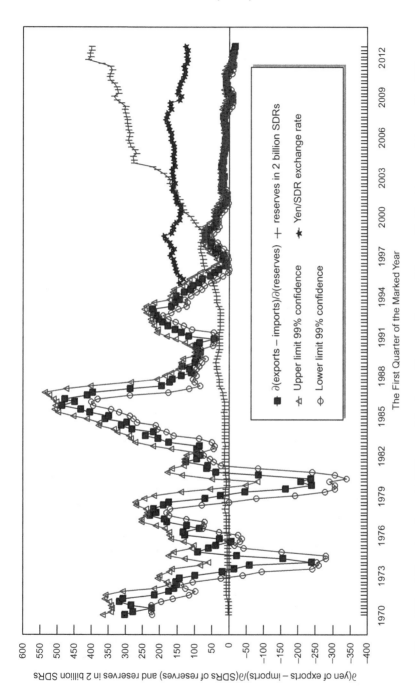

Figure 6.17: $\partial(\text{Exports} - \text{Imports})/\partial(\text{Reserves})$ for Japan: Exports − Imports Measured in Yen, Reserves Measured in SDRs

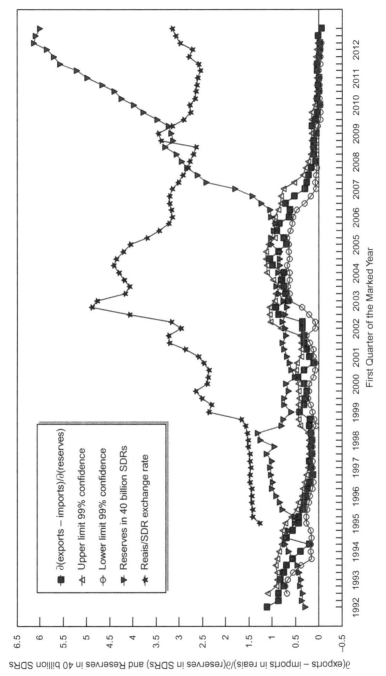

Figure 6.18: ∂(Exports − Imports)/∂(Reserves) for Brazil: Exports − Imports Measured in Reais, Reserves Measured in SDRs

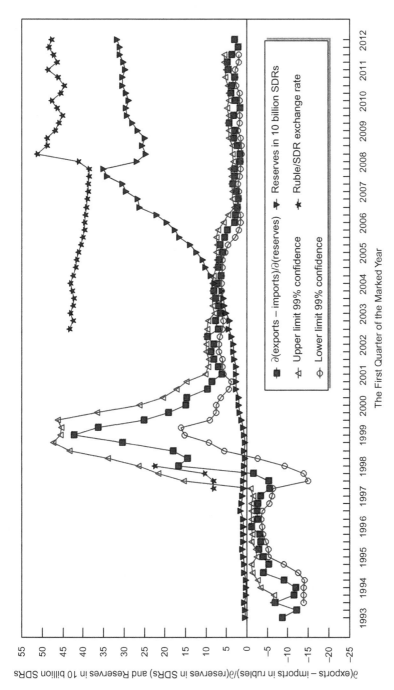

Figure 6.19: ∂(Exports − Imports)/∂(Reserves) for Russia: Exports − Imports Measured in Rubles, Reserves Measured in SDRs

exceeded the value of the foreign reserves they accumulated after the second quarter of 1997.

Recall that I found that ∂exports/∂reserves exceeded the SDR exchange rate for the USA and the UK. However, Table 6.2 and Figures 6.15 and 6.16 show that a similar result is not true for the USA's and the UK's ∂(exports − imports)/∂reserves. Indeed ∂(exports − imports)/∂reserves were less than zero after the second quarter of 1998 for the USA and the UK. This implies that accumulating another dollar of foreign reserves was correlated with a fall in exports minus imports and, thus, a fall in GDP.[11] Furthermore, Figures 6.17–6.19 show that ∂(exports − imports)/∂reserves were noticeably below the SDR exchange rate for Japan, Brazil, and Russia for all quarters after 1995. Indeed, I found only one quarter for one country in which ∂(exports − imports)/∂reserves exceeded the SDR exchange rate and that was for the USA in the second quarter of 1997. Trying to increase GDP by accumulating foreign reserves in order to sustain an exchange rate below equilibrium that will increase exports and decrease imports is not a viable policy strategy in today's world.

---

[11] Recall that GDP $= C + I + G + X - M$ where $X =$ exports and $M =$ imports.

Chapter 7

CHINA AND EXPORT VERSUS CONSUMPTION-DRIVEN GROWTH[1]

My thesis is that a global surplus of savings is plaguing the world today. Instead of being invested in ways that would expand production, this savings is flitting around the world funding speculative bubbles,[2] seeking a return from rent or deception, or sitting idle. The reason the savings is not being sufficiently invested in the expansion of production is that there is too little consumption to justify such investment. Some nations, like several of the European countries that are in the deepest crises, hope to reduce wages and labor power so that they can drive their economies off of increased exports. However, such strategies reduce the total amount of consumption in the world, making the global surplus of savings worse. The consequences of this surplus of savings are a fall in the effectiveness of monetary policy (Chapter 3), fiscal policy (Chapter 4), trade policy (Chapter 5), and currency policy (Chapter 6). The solution to this problem is to give more income to those who would consume which would provide a reason to invest the surplus savings in ways that expand production. In 2013, China

---

[1] Sections on "China's Export-Driven Growth Model," "Reforms Needed for a Successful Chinese Consumption Growth Model," and "A Fork in the Road: China's International Capital Choices" are similar, but not identical, to Leightner (2013b) and to Sections I and III of Leightner (2009) and Leightner (2012).

[2] Recall that Chapter 2 provided examples of this global surplus of savings funding speculative bubbles in Thailand and Ireland.

is the only major economy that is advocating such a strategy.[3] This chapter discusses China's 1986–2007 Export-Driven Growth Model, explains why after 2008 China decided to switch to a Domestic Consumption-Driven Growth Model, uses empirical estimates to evaluate the success (as of today) of China's efforts to switch growth models, explains what China needs to do to successfully switch to a Domestic Consumption-Driven Growth Model, and discusses a fork in the road that China faces concerning international capital flows.

China's Export-Driven Growth Model

As mentioned in Chapters 5 and 6 of this book, China used an export-driven growth model between 1986 and 2007. Even in 2013, China's exchange rate is fixed at a level less than market clearing which generates a shortage of China's currency, the yuan. In order to eliminate this shortage, China prints more yuan and exchanges it for US dollars or US treasury bonds (or for other foreign assets). China attempts to "sterilize" (neutralize) the resulting increase in the supply of yuan by imposing strong capital controls and by forcing Chinese banks to purchase government bonds. When Chinese banks purchase government bonds, excess yuan is removed from the market. However, sterilization interferes with bank profit maximization and its effectiveness is subject to debate. Irrefutable evidence that China has continued to keep its exchange rate below market clearing levels is China's foreign reserves increasing from US$1.9 trillion in January 2009 to US$3.66 trillion dollars in September 2013.[4] No other country in all of known history has held such a large amount of foreign reserves.

China also promoted labor-intensive exports by suppressing labor unions and the wage rate.[5] The dual strategy of suppressing both the wage

---

[3] Japan has also mentioned consumption-driven growth; however, Japan's plan to increase the national sales tax is in direct opposition to consumption-driven growth. Taxing sales reduces consumption.

[4] *Source*: People's Bank of China http://www.pbc.gov.cn/publish/html/2013s09.htm and /2009s09.htm. Accessed respectively on December 13, 2013 and June 17, 2011.

[5] Since 2008, China has loosened up on these labor-suppressing strategies. As a consequence, manufacturing wages in China have risen by 71% between 2008 and 2013. The average private sector wage rose 12.3% and 14% in 2011 and 2012 respectively (Orlik, 2013).

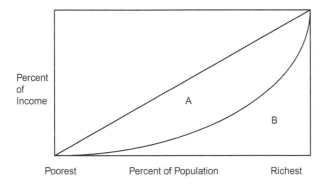

Figure 7.1:   The Lorenz Curve and the Gini Coefficient

rate and the exchange rate caused the domestic market to develop very slowly, or not at all. This dual strategy also made it possible for wealthy owners of export industries to keep most of the returns as profits (thus enriching themselves) while most laborers remained in poverty. The resulting rise in Chinese income inequality is dramatically illustrated by the Gini coefficient.

Figure 7.1 illustrates how the Gini coefficient is calculated from a Lorenz Curve. The diagonal line from the lower left corner to the upper right corner shows the line of perfect equality — if an economy was on this line, then the poorest 10% of the population would have 10% of the country's income and the richest 10% of the population would have only 10% of the income. The line that is bowed downward shows the actual income distribution for this country. The closer this bowed line is to the diagonal line, the more equal the society; the further away from the diagonal line, the less equal. The Gini coefficient is calculated as the area designated with an "A" divided by the areas "A + B." If the Gini coefficient is "0," then area "A" must be "0" making the bowed downward line the same as the diagonal line. Thus, a Gini coefficient of "0" indicates perfect equality. A Gini coefficient of "1" would occur if area "B" did not exist. This would be the case of complete inequality. Therefore, the Gini coefficient ranges from 0, indicating perfect equality, to 1, indicating complete inequality.

China's Gini coefficient was only 0.28 in 1983, making China one of the most equal countries on the earth. This is especially significant because it is easier to improve and sustain equality in small countries, like Japan and Sweden, and harder in large countries like China. However, the degree of inequality skyrocketed in China after 1983. By 2001, China's Gini was 0.447, making China less equal than Thailand (Gini = 0.43), Korea (Gini = 0.32), Indonesia (Gini = 0.34), India (Gini = 0.325), and the USA (Gini in 2000 = 0.408). Although China is not yet as unequal as Mexico (Gini = 0.55) or Brazil (Gini = 0.59), there is probably "no other case where a society's income distribution has deteriorated so much, so fast" (Naughton, 2007, pp. 217–218). Furthermore, China's Gini has continued to rise; as of 2006, it was 0.47 (Xin, 2008) and this author has heard unofficial estimates that in 2009, China's Gini was 0.50.

With a highly unequal income distribution, Chinese producers did not have a domestic market for what they produced; thus, China had to export. For trade to occur, there must be both a buyer and a seller — if China exports, then other countries have to import. China enticed other countries to buy Chinese goods and services by keeping the prices of its exports extremely low. Prices were kept low by keeping the cost of Chinese production low via wage repression and by fixing the exchange rate below its market clearing level (and thus accumulating foreign reserves). China's net "exports" (exports minus imports or "trade surplus") equals the amount that China produces in excess of what it consumes domestically and, thus, it equals China's "excess savings." Excess savings (trade surpluses) can be maintained only if other countries have off-setting excess consumption (trade deficits). Thus, China's 1986–2007 "Export Promotion" strategy could have been named China's "Excess Savings Strategy" and this strategy necessarily implies that there must be countries with offsetting excess consumption (Leightner, 2009; 2010b; 2012).

Modigliani and Cao (2004, pp. 165–166) state:

> By the early 90s, the Chinese personal saving rate had reached a remarkable level of nearly 30% .... This occurred despite the fact that, even with the high growth rate, the per-capita income remained one of the lowest in the world. The saving rates are stunningly high in comparison with those of the United States, one of the world's richest nations. During those same years, the personal saving rate in the United States was 7.6%: and even the "private" saving rate, which is the sum of personal saving and corporate saving (profit retention), rises to only 10% .... Since then the saving rate has slipped further with the personal down to 3% and the private down to 5%.

If corporate savings is added to household savings, then China is saving approximately 50% of the income it generates.

"An 'Excess Savings' strategy can be maintained if and only if, year after year (forever more), a country accumulates more and more savings" (i.e., if they never use the US dollars they continue to accumulate). If a country was to spend the foreign reserves they had previously accumulated on buying goods and services, then that country would run a trade deficit.[6] When the rest of the world produces goods and services and exports them to the USA but never uses what it is paid for those goods and services, it is equivalent to the world giving the USA a huge gift. It is equivalent to you never cashing the pay checks your employer gives to you: lucky employer, lucky USA. The USA has gained tremendously from this situation. The big losers were the Chinese consumer and worker. The winners in China were the rich who own the companies that exported — they got to keep the profits which were artificially high due to the suppression of labor and wages (Leightner, 2012).

The USA has gained tremendously from the world's increased appetite for US dollar reserves between 1997 and 2007. However, the world's savings pouring into the USA funded the speculative housing bubble that led to the worse recession the USA has suffered since the great depression. Once that bubble burst, the USA reduced its imports, creating problems for China's Export-Driven Growth Model. Recall that an export promotion strategy requires an importer.

China could return to its pre-crisis export promotion strategy if and only if two unlikely conditions occurred after the crisis. First, the USA would have to return to its excess consumption. However, this is unlikely in the near future since many Americans have been scared by the crisis into saving more. Second, China would have to return to its perpetual accumulation of US dollar reserves. Although China has continued to accumulate **foreign**

---

[6]Even if China was to use its US dollar foreign reserves to purchase foreign property (which China is now doing), the increase in the supply of dollars being used internationally would decrease the value of the dollar, *ceteris paribus*. If China did not maintain its fixed exchange rate, then a falling dollar would cause a rising yuan (if yuan/dollar is falling, then the dollar/yuan is rising). A rising yuan would cause China's exports to fall and imports to rise, *ceteris paribus*. If, instead, China wanted to maintain its fixed exchange rate, it would need to print more yuan and exchange it for dollars; i.e., accumulate more foreign reserves.

reserves after the crisis, China's previous top leadership — Hu Jintao, Wen Jiabao, and Zhou Xiaochuan — have made it very clear that China will not continue to accumulate **US dollars** for very long (Leightner, 2012; Xin and Fion, 2013). China's holdings of US Treasuries have not been steadily increasing since 2009. They were 939.9 billion in July 2009, only 843.7 billion in June 2010 (for a more than 10% reduction), climbed to 1,175.3 billion by October 2010, and then fell to 1,144.9 billion in March 2011, climbed to 1,297 in May 2011, fell to 1,153.6 billion in September 2012, and rose to 1,304.5 billion in October 2013.[7] Furthermore, China continues to diversify its foreign reserves — adding more Euro, Japanese, and South Korean assets.

The USA and Europe significantly decreased their imports from China when they went into crises in 2007–2008. This greatly hurt China which was dependent on exporting goods to the USA and Europe.[8] Not wanting to be so vulnerable to forces outside of its control, China announced that it would switch from an export-driven growth model to a domestic consumption-driven growth model.

An Empirical Evaluation of China's Consumption-Driven Growth Model

In this Section, I estimate $\partial GPP/\partial(w/(p + r))$ for 30 of China's 31 provinces and/or administrative areas where GPP is Gross Provincial Product (measured in units of 100 million yuan) and $w/(p + r)$ is the ratio of wages to profits plus rent. The one province that I do not include is Tibet because the reliability of the data for Tibet is very questionable.[9] Under a consumption-driven growth model, an increase in wages

---

[7]Available at http://www.ustreas.gov/tic/mfh.txt [accessed December 2013, October 2012, July 2011, and August 2010].

[8]Recall that in Chapter 5, we discovered that decreases in exports tend to reduce GDP much more than increases in exports increase GDP for most of the countries examined in this book.

[9]I would have liked to have included estimates from China throughout this entire book. Unfortunately, quarterly data on China's GDP is not available. The data I use in this chapter is annual data on a provincial basis. Using provincial data provides sufficient observations to make the estimates. However, the data on Tibet is not credible. For example, per capita annual income of urban households in Tibet from rent is listed as 1 yuan in 2004, 10 yuan

increases the purchasing ability of consumers which increases growth. In contrast, under an export-driven growth model, an increase in wages reduces the international competitiveness of the producer, reducing exports and growth. Thus, the ratio of wages to profits and rents $(w/(p+r))$ should be positively related to GPP under a consumption-driven growth model $[\partial\text{GPP}/\partial(w/(p+r)) > 0]$, but negatively related $[\partial\text{GPP}/\partial(w/(p+r)) < 0]$ under an export-driven growth model.[10]

I separated the empirical results into two groups: provinces for which $\partial\text{GPP}/\partial(w/(p+r))$ is increasing versus provinces for which $\partial\text{GPP}/\partial(w/(p+r))$ is decreasing over time. Panel A of Table 7.1 lists the estimates and Figure 7.2 graphs the estimates for the increasing $\partial\text{GPP}/\partial(w/(p+r))$ group. As of 2011, only six provinces had positive $\partial\text{GPP}/\partial(w/(p+r))$: Beijing, Inner Mongolia, Heilongjiang, Jiangsu, Gansu, and Xinjiang. In addition to these six provinces, Shanghai, Hubei, Hainan, Guizhou, Yunnan, Shaanxi, Qinghai, and Ningxia have $\partial\text{GPP}/\partial(w/(p+r))$ that are still negative in 2011, but which have been increasing over time. These 14 provinces appear to be moving toward a consumption-driven growth model, although only the first 6 appear to have gotten there. In contrast, there are 16 provinces for which $\partial\text{GPP}/\partial(w/(p+r))$ appears to be declining over time and the estimates for these provinces are listed in Panel B of Table 7.1 and depicted in Figure 7.3.[11]

---

in 2005, but 218 yuan in 2006. Per capita income from profits in Tibet is listed as 43 yuan in both 2004 and 2005, but jump to 390 yuan in 2006. All the data used in this chapter comes from *China's Statistical Yearbook*.

[10]Appendix 1 explains how Reiterative Truncated Projected Least Squares (RTPLS) handles cases where the estimated relationship could be positive or negative (or even change from negative to positive (or vice versa) due to omitted variables). The appendix also explains why and how, for the estimates in this chapter, I eliminated the influence of government consumption before doing the estimates.

[11]Tianjin and Jilin appear to be border-line cases but were included in the second group. I do not provide confidence intervals for the Chinese results because, as Appendix 1 explains, the construction of confidence intervals involves applying the central limit theorem to a particular RTPLS estimate and the two estimates before and the two estimate after it. The resulting 99% confidence interval tells the researcher that there is only a 1% chance that the true "average" value for the five estimates included lies outside of the 99% confidence interval. Finding an "average" value for a five-year period (which is what China's *annual* data would force us into) when China's economy is changing so rapidly, does not make sense.

Table 7.1:   ∂GPP/∂(Wages/(Profits + Rents)) and the Ratio of Wages/(Profits + Rents)

	2011	2010	2009	2008	2007	2006	2005	2004	2003	2002
A $\partial GPP/\partial(w/(p + r))$										
Beijing	543.53	381.06	353.00	306.96	248.94	505.10	268.15	−334.03	−38.62	−49.23
Inner Mongolia	19.91	18.41	11.21	−46.07	−59.96	−64.75	−60.80	−54.65	−66.19	−70.31
Heilongjiang	151.44	116.99	103.27	44.17	−5.10	−34.25	−58.82	−68.83	−78.91	−80.04
Shanghai	−61.17	−123.38	−54.38	−108.67	−85.56	−115.64	−123.71	−179.74	−245.87	−172.47
Jiangsu	139.91	179.44	111.43	38.74	−8.69	−84.07	−124.72	−122.58	−96.81	−128.78
Hubei	−54.14	−37.74	−41.22	−44.44	−82.72	−54.33	−103.90	−129.07	−147.95	−167.63
Hainan	−72.90	−77.99	−81.63	−82.20	−90.43	−89.55	−90.29	−102.99	−99.76	−102.51
Guizhou	−50.52	−48.40	−50.25	−60.07	−52.49	−50.65	−52.87	−70.32	−84.10	−82.72
Yunnan	−4.77	−12.89	−20.47	−32.38	−24.35	−15.38	−32.99	−41.05	−54.10	−45.73
Shaanxi	−41.93	−58.19	−56.12	−78.44	−134.72	−192.59	−236.79	−180.02	−174.35	−220.95
Gansu	20.37	0.28	−17.77	−36.14	−69.08	−93.85	−103.48	−112.82	−135.84	−147.52
Qinghai	−58.43	−62.43	−70.71	−63.22	−71.84	−71.23	−79.56	−99.11	−107.12	−116.67
Ningxia	−72.89	−75.24	−87.47	−70.02	−71.02	−75.80	−76.06	−89.22	−87.50	−89.28
Xinjiang	108.38	73.56	28.21	7.81	−22.07	0.01	−55.50	−63.47	−74.56	−94.85
Mean	**40.49**	**19.53**	**9.08**	**−16.00**	**−37.79**	**−31.21**	**−66.52**	**−117.71**	**−106.55**	**−112.05**
B Tianjin	−75.81	−80.37	−82.57	−91.13	−79.22	−77.55	−87.23	−84.25	−84.80	−87.20
Hebei	−182.94	−92.82	−100.26	−55.36	−36.19	−65.69	−72.14	−98.91	−133.95	−120.36
Shanxi	−126.14	−96.91	−69.51	−78.59	−116.77	−122.13	−112.84	−106.40	−106.20	−107.42
Liaoning	−290.05	−216.53	−178.00	−169.02	−124.27	−93.56	−73.89	−93.07	−62.33	−51.38
Jilin	−80.00	−69.93	−62.12	−59.52	−80.22	−107.01	−85.11	−73.93	−67.57	−63.89
Zhejiang	−251.84	−215.89	−173.28	−152.37	−149.92	−103.37	−96.20	−83.16	−76.81	−49.70
Anhui	−173.21	−156.12	−177.26	−158.42	−154.59	−132.68	−119.97	−105.60	−87.73	−90.74
Fujian	−210.09	−157.49	−126.02	−113.86	−101.76	−91.21	−74.50	−68.83	−71.79	−77.72

(Continued)

Table 7.1: *(Continued)*

	2011	2010	2009	2008	2007	2006	2005	2004	2003	2002
Jiangxi	−127.42	−160.59	−141.66	−126.46	−102.64	−108.36	−117.50	−122.25	−113.59	−104.39
Shandong	−261.71	−282.82	−272.22	−280.01	−276.23	−49.75	−61.32	−91.25	−127.32	−337.66
Henan	−148.95	−123.06	−87.23	−105.35	−66.87	−18.21	−42.33	−68.91	−60.05	−54.37
Hunan	−166.86	−140.42	−106.22	−94.50	−62.69	−45.60	−50.32	−61.09	−61.88	−74.50
Guangdong	−384.06	−357.06	−366.70	−355.91	−361.07	−212.59	−181.14	−162.86	−78.15	−70.99
Guangxi	−122.65	−94.67	−84.60	−79.29	−44.50	−49.84	−62.79	−76.17	−63.75	−70.34
Chongqing	−107.49	−93.06	−105.03	−111.32	−100.23	−91.69	−89.83	−152.28	−556.01	−158.08
Sichuan	−143.88	−150.75	−143.51	−92.25	−82.89	−83.10	−81.76	−87.07	−79.46	−79.86
Mean	**−178.32**	**−155.53**	**−142.26**	**−132.71**	**−121.25**	**−90.77**	**−88.05**	**−96.00**	**−114.46**	**−99.91**
C $w/(p + r)$										
Beijing	13.33	12.64	12.55	15.22	20.87	32.12	33.83	35.77	20.76	16.48
Inner Mongolia	5.22	5.15	5.36	5.47	6.94	6.48	6.54	6.88	7.50	7.89
Heilongjiang	6.13	6.64	6.36	5.42	6.82	5.33	5.88	7.66	8.16	8.97
Shanghai	10.87	11.89	12.14	12.33	12.44	12.72	13.10	18.22	22.73	16.93
Jiangsu	4.81	4.96	5.35	5.34	5.66	6.25	6.62	7.20	7.71	13.84
Hubei	5.58	6.47	6.76	6.97	10.74	12.42	12.36	15.40	18.05	19.19
Hainan	4.48	4.81	4.95	5.27	8.29	7.26	7.06	10.56	9.46	10.17
Guizhou	5.46	6.94	7.10	8.86	8.37	6.46	6.26	8.15	10.73	10.33
Yunnan	4.06	4.75	4.51	4.27	6.90	6.85	6.03	7.20	15.69	15.56
Shaanxi	14.25	15.89	15.48	14.09	20.68	14.38	20.22	16.89	18.60	22.85
Gansu	10.40	13.00	12.26	11.87	14.41	16.07	15.67	15.89	16.94	18.57
Qinghai	10.06	9.88	10.60	10.57	12.87	10.07	9.76	13.72	13.74	15.03
Ningxia	4.83	4.46	4.14	4.31	5.77	6.04	5.65	9.31	8.93	9.79
Xinjiang	8.11	8.82	9.38	8.72	13.37	11.47	11.36	14.70	16.90	19.20
Mean	**7.68**	**8.31**	**8.35**	**8.48**	**11.01**	**10.99**	**11.45**	**13.40**	**13.99**	**14.63**

(Continued)

Table 7.1:   (Continued)

	2011	2010	2009	2008	2007	2006	2005	2004	2003	2002
D Tianjin	12.36	13.26	12.49	11.46	10.52	10.20	10.04	10.37	11.79	10.29
Hebei	5.43	7.72	8.40	6.82	10.23	7.91	8.34	12.62	12.37	13.79
Shanxi	11.44	8.67	8.14	7.61	14.63	14.70	14.59	13.29	14.21	14.17
Liaoning	5.00	5.72	5.81	5.49	7.98	7.92	10.49	14.09	13.77	13.49
Jilin	5.83	6.95	6.53	6.93	8.74	7.28	7.44	6.32	7.14	7.74
Zhejiang	3.41	3.58	3.55	3.46	3.93	4.25	4.82	6.25	6.27	8.86
Anhui	5.28	7.16	8.00	7.42	9.26	8.97	8.61	8.85	10.06	12.40
Fujian	3.68	4.41	4.40	4.04	5.73	6.93	6.83	7.42	8.99	10.38
Jiangxi	5.31	6.59	7.03	6.64	10.37	9.08	10.14	10.60	11.88	12.40
Shandong	6.06	7.17	7.80	8.40	11.41	13.40	14.02	19.97	21.95	28.65
Henan	4.72	6.36	7.24	6.86	8.23	7.62	8.05	9.59	10.62	11.38
Hunan	3.35	4.45	4.56	4.80	6.32	6.08	6.37	11.60	13.10	15.63
Guangdong	4.93	5.22	5.29	4.89	7.40	6.84	8.39	10.50	11.20	11.77
Guangxi	5.32	5.88	5.96	5.88	6.77	6.86	10.02	13.06	10.77	11.74
Chongqing	6.25	8.08	9.29	11.02	10.98	12.91	11.54	21.13	32.25	22.18
Sichuan	5.78	7.17	7.05	7.00	7.74	7.38	8.04	8.59	9.20	9.62
Mean	**5.88**	**6.77**	**6.97**	**6.80**	**8.77**	**8.65**	**9.23**	**11.51**	**12.85**	**13.41**

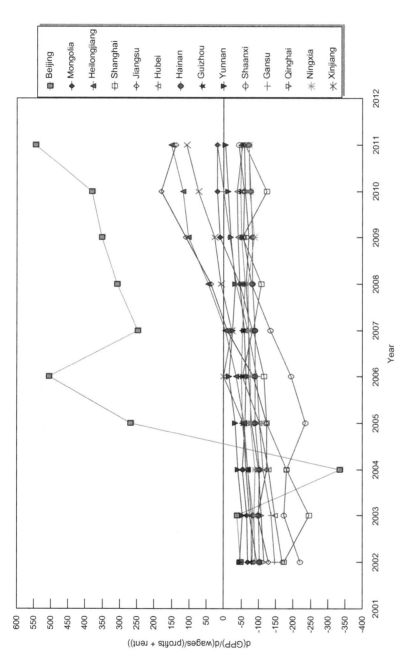

Figure 7.2: Change in GPP due to a Change in Ratio of Wages to Profits and Rent: Provinces Moving toward Consumption-Driven Growth

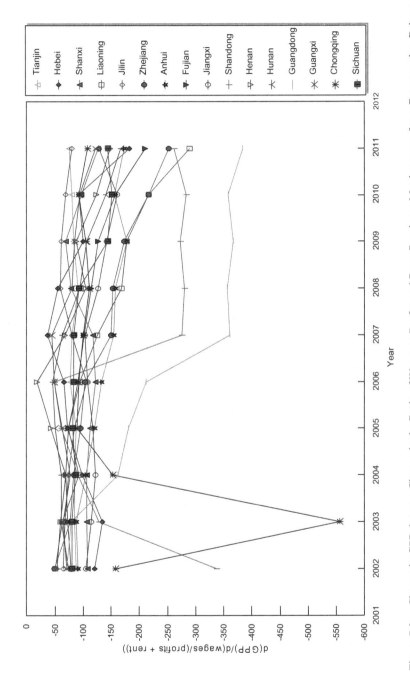

Figure 7.3:　Change in GPP due to a Change in the Ratio of Wages to Profits and Rent: Provinces Moving away from Consumption-Driven Growth

The six provinces with positive $\partial GPP/\partial(w/(p+r))$ in 2011 show that consumption-driven growth is possible in China; the 24 provinces with negative $\partial GPP/\partial(w/(p+r))$ show that China has a significant way to go before consumption-driven growth takes firm root and drives the entire Chinese economy. Beijing's 2011 $\partial GPP/\partial(w/(p+r))$ estimate of 543.53 implies that if the ratio of per capita wages to per capita profits plus rent increased by 1, then Beijing's GPP would increase by 54.353 billion yuan.[12] Panels C and D of Table 7.1 put the $\partial GPP/\partial(w/(p+r))$ estimates into better perspective by giving the actual ratios for wages to profits plus rent. Beijing's $w/(p+r)$ ratio was 12.64 in 2010 and it grew to 13.33 in 2011 for an increase of 0.69 which multiplied by 54.353 produced a 37.5 billion yuan increase in GPP for Beijing in 2011. Unfortunately, only two of the six provinces with positive values for $\partial GPP/\partial(w/(p+r))$ had increases in $w/(p+r)$ between 2010 and 2011 — Beijing and Inner Mongolia. Indeed, Figures 7.4 and 7.5 show that the ratio of wages to profits plus rents is falling over time for the vast majority of China's provinces, and this is true for both those provinces moving toward and those moving away from consumption-driven growth.

Figure 7.2 shows that consumption-driven growth has made some progress in approximately half of China's provinces; however, if the actual ratio of wages to profits plus rent declines, then consumption-driven growth will die before it has a chance to firmly take root. The last row of Panels C and D of Table 7.1 show that the average ratio of wages to profits plus rent has fallen between 2002 and 2011 from 14.63 to 7.68 for the provinces moving toward consumption-driven growth and has fallen from 13.41 to 5.88 in the provinces moving away from consumption-driven growth. Wages have risen in China since 2008 (Orlik, 2013),[13] but profits and rents have risen even more.

Perhaps, the strongest evidence that consumption-driven growth has not yet succeeded in China is that the consumption to GPP ratios have been falling in most of China's provinces as shown in Table 7.2, Panels A and B,

---

[12]GPP is measured in units of 100 million yuan, thus the movement of the decimal point.

[13]According to Orlik (2013), manufacturing wages in China have increased 71% since 2008. Furthermore, average private sector wages increased by 12.3% and 14% in 2011 and 2012 respectively.

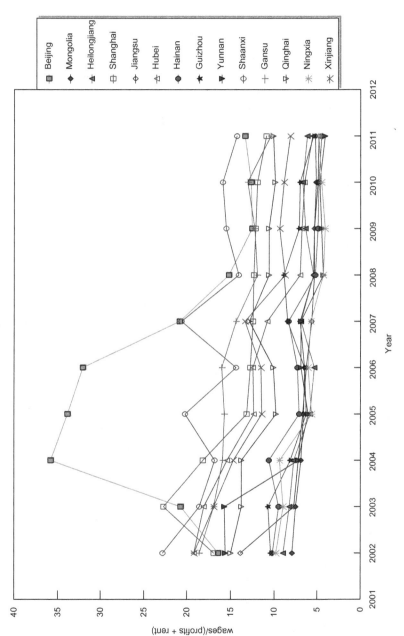

Figure 7.4: Ratio of Wages to Profits and Rent: Provinces Moving toward Consumption-Driven Growth

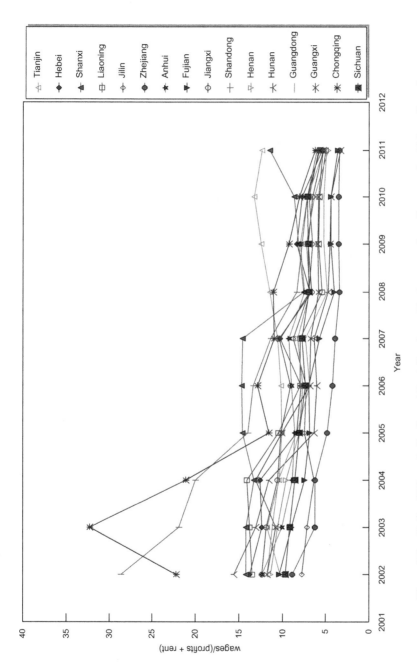

Figure 7.5:   Ratio of Wages to Profits and Rent: Provinces Moving away from Consumption-Driven Growth

Table 7.2:   C/GPP and (Exports − Imports)/GPP Ratios

	2011	2010	2009	2008	2007	2006	2005	2004	2003	2002
A C/GPP										
Beijing	0.3400	0.3293	0.3145	0.3030	0.3043	0.3323	0.3265	0.3318	0.3487	0.3564
Inner Mongolia	0.2288	0.2323	0.2400	0.2339	0.2637	0.2893	0.3075	0.3167	0.3551	0.4091
Heilongjiang	0.3239	0.3289	0.3447	0.3238	0.3222	0.3175	0.3340	0.3376	0.3685	0.3684
Shanghai	0.4293	0.4242	0.3744	0.3772	0.3690	0.3630	0.3570	0.3554	0.3641	0.3719
Jiangsu	0.2756	0.2642	0.2680	0.2720	0.2816	0.2881	0.2917	0.2952	0.3142	0.3276
Hubei	0.3095	0.3175	0.3366	0.3602	0.3885	0.4160	0.4271	0.4355	0.4455	0.4419
Hainan	0.3195	0.3167	0.3476	0.3466	0.3772	0.3742	0.3810	0.3917	0.4055	0.4148
Guizhou	0.4502	0.4644	0.4891	0.4893	0.5343	0.6047	0.6215	0.6305	0.6403	0.6846
Yunnan	0.4297	0.4266	0.4378	0.4311	0.4402	0.4542	0.4785	0.4727	0.4405	0.4591
Shaanxi	0.3004	0.3068	0.3259	0.3300	0.3547	0.3274	0.3536	0.3750	0.4115	0.4288
Gansu	0.3825	0.3805	0.4106	0.4032	0.4127	0.4352	0.4617	0.4597	0.4771	0.4830
Qinghai	0.2964	0.3000	0.3340	0.3160	0.3438	0.3598	0.3867	0.3970	0.4231	0.4370
Ningxia	0.3311	0.3349	0.3607	0.3605	0.3798	0.4318	0.4472	0.4209	0.4247	0.4324
Xinjiang	0.2956	0.2904	0.3004	0.2799	0.2886	0.2805	0.2949	0.3038	0.3309	0.3819
Mean	**0.3366**	**0.3369**	**0.3489**	**0.3448**	**0.3615**	**0.3767**	**0.3906**	**0.3945**	**0.4107**	**0.4283**
B Tianjin	0.2421	0.2437	0.2421	0.2413	0.2509	0.2567	0.2650	0.2819	0.3029	0.3287
Hebei	0.2812	0.2810	0.2926	0.2827	0.2882	0.2915	0.2916	0.3009	0.3192	0.3440
Shanxi	0.3108	0.3103	0.3150	0.3026	0.3198	0.3406	0.3402	0.3513	0.3574	0.3841
Liaoning	0.3080	0.3046	0.3078	0.3040	0.3045	0.3180	0.3361	0.3471	0.3618	0.3923
Jilin	0.2662	0.2751	0.3018	0.3101	0.3290	0.3128	0.3743	0.4133	0.4342	0.4343
Zhejiang	0.3603	0.3500	0.3537	0.3380	0.3416	0.3502	0.3502	0.3357	0.3440	0.3592
Anhui	0.3918	0.3943	0.4162	0.4156	0.4383	0.4415	0.4486	0.4440	0.4841	0.4776
Fujian	0.3092	0.3185	0.3143	0.3256	0.3352	0.3581	0.3643	0.3731	0.3854	0.3926

(Continued)

Table 7.2: (Continued)

	2011	2010	2009	2008	2007	2006	2005	2004	2003	2002
Jiangxi	0.3642	0.3752	0.3594	0.3618	0.3533	0.3861	0.4042	0.4130	0.4160	0.4533
Shandong	0.2866	0.2823	0.2924	0.2937	0.2950	0.2952	0.2935	0.3000	0.3280	0.3460
Henan	0.3200	0.3206	0.3208	0.3065	0.3211	0.3480	0.3606	0.3940	0.4179	0.4055
Hunan	0.3530	0.3610	0.3881	0.3941	0.4207	0.4600	0.4694	0.4752	0.4914	0.4998
Guangdong	0.3853	0.3634	0.3715	0.3600	0.3645	0.3822	0.4019	0.4216	0.4126	0.4036
Guangxi	0.3624	0.3821	0.4297	0.4165	0.4166	0.4206	0.4470	0.4479	0.4821	0.4956
Chongqing	0.3429	0.3523	0.3625	0.3650	0.3869	0.4256	0.4246	0.4193	0.4295	0.4436
Sichuan	0.3789	0.3863	0.3958	0.3919	0.4057	0.4268	0.4558	0.4630	0.4836	0.4948
Mean	**0.3289**	**0.3313**	**0.3415**	**0.3381**	**0.3482**	**0.3634**	**0.3767**	**0.3863**	**0.4031**	**0.4159**
C net X/GPP										
Beijing	0.0049	0.0077	0.0118	0.0372	0.0288	−0.0389	−0.0340	−0.0365	−0.0742	−0.0734
Inner Mongolia	−0.1519	−0.1674	−0.1761	−0.0537	−0.1095	−0.1609	−0.1861	−0.1302	−0.0871	−0.0294
Heilongjiang	−0.0709	−0.0738	−0.1421	0.0245	0.0778	0.1443	0.1618	0.1635	0.1649	0.1232
Shanghai	0.0337	0.0195	0.0374	0.0511	0.0311	0.0505	0.0609	0.0567	0.0598	0.0730
Jiangsu	0.0695	0.0728	0.0728	0.1007	0.0992	0.0908	0.0794	0.0546	0.0624	0.0939
Hubei	0.0104	0.0174	0.0066	0.0102	0.0105	−0.0406	−0.0106	−0.0142	0.0110	0.0025
Hainan	−0.0610	−0.0358	−0.0417	−0.0266	−0.0112	0.0076	0.0022	0.0013	−0.0043	−0.0080
Guizhou	−0.1694	−0.1869	−0.1942	−0.1555	−0.2171	−0.3146	−0.3401	−0.3480	−0.3738	−0.4224
Yunnan	−0.3957	−0.3663	−0.2160	−0.1256	−0.0633	−0.2483	−0.2416	−.1334	−0.1131	−0.0821
Shaanxi	−0.1237	−0.1279	−0.1438	−0.1028	−0.0980	−0.0323	−0.0072	−0.0157	−0.0734	−0.0413
Gansu	−0.1631	−0.1597	−0.1889	−0.1162	−0.0865	−0.0887	−0.1039	−0.1043	−0.0979	−0.1015
Qinghai	−0.3527	−0.3348	−0.3080	−0.2139	−0.2622	−0.3271	−0.3444	−0.3584	−0.4077	−0.4135
Ningxia	−0.3202	−0.4136	−0.4494	−0.3447	−0.3351	−0.3826	−0.4455	−0.3985	−0.3820	−0.3952
Xinjiang	−0.1620	−0.1469	−0.1260	−0.0457	−0.0564	−0.1550	−0.1048	−0.1209	−0.1379	−0.1333
Mean	**−0.1323**	**−0.1354**	**−0.1327**	**−0.0686**	**−0.0708**	**−0.1068**	**−0.1081**	**−0.0989**	**−0.1038**	**−0.1005**

(Continued)

Table 7.2: (Continued)

	2011	2010	2009	2008	2007	2006	2005	2004	2003	2002
D Tianjin	-0.1391	-0.1336	-0.1078	0.0266	0.0611	0.0532	0.0600	0.0341	0.0279	0.0288
Hebei	0.0405	0.0506	0.0435	0.0649	0.0753	0.1001	0.1141	0.1346	0.1490	0.1246
Shanxi	-0.0785	-0.1272	-0.1154	0.0134	0.0166	-0.0127	-0.0073	-0.0026	0.0054	-0.0009
Liaoning	-0.0257	-0.0245	-0.0311	-0.0335	-0.0178	0.0131	0.0228	0.0394	0.0943	0.1083
Jilin	-0.1315	-0.1991	-0.2392	-0.2511	-0.1567	-0.0095	-0.0085	-0.0096	-0.0128	-0.0115
Zhejiang	0.0784	0.0758	0.0742	0.1141	0.0839	0.0642	0.0458	0.0415	0.0431	0.0592
Anhui	-0.0019	-0.0020	-0.0030	-0.0045	-0.0050	-0.0037	-0.0020	-0.0025	-0.0005	-0.0011
Fujian	0.0311	0.0316	0.0302	0.0352	0.0392	0.0446	0.0502	0.0552	0.0512	0.0513
Jiangxi	0.0103	0.0113	-0.0071	-0.0099	-0.0104	-0.0113	-0.0094	-0.0159	-0.0114	0.0008
Shandong	0.0512	0.0597	0.0653	0.0962	0.0899	0.0780	0.0691	0.0664	0.0663	0.0533
Henan	-0.1492	-0.1340	-0.1317	-0.0252	-0.0123	-0.0046	0.0202	0.0281	0.0277	0.0290
Hunan	-0.0169	-0.0216	-0.0274	-0.0077	-0.0127	-0.0345	-0.0154	-0.0149	0.0030	0.0012
Guangdong	0.1152	0.1406	0.1507	0.2090	0.2025	0.1408	0.1095	0.0789	0.0814	0.1076
Guangxi	-0.3302	-0.3309	-0.3062	-0.1323	-0.0884	-0.0487	-0.0366	-0.0058	-0.0245	-0.0214
Chongqing	-0.0388	-0.0584	-0.0724	-0.0497	-0.0926	-0.1926	-0.1886	-0.1572	-0.1494	-0.0913
Sichuan	-0.0221	-0.0375	-0.0536	-0.0408	-0.0333	-0.0391	-0.0405	-0.0241	-0.0461	-0.0455
Mean	**-0.0380**	**-0.0437**	**-0.0457**	**0.0003**	**0.0087**	**0.0086**	**0.0115**	**0.0153**	**0.0190**	**0.0245**

and depicted in Figures 7.6 and 7.7. These tables and figures show that between 2008 and 2011, the consumption to GPP ratio has been consistently rising in only Beijing and Shanghai. The last row of Panels A and B of Table 7.2 show that the average consumption to GPP ratio has steadily fallen between 2002 and 2011 from 0.4283 to 0.3366 and from 0.4159 to 0.3289 in the provinces moving toward and away from consumption-driven growth respectively. Clearly, consumption-driven growth is not occurring in most of China.

Remember that China's leaders after 2008 declared that China would shift from an export-driven growth model to a consumption-driven model. Table 7.2, Panels C and D, and Figures 7.8 and 7.9 depict the ratio of net exports to GPP where net exports are exports minus imports. It is relevant that, on average, the ratio of net exports to GPP is more negative for the provinces moving toward consumption-driven growth than it is for the provinces moving away from consumption-driven growth for every year in my data (see last line of Panels C and D of Table 7.2). This makes sense because the provinces most dependent on exports before 2008 are likely to be the ones that have the most difficulty shifting to consumption-driven growth.

Part of the fall in the net exports to GPP ratios for Heilongjiang, Jiangsu, Yunnan, Gansu, Qinghai, Xinjiang, Guangdong, Tianjin, and Guangxi provinces depicted in Figures 7.8 and 7.9 could be due to the efforts of the governments of those provinces to shift their economies away from a dependence on exports; however, most of it is probably due to falling demand for China's exports in the wake of the crisis that began in 2007–2008. It was this falling demand that spurred China's leaders to declare a shift from an export-driven growth model to a consumption-driven model. However, China has a long way to go to make that declared shift a reality.[14]

---

[14]Given the earlier discussion on what China could do with its accumulated foreign reserves if it every successfully established a consumption-driven growth model, this is good news for the US dollar but bad news for the masses of Chinese workers.

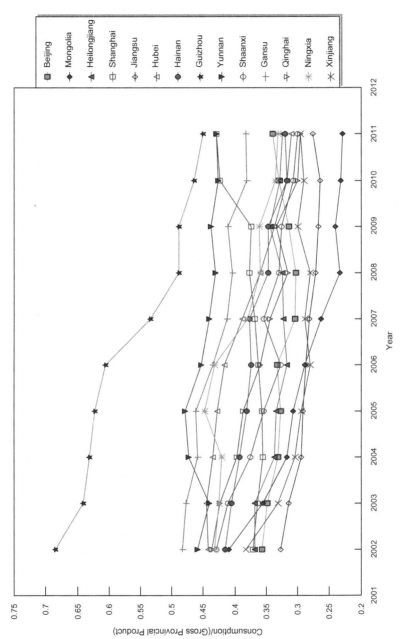

Figure 7.6:   Ratio of Consumption to Gross Provincial Product: Provinces Moving toward Consumption-Driven Growth

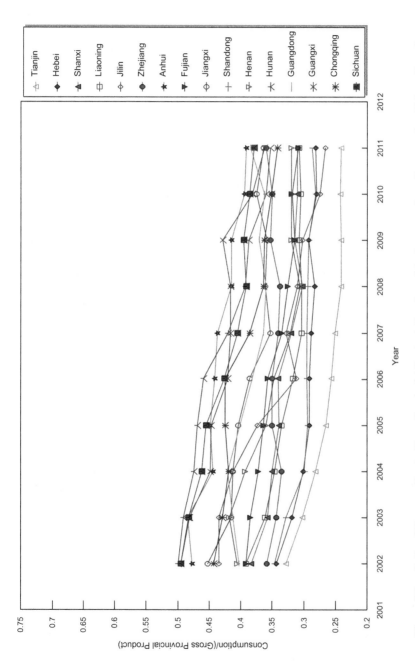

Figure 7.7:   Ratio of Consumption to Gross Provincial Product: Provinces Moving away from Consumption-Driven Growth

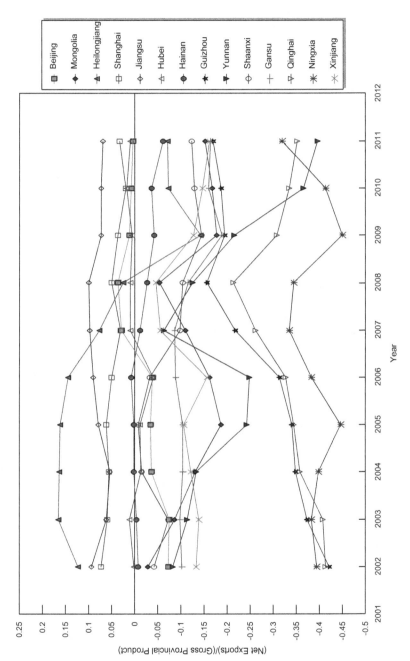

Figure 7.8:   Ratio of Net Exports to Gross Provincial Product: Provinces Moving toward Consumption-Driven Growth

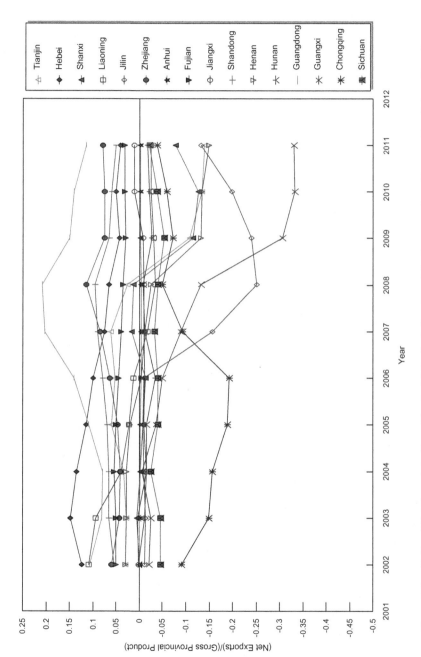

Figure 7.9: Ratio of Net Exports to Gross Provincial Product: Provinces Moving away from Consumption-Driven Growth

Reforms Needed for a Successful Chinese Consumption Growth Model

The international financial crisis that began in 2008 convinced China that it cannot rely upon US and European demand for its exports. China wants a new and more reliable buyer for its goods. The currently under-developed massive domestic market in China is the greatest source of potential buyers for Chinese goods on this earth. Realizing that, Hu Jintao and Wen Jiabao, China's previous top leadership, actively advocated a domestic consumption-driven growth model for China's future. China's current top leadership, Xi Jinping and Li Kequing, have added to Hu Jintao's ideas by arguing that urban areas consume more than rural areas, and, therefore, China needs to accelerate its urbanization. As of 2012, more than 50% of China's population lives in urban areas for the first time in history. However, for the full potential of this market to be realized, major reforms will need to be made in China.

Buyers need income in order to be able to buy. Thus, China must redistribute income from the wealthy (who tend to save more of their income) to the poor (who spend a larger percent of their income). In 2010, China's top legislature (the National People's Congress) proposed a major reform in income distribution to "be launched as soon as possible," which aims to increase incomes, reduce the wealth gap, and make the middle class the largest sector of society ("Legislature," 2010).

Until recently, the Chinese communist party suppressed labor strikes. Thus, it surprised many when, in response to a 2010 labor dispute at a Japanese owned factory in China, Wen Jiabao told a Japanese delegation that "Labor disputes are occurring at some foreign companies [located in China], where there is a problem of relatively low wages. We would like (Japan) to address this issue" (Chang, 2010). Apparently, China is now allowing labor strikes and slow-downs in foreign-owned factories located in China in an effort to get higher wages for Chinese workers.

China began making policy shifts to help workers, at the expense of the factory owners, even before the 2008 financial crisis. For example, China's new labor law officially took effect in January 2008.[15] This law requires that

---

[15]I do not know to what extent this new labor law is enforced.

all employers give their employees written contracts and that an employee can be given a maximum of two contracts with fixed ending dates. At the end of the second fixed ending date contract, the employee must be fired or given a permanent labor contract. Under a permanent labor contract, the worker can only be fired if the worker breaks his obligations as outlined in the written contract.

The policy shifts discussed above should increase disposable income for China's relatively poorer masses. However, China needs to do more than just increase disposable income. China needs to eliminate the fear that is the primary driving force behind China's excess savings rate. The Chinese people are afraid of getting sick and of not having enough money to pay the doctor. Many Chinese medical doctors enthusiastically embraced Deng Xiaoping's sayings, "to get rich is glorious," "some will get rich before others," and "whatever makes profits is good for China," A doctor maximizes his profits by giving his patients expensive treatments that keep the patients alive but still sick. If a patient gets well, they stop going to the doctor and the doctor loses them as a source of income. Furthermore, until very recently, health insurance only covered a small percent of China's population and the limited health insurance that did exist required payment by the insured upfront. The Chinese people are afraid that they will get sick and not have enough money to pay their medical expenses.

The Chinese people also are afraid that corrupt government officials or corporate leaders will misuse and lose their pension funds.[16] People can either save or consume their disposable income. Chinese households save almost 30% of their disposable income out of fear of major health care problems and/or pension funds failing (Leightner, 2010b; Prasad, 2009). Until China's health care system and pension system problems are fixed, the Chinese people will continue to save, limiting (or preventing) the success of any consumption promoting strategies of the government.

China's one-child policy has also contributed to the fear that causes the Chinese to save. Many one-child couples worry about what would happen to them in their old age if their one child died, perhaps from an earthquake causing schools to collapse. Furthermore, China's dependency

---

[16]The problems with Detroit, Michigan's 2013 bankruptcy and its pension obligations implies that even citizens of the USA should worry about the safety of their pension funds.

rate is projected to grow from under 40% in 2010 to almost 70% in 2050 (Naughton, 2007). The dependency rate is the ratio of the total population that is either too old or too young to work divided by the number of people who are the right age to work. A dependency ratio of 40 means everyone of working age must produce enough goods and services to support themselves and 40% of another person. If China had not changed its one-child policy, by 2050, every person of working age would have had to support themselves and 70% of another person. Such an increased burden on workers requires much savings. China's leaders realized this problem and relaxed China's one-child policy in November 2013; now couples can have two children if either the mother or father was a single child. However, this change is too late for the many women who were automatically sterilized when their first child was born. While Japan, the USA, and Europe face problems from a graying population, China's one-child policy has exacerbated its graying process. Hopefully, the recent changes in the one-child law will help reverse this process, but the question remains, "Are these changes too little and too late?" As countries gray, they save more and consume less.

If China could also prevent the exploitation of rural migrants in urban areas and the taking of farm land by local governments (Leightner, 2010a), then a consumption-driven model would get a boost from rural spending. Most importantly, if the Chinese people could trust each other because any form of corruption or illegal activity was vigorously prosecuted in a fair, transparent, and efficient legal system that was accessible to all, regardless of wealth, then the Chinese would fear less and consume more. Finally, it is essential that China ensures that the products it produces are safe. Repeated cases of lead paint on toys, melamine in milk, and lyme in flour reduce the consumption of domestically produced goods.

China also needs to solve problems with its state-owned banks. These banks have historically loaned to China's state-owned enterprises, which tend to emphasize exports, and have ignored China's small and medium firms, which would be more likely to cater to the domestic market. The small and medium firms have often felt starved of credit. Chinese citizens are not allowed to invest abroad, and, therefore, many Chinese put their savings into accounts in Chinese banks which pay very low interest rates. Recently, the banks have devised "wealth management" products for their rich clients, which make it possible for the rich to earn a much higher rate of return. However, there are serious concerns that some of these wealth management products are Ponzi schemes or have problems similar to the problems of derivatives that caused the sub-prime crisis in the USA.

If the above problems were significantly reduced, then increased consumption could lead to several waves of domestic investment and, thus, growth. Both Japan and the USA have enjoyed periods of consumption-driven growth. During the 1960s, a substantial increase in the real income for Japan's working class led to several waves of domestic demand-driven investment and growth (Ozawa, 1985). During the first wave, Japan's working class purchased automatic rice cookers, washing machines, air conditioners, TVs, and automobiles. In response, Japanese companies expanded old factories and built new factories to increase their production of these consumer products. These products also increased the leisure time for Japanese housewives. By 1969, the average Japanese housewife spent less than 8 hours per day on household chores, in contrast to before the war spending 11 hours. Increased leisure time produced increased purchases of, and investment in, the production of domestically made leisure goods and services (Leightner, 1992).

In the 1920s, the USA enjoyed several waves of demand-driven growth. Rosenberg (2003, p. 4) explains:

> Though invented earlier, the full impact of the automobile on the US economy was not felt until the 1920s. Car production increased three-fold during this decade. This generated strong demand for investment in the automobile industry as well as in other industries dependent on car production such as tires, auto parts, plate glass and steel. Roads and traffic lights needed to be built and gas stations soon followed. The automobile fostered the growth of the suburb. With suburbanization came increased spending on new housing. Many of the new homes would be electrified and have telephones and radios. Thus, investment spending in the electric power, telephone and communications industries took off.

The USA and Japan enjoyed periods of consumption-driven growth and so could China, if China would implement the key reforms discussed above.

Finally, notice that a consumption-driven growth model is not anti-trade. Instead, giving more income and security to labor and the poor will cause an increase in the domestic demand for goods which will cause production for goods sold domestically to increase, *ceteris paribus*. As this happens, the percent of the economy dependent on trade will naturally decline without any anti-trade policies imposed. As a country becomes less dependent on trade, the probability falls that it will face a crisis due to declining foreign demand.

A Fork in the Road: China's International Capital Choices

Zheng Xinli (a member of the National Committee of the Chinese People's Political Consultative Conference and deputy director of the Subcommittee of Economy of the advisory body) wrote in July 2011,

> As part of world's ongoing economic adjustments, global inflation triggered by the depreciation of the dollar will continue into the future, which will increase imported inflationary pressures on China, threaten the country's foreign reserve security and constitute an immediate, and indeed, the biggest challenge to its development over the next five years. The quantitative easing policy adopted by the US Federal Reserve, aimed at shifting the US' economic losses to other countries, has fuelled sharp devaluations of the dollar and global inflation. Given that 70% of China's foreign reserves are dollar-denominated assets, every one percent depreciation of the dollar will lead to more than $10 billion of its foreign reserves evaporating. Also, the dramatic price rises of bulk commodities such as oil, iron ore, beans and cotton in recent years, as a result of the US' adoption of the weak dollar policy, have brought huge pressures to China's manufacturers that are heavily dependent on imports of these commodities. China has achieved success in fending off the first impacts of the global financial crisis, but it has yet to come up with effective measures to better resist the new wave of global inflation in a bid to maintain the safety of its financial assets.

China, like most countries, attempts to fight inflation by decreasing its money supply which causes domestic interest rates to rise. In contrast, interest rates in the USA are stuck at approximately 0% due to the US Federal Reserves' continuing policy of quantitative easing. People like to put their assets into countries that have the highest interest rates because they earn the greatest possible return there. Thus, as China's interest rate rises, there will be increasing demand for the Chinese yuan and increasing pressure for the Chinese yuan to appreciate. In essence, China's increased interest rate causes China's Demand Total line in Figure 7.10 to increase. In response, China will either have to purchase even more foreign reserves in order to keep the yuan fixed or it will have to allow the yuan to appreciate.

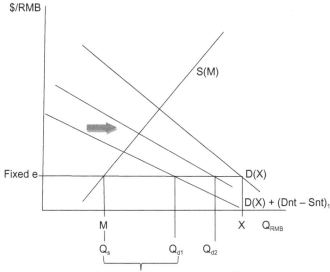

Figure 7.10:   Effect of China's Rising Interest Rates on the International Currency Market

In this situation, China has several conflicting goals. First, China would like to shift to a consumption-driven growth model, without damaging their exports. However, purchasing additional foreign reserves would continue the past policies that aided the producer and exporter at the expense of the consumer (see Chapter 5). Allowing the yuan to appreciate would hurt exporters, but help consumers. Furthermore, China would like to control the value of the yuan, while simultaneously increasing its international use and prestige. Lingling Wei and Robert Davis (2011) writes,

> The [yuan internationalization] move had important unintended side effects, including giving companies and investors a way to profit from the difference in interest rates between China and other countries, and opening a path for "hot money" to flood the country. . . . China's stumble in trying to get its currency more widely accepted outside its borders underlie a fundamental contradiction at the heart of Beijing's plans: the Chinese authorities want to keep a tight grip on the value of the yuan to keep exports booming, while at the same time encourage more foreign companies and investors to use it. . . . There is a "tension in the short run between managing yuan appreciation and increasing the yuan's prominence in global trade and finance transactions," says Brooking Institute China scholar Eswar Prasad.

Moreover, China has advocated the world shifting away from using the US dollar as the dominant world reserve currency (Leightner, 2013b). China has also made it clear that they would like for the yuan to be included in a basket of currencies that would replace the US dollar. Some Chinese scholars have openly advocated the world switching from primarily using the US dollar to the world using the Chinese yuan as the reserve currency. For the Chinese yuan to be considered a reserve currency, it must be more freely floating. China's progressive and steady stream of currency reforms of the last three years indicate that China's dominating goal is to make China's yuan a reserve currency (Blumenstein *et al.*, 2010; LeVine, 2009).

The stronger China's capital controls, the less foreign capital flows into China, and, thus, the lower the risk of foreign capital funding a speculative bubble, *ceteris paribus*. The more China dismantles those capital controls in an effort to move the Chinese yuan closer to a free float and, thus, closer to being a world reserve currency, the greater the risk of foreign capital flows funding a speculative bubble (Wei and Davis, 2011). Therefore, if China wants to reduce its risk of an externally originating crisis from foreign capital flows, then it must stop (and possibly reverse) its steady and progressive liberalization of its capital account.

The Thai 1997 crisis illustrates the danger that China faces as it eliminates its capital controls while its interest rate rises relative to world interest rates. Thailand opened an international banking sector in 1996 which (for all practical considerations) eliminated Thailand's capital controls. Because interest rates in Thailand, at that time, were 5% higher than world interest rates, foreign capital came flooding into Thailand. Those foreign funds financed the speculative bubble in the Thai real estate market which led to the Bangkok Bank of Commerce case, the soiling of the reputation of the central bank of Thailand, Somgprasong Land company defaulting on a 3 million dollar interest payment for some European debentures, and a temporary shutdown of the Thai stock market so that Thai regulators could increase the reserve requirements for Thai financial institutions. These events gave George Soros the ammunition he needed to lead a successful speculative attack against the Thai baht (Leightner, 1999; 2007b).

If China wants the Chinese yuan to become a world reserve currency, then it needs to liberate its capital controls. However, liberating its capital controls while Chinese interest rates are much higher than world interest rates could lead to a flood of foreign capital entering China, which then might fund a speculative bubble in China's real estate market. Furthermore, the current global surplus of savings increases the risk China faces if it dismantles its capital controls. China is facing a difficult fork in the road — does it liberate or not liberate its capital controls?

In recent years, China has projected two very different images to the world community. On the one hand, China looks like a successful world power when it hosts the summer Olympics and the World Fair and puts men in outer space. On the other hand, China claims that it is just a developing country, and not a world leader, when challenged to take a leadership role on global moral issues like genocide in the Sudan.

The branch of political economy called "Realism" would argue that China is out to increase its power as much as possible and would dominate the world if it could. China is now the second largest economy on the earth. Indeed, China sees the USA as its only major remaining rival. If China could cause the USA to fall, then China could assume the top, most powerful, position.

China's holdings of US dollar assets, which China accumulated while under its export promotion strategy, is the bullet that China could use to shoot the USA. If China successfully switches to a domestic consumption-driven growth model, then China would no longer need the USA as a buyer of its goods and China could then cause a fall of the US dollar (by dumping their US dollar assets) without significantly hurting itself.

Some scholars believe that China will not sell its US dollar assets because such a sell would drive down the value of their remaining US dollar assets (Wines *et al.*, 2009). Leightner (2010d, p. 35) finds that the value of the US dollar would fall by 4.42% in Europe and Asia if China sold 10% of its foreign reserves.

[Thus] if 1.27 trillion of China's reserves are in US dollar assets (or 65% of the total reserves as estimated by Molinski, 2007), then China selling ten percent of its reserves (for 195.4 billion dollars) could cause the value of China's remaining reserves to fall by 50.5 billion dollars ($1.27 \times 0.90 \times 0.0442$), greatly diminishing China's return. Given this large effect, China has the incentive to either sell none of its US dollar reserves or to sell all of its US dollar reserves. If China was convinced that the value of the US dollar would fall by a significant amount, no matter what China did, then it would be rational for China to sell as many of its US dollar assets as possible and as quickly as possible. If China sold all of its US dollar reserves then the value of the US dollar would plummet by at least 44% which would cause the value of US exports to fall by 44% (as measured in other currencies) and the dollar price the US pays for imports to increase by 44%. Such changes in exports and imports would drive the US economy much further into recession.

This author has heard several Chinese scholars say that China's currency, the yuan, should move "from the periphery to the center where it belongs." China is now steadily implementing currency reforms (Blumenstein *et al.*, 2010) which could be viewed as a preparation for the yuan to make a bid to replace the dollar as the world's reserve currency (LeVine, 2009). If China wants the yuan to replace the dollar as the world's reserve currency, then China might want to orchestrate a massive fall in the value of the dollar (by selling all of its holdings of US dollar assets at one time), once the yuan is ready.

China would minimize its own losses from a massive selling of its US dollar reserves if it arranged to sell parts of those reserves at the same time in different locations. If timed well, then most of China's reserves could be sold at the exchange rate that prevailed immediately before China began its selling. For this to work, China must not tell anyone else about its plans. For the rest of Asia, such a move would destroy the value of their US dollar reserves, causing a fall in international confidence in the rest of Asia. Such a move could throw Asia, and indeed the entire international financial system, into crisis.

Conclusion

In 2008–2009, China faced an externally originating crisis due to its declining exports to the USA and Europe. In order to reduce the possibility of being hurt in a similar way in the future, China's government is advocating a switch from an export-driven growth model to a domestic consumption-driven growth model. Whether or not China will be able to successfully make this switch is not yet obvious. China will have to fix some major problems (like its broken health care and pension systems) before such a switch could occur.

However, what China is advocating is exactly what the world needs. The world needs consumption to increase so that there is a reason to invest the global surplus of savings into increasing production. Until world consumption increases, the global economy will be buffeted by speculative bubbles, by investors seeking a return from rent or deception, and by financial/currency crises.

Chapter 8

INCOME DISTRIBUTION

Income distribution in the world is becoming less equal. This is clearly shown in Table 8.1 which provides Gini Coefficient[1] estimates for 45 countries. Of these countries, only Ecuador, Lithuania, Mexico, Spain, and Venezuela had Gini Coefficients that were falling and only France had a stable Gini Coefficient. The other 39 countries had rising Gini Coefficients indicating a decrease in income equality. The mean Gini Coefficient in Table 8.1 increased from 31.4 to 35.2 for a 12% fall in income equality, but that average weighs each country the same no matter what their population is. Consider the world's two largest economies as of 2013: the USA and China. The Gini Coefficient for the USA increased from 34.4 in 1979 to 40.1 in 2000 for a 16.6% increase. China's Gini Coefficient more than doubled from 22.4 in 1985 to 44.9 in 2003. Furthermore, the most recent Gini Coefficient estimates in Table 8.1 are from 2006, before the current crisis and before the current austerity measures aimed at reducing labor's share of income.

Figures 8.1 and 8.2 show how labor's share of income has fallen between 1970 and 2010 for the non-Euro (17) countries and for the Euro (17) countries respectively.[2] Note that, in Figure 8.2, labor's share of income fell between 2009 and 2010 for all the Euro (17) countries for which I have data. This fall is partially due to the anti-labor austerity programs being

---

[1] Recall that Chapter 7 included an explanation of how Gini Coefficients are calculated.
[2] The data underlying these figures is provided in Table A4.1 in Appendix 4.

Table 8.1:   Gini Coefficients[3]

Country	Year 1	Gini 1	Year 2	Gini 2
Argentina	1980	40.8	1998	49.4
Australia	1986	36.4	1998	39
Austria	1997	23.7	2006	25
Belgium	1985	24.7	2000	32.2
Bolivia	1996	58.8	1999	60.1
Bulgaria	1992	30.9	2006	31
Canada	1989	27.8	2000	30.1
Chile	1992	53.3	2000	59.5
China	1985	22.4	2003	44.9
Croatia	1987	21.1	1993	26.5
Denmark	1995	20	2006	24
Ecuador	1994	62.5	1999	58.8
El Salvador	1997	52	1999	54.6
Estonia	1996	35.5	2005	36.1
Finland	1987	19.6	2003	25.6
France	2002	27	2006	27
W. Germany	1987	28.6	2004	31.7
E. Germany	1990	18.5	2004	26
Greece	2000	32.3	2006	34
Hungary	1991	20.3	2006	26.2
Iceland	2004	24	2006	26
Ireland	2001	28.9	2006	32
Israel	1986	34.8	2001	37.2
Italy	2001	29.2	2006	32
Japan	1986	29.3	1998	31.9
Korea	1993	32.4	1998	36.9
Republic of Latvia	1997	31.5	2004	39.1
Lithuania	1997	32.3	2004	30.9
Luxembourg	1997	25.1	2006	28
Macedonia, FYR	1990	22.3	2006	32
Mexico	1992	54.7	2005	51
Netherlands	1997	25	2006	26

(*Continued*)

[3]The data for this table comes from the United Nations University data set available at http://www.wider.unu.edu/research/Database/. I used data for disposable or net income that had a quality rating of 1 or 2 (1 where available), from the research group that had done the most estimates over the longest time period. The last column has that group's most recent estimate. The third column has that group's lowest estimate if the Gini Coefficient was rising or highest estimate if falling.

Table 8.1: (*Continued*)

Country	Year 1	Gini 1	Year 2	Gini 2
New Zealand	1986	27	2004	33.5
Norway	1988	31.2	2002	37
Poland	1993	31.5	2005	36.6
Portugal	1996	36.8	2006	38
Romania	1990	22.9	2006	36.4
Slovak Republic	1997	23.2	2006	24.2
Slovenia	1994	21.9	2005	24.2
Spain	1997	34.9	2006	31
Sweden	1991	23	2003	25.2
Taiwan	1980	27.7	2003	33.9
United Kingdom	1977	23.3	2002	34.2
United States	1979	34.4	2000	40.1
Venezuela	1996	49.7	2000	45.8
Mean	1992	31.4	2003	35.2

used in Europe. In the USA, labor's share of income fell from 71% in 1970 to only 51% in 2011. In Japan, labor's share of income rose from 48% in 1970 to 62% in 1975 but then fell to 58% in 2011. Recall Figure 4.1 which shows that Japan enjoyed the highest $\partial GDP/\partial G$ of all the countries studied between 1965 and 1978 due to its pro-labor policies. Giving more income to labor, which has a much higher marginal propensity to consume (MPC)[4] than capital has, would increase the multiplier effect from increases in government spending or increases in the money supply in a Keynesian Macroeconomic model. Likewise, giving more income to capital would decrease the MPC and thus decrease the effectiveness of fiscal and monetary policy in a Keynesian model. Thus, the fall in labor's share of income depicted in Figures 8.1 and 8.2 fits theoretically with a falling effectiveness of monetary policy (Chapter 3), fiscal policy (Chapter 4), and trade policy (Chapter 5).

In spite of the above theoretical result, income distribution has not received the attention it deserves in economics. This insufficient attention

---

[4]The MPC is the additional consumption that results from increasing after tax income (disposable income = DI) by one unit. MPC = $\partial C/\partial DI$. It is the slope of the consumption function.

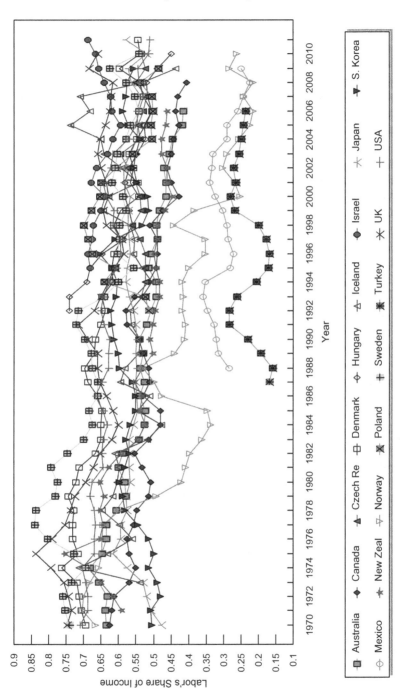

Figure 8.1:   Labor's Share of Income: Non-Euro(17) Countries

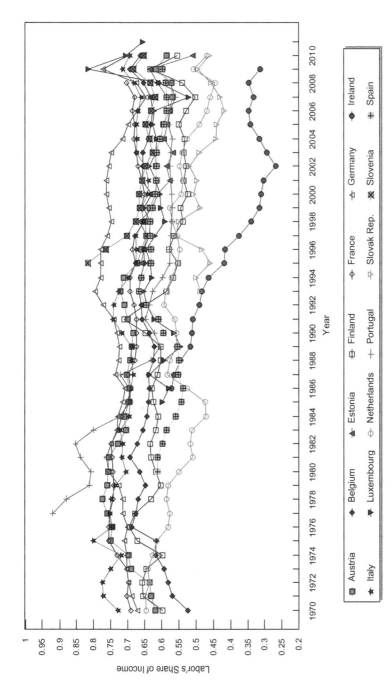

Figure 8.2:   Labor's Share of Income: Euro(17) Countries

is partly because, in both the mathematical Classical and Keynesian Macroeconomic models, each worker is assumed to earn a nominal wage equal to the value of the output he or she adds[5] which implies that the wage is both fair and efficient. The assumption that the wage is equal to the value of the output the worker adds is based on the two underlying assumptions that (1) firms compete with each other when hiring labor and that (2) firms have perfect information about the productivity of each potential employee. However, even if these extremely dubious underlying assumptions are true, this book has argued that the economy as a whole gains a benefit[6] from labor being paid more because increasing labor's income increases the average MPC, increasing the effectiveness of fiscal, monetary, and trade policies. Since the firm making a given hiring decision does not directly acquire this macrolevel additional benefit, it does not consider this macrolevel benefit when making a wage offer. This results in labor being paid less than the additional benefits it provides society (where societal benefits include the value of the output the worker produces and the effects of that worker's consumption on the macroeconomy and on the effectiveness of government policies).

Microeconomic analysis usually assumes the current income distribution and ignores the question of what is the optimal income distribution. Indeed, microeconomics likes to use a concept called "Pareto Optimality." A situation is considered Pareto Optimal if you cannot make someone better off without making someone else worse off. However, if one person had the entire wealth and income of a country, such a situation is "Pareto Optimal" because taking even one dollar from this rich person to give to a person with nothing would make the rich person worse off.

---

[5]Nominal wage $= MP_L \times P_{output}$ where $MP_L =$ the marginal product of labor or $\partial Q/\partial L$. This equation when re-arranged becomes $W/P = MP_L$. The Classical and Keynesian views of labor demand contrast sharply with the Marxian view. According to Karl Marx, the capitalist will pay a given worker the minimum amount that will keep that worker alive and able to have a child. The difference between the true value of the output a worker produces and the amount he or she is paid is the surplus value that the capitalist, or a middle man or the government, steals from labor. Thus, according to Marx, labor is not paid a "fair" wage.

[6]This is a benefit external to the hiring decision of the firm and, thus, would not be considered when the firm makes its hiring decision. This is an important example of what economists call an externality. Free markets do not produce the socially optimal amount of goods and services when there are externalities.

The only branch of economics that gives income distribution sustained and serious consideration is economic development. Appendix 4 contains a brief literature survey of some of the most important writings on income distribution in economic development. Several of the earliest and most influential economic growth models treated the accumulation of capital as a major driver of growth and argued that limited saving constrains the accumulation of capital. In essence, these growth models contained a mathematical formulation of the anti-equality argument.

The Anti-Equality Argument

1. The rich save more out of additional income than the poor save.
2. If the rich save more out of additional income than the poor save, then increasing the share of total income going to the rich will increase private saving.
3. If private saving increases, then investment increases.
4. If investment increases, then growth increases.
5. Increasing the share of total income going to the rich will increase private saving (from steps 1 and 2 by *Modus Ponens*).
6. Increasing the share of total income going to the rich will increase investment (from steps 5 and 3 by Hypothetical Syllogism).
7. Increasing the share of total income going to the rich will increase growth (from steps 6 and 4 by Hypothetical Syllogism).

The third step of this anti-equality argument makes no sense in a world with a surplus of savings — clearly, savings that are sitting idle are not funding growth producing investment. Furthermore, saving that is funding speculative bubbles or is seeking a return from rent or deception is also not funding long-term sustainable growth. The antithesis of the anti-equality argument is the pro-equality argument.

The Pro-Equality Argument

1. The poor consume more out of additional income than the rich.
2. If the poor consume more out of additional income than the rich, then increasing the share of total income going to the poor will increase private consumption.

3. If private consumption increases, then investment increases.
4. If investment increases, then growth increases.
5. Increasing the share of total income going to the poor will increase private consumption (from steps 1 and 2 by *Modus Ponens*).
6. Increasing the share of total income going to the poor will increase investment (from steps 5 and 3 by Hypothetical Syllogism).
7. Increasing the share of total income going to the poor will increase growth (from steps 6 and 4 by Hypothetical Syllogism).

The first step of both arguments is logically the same. The key difference in the two arguments is their third step. If saving constrains productive investment (third step of anti-equality argument), then increased inequality may drive growth; however, if consumption drives productive investment (third step of pro-equality argument), then increased equality will drive growth. To test which argument's third step fits reality, I estimated $\partial I/\partial(C/S)$ where "I" is investment, "C" is private consumption, and "S" is private saving.[7] A $\partial I/\partial(C/S)$ greater than zero would imply that moving a dollar from saving to consumption would result in an increase in investment. A $\partial I/\partial(C/S)$ less than zero would imply that moving a dollar from consumption to saving would result in an increase in investment.

Figures 8.3 and 8.4 show that the $\partial I/\partial(C/S)$ estimates were positive for the USA, the UK, Italy, and Spain providing evidence for the pro-equality argument in those countries, but Figures 8.5–8.7 show that the $\partial I/\partial(C/S)$ estimates were negative for Estonia, Finland, and Germany providing

---

[7]The IMF provided sufficient quarterly data on saving for only Estonia, Finland, Germany, Italy, Spain, the UK, and the USA. As explained in Appendix 1, RTPLS techniques have been developed that can handle more than one explanatory variable if only one of the explanatory variables is affected by omitted variables. However, RTPLS techniques have not yet been developed that can handle two or more right-hand side variables that are affected by omitted variables. In this case, both $\partial I/\partial C$ and $\partial I/\partial S$ would be affected by omitted variables. Furthermore, C and S are collinear because an increase in income will increase both C and S, holding everything else constant. To reduce the number of explanatory variables to only one that is affected by omitted variables and to handle the collinear relationship between C and S, I used the C/S ratio as the single explanatory variable. Furthermore, since theory does not require that $\partial I/\partial(C/S)$ be always negative or always positive, I had to run a preliminary regression to determine whether to assume a positive or negative relationship. This preliminary regression produced a positive $\partial I/\partial(C/S)$ for Italy, Spain, the UK, and the USA but a negative one for Estonia, Finland, and Germany. See Appendix 1 for more details.

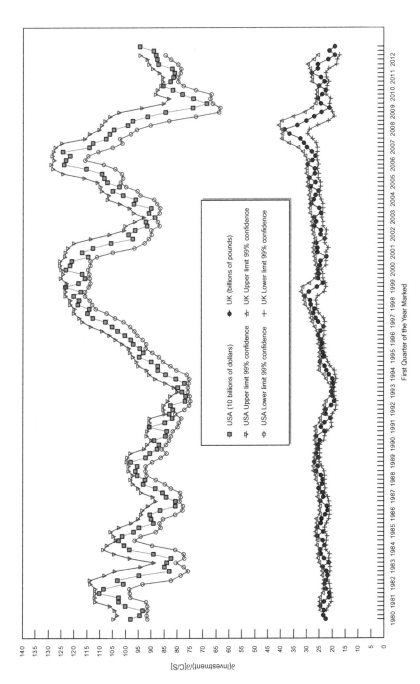

Figure 8.3:   The Change in Investment due to a Change in the Consumption/Savings Ratio: USA and UK

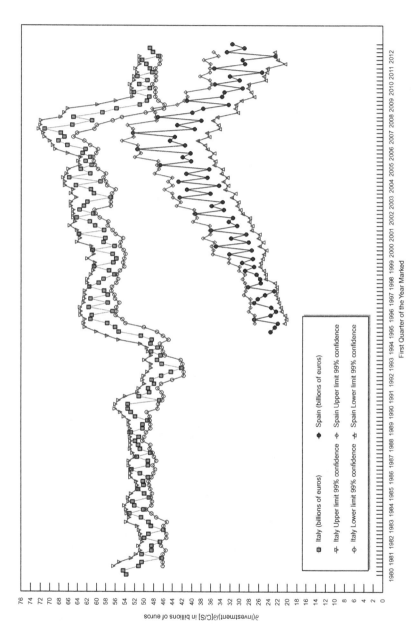

Figure 8.4:   The Change in Investment due to a Change in the Consumption/Savings Ratio: Spain and Italy

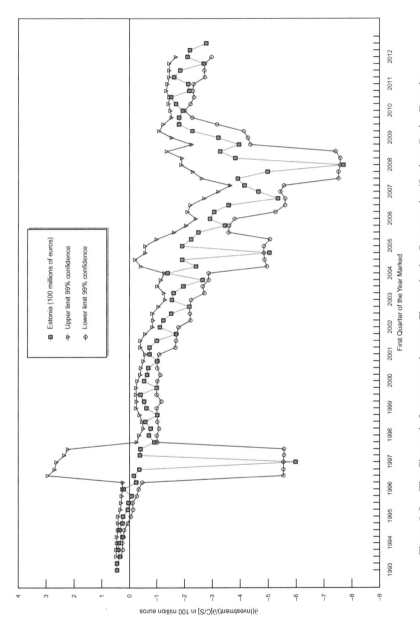

Figure 8.5: The Change in Investment due to a Change in the Consumption/Savings Ratio: Estonia

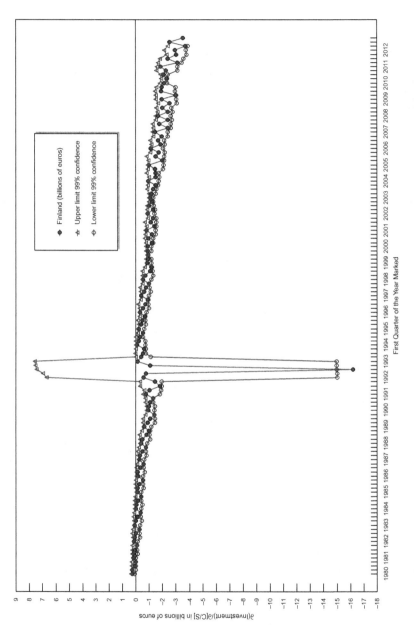

Figure 8.6:   The Change in Investment due to a Change in the Consumption/Savings Ratio: Finland

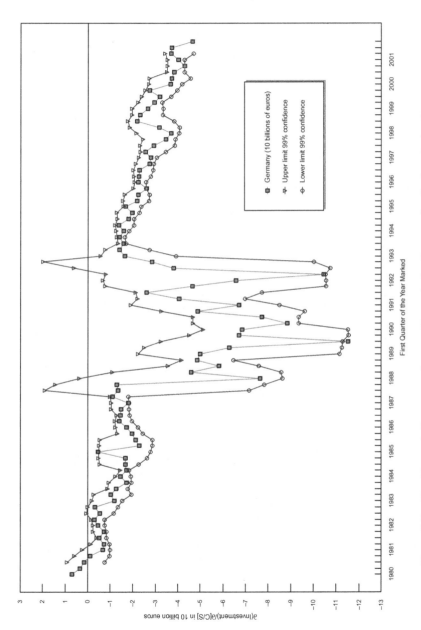

Figure 8.7: The Change in Investment due to a Change in the Consumption/Savings Ratio: Germany

evidence for the anti-equality argument in those countries.[8] Therefore, the first conclusion that we can draw is that we should not assume that the pro- or anti-equality argument always functions in every country. Indeed, it makes logical sense that investment requires two things — saving to invest and a reason to invest which is provided by sufficient consumption. It is possible to push either argument too far. If all income was taken from the consumers and given to the savers (which the anti-equality argument implies would produce the most growth), then there would not be a reason to invest — investors have to have the hope that someone will purchase what the investment produces. On the other hand, if all income is taken from the savers and given to the consumers (which the pro-equality argument implies would produce the most growth), then there would be no saving to fund investment. The real world is always more complex than our economic models imply. In the real world, there must be an optimal mix of saving and consumption that would produce the most investment and thus the greatest growth.

However, in the world today, there is a global surplus of savings implying that worldwide investment is not constrained by saving. On a global scale, the pro-equality argument is more logical in today's world. Shifting back to the perspective of an individual country, domestic consumption is not needed if there is sufficient foreign demand to drive domestic investment. Thus, the anti-equality argument is more likely to function in countries that depend heavily on exports.[9] It is interesting that the average exports to GDP ratios between 1980 and 2012 for the pro-equality countries shown in Figures 8.3 and 8.4 were 0.238 for Italy, 0.229 for Spain, 0.267 for the UK, and 0.102 for the USA. These pro-equality exports to GDP ratios are much smaller than the exports to GDP ratios for the anti-equality countries shown in Figures 8.5–8.7 which were 0.737 for Estonia (1993Q1–Q4 2012Q4), 0.357 for Finland (1985Q1–2012Q4), and 0.3979 for Germany (1997Q1–2012Q4). Germany is an especially interesting case as its exports to GDP ratios have steadily increased from 0.230 in 1994 to 0.516 in 2012.

---

[8]Table A4.2 in Appendix 4 provides the numerical values for $\partial I/\partial(C/S)$ from 1980 to 2012.
[9]In this case, the anti-equality argument also requires some barriers to foreign saving entering the country.

The results depicted in Figures 8.3–8.7 contain some additional noteworthy characteristics. First, the $\partial I/\partial(C/S)$ estimates fell in all the pro-equality countries starting sometime between the fourth quarter of 2006 and the first quarter of 2008 (see Figures 8.3 and 8.4). It makes sense that the importance of saving to investment would increase when financial crises cause banks to significantly reduce their lending as the USA and European banks did at the beginning of the crisis in 2007. The dramatic fall in $\partial I/\partial(C/S)$ for Finland in the third quarter of 1992, as shown in Figure 8.6, corresponds to Finland's hosting of the winter Olympics. In preparation for this Olympics, the role of domestic consumption in providing a reason for domestic investment was lost as Finland focused on the anticipated increase in world demand that comes with hosting an Olympics. The big fall in $\partial I/\partial(C/S)$ for Estonia in the first quarter of 1997 in Figure 8.5 corresponds to when Estonia's Prime Minister, Tiit Vähi resigned due to a scandal. The fluctuations in Estonia's $\partial I/\partial(C/S)$ between 2004 and 2011 correspond to the time period between Estonia joining the European Union in 2004 and adopting the euro in 2011. The fluctuations in Germany's $\partial I/\partial(C/S)$, which began in the first quarter of 1999, correspond to when the euro was first established (see Figure 8.7).

Establishing the euro increased trade by eliminating the transactions costs associated with exchanging different European currencies. However, in the wake of the 2007–2008 crisis, the common currency has been criticized for preventing needy countries from devaluing their individual currencies in order to increase their exports and drive growth (see Chapters 5 and 6). Because crisis countries using the euro cannot devalue their currencies, they have been told that they must go through "internal devaluations."

"Internal devaluation" is a euphemism for cutting wage rates and reducing labor's power. Internal devaluations may work for a few individual countries, but the more countries that try it, the less likely it is to succeed. A country that is internally devaluing is cutting wage rates, thus domestic demand, so they have to hope that sufficient external demand exists. Two countries attempting internal devaluations have to split any increase in external demand into two parts, but 10 countries attempting internal devaluations have to split any increase in external demand into 10 parts. Furthermore, the crisis that began in 2007 is shrinking the amount of external demand available. Thus, as more countries attempt internal devaluations, they are fighting for ever smaller pieces of external demand that is simultaneously shrinking. Moreover, by cutting wage rates, they are making global demand shrink even more.

Instead of nations fighting over a shrinking pie of external demand, it makes much more sense for nations to improve their income distributions thereby increasing the domestic demand for their goods. External demand is more risky than domestic demand, as China discovered in 2008. Furthermore, improving income distribution increases the MPC, and thus increases the multiplier effect from fiscal and monetary policy. Nations can enjoy both greater equality and greater growth. This conclusion is consistent with some recent studies of the relationship between growth and inequality. For example, Berg and Ostry (2011) find that

> longer growth spells are robustly associated with more equality in the income distribution. For example, closing, say, half the inequality gap between Latin America and emerging Asia would, according to our central estimates, more than double the expected duration of a growth spell. Inequality typically changes only slowly, but a number of countries in our sample have experienced improvements in income distribution of this magnitude in the course of a growth spell.

Chapter 9

CONCLUSION

The most important empirical findings from Chapters 3–5 are summarized in Table 9.1.[1] This table is divided into three sets of columns one for each of the multipliers: $\partial GDP/\partial$(Government Consumption), $\partial GDP/\partial$Exports, and $\partial GDP/\partial$(Money Supply).[2] The first column for each set gives the year that the corresponding multiplier hit is maximum between 1981 and 2012. The second column gives the year (subsequent to the max year) that the multiplier hit its minimum.[3] The third column gives the maximum value for the multiplier, and the fourth column gives its minimum value. The fifth column gives the percentage change from the maximum value to the minimum value. This fifth column shows that $\partial GDP/\partial G$, $\partial GDP/\partial X$, and $\partial GDP/\partial$Money have all fallen noticeably for all the countries studied.

In Japan (Row 1, Table 9.1), the effectiveness of fiscal policy ($\partial GDP/\partial G$) fell by 35% between 1990 and 2012, the effectiveness of monetary policy ($\partial GDP/\partial$Money) fell by 78% between 1991 and 2012, and the effect of an increase in exports ($\partial GDP/\partial X$) fell by 49% between 1994 and 2007. In the USA (Row 3), the effectiveness of fiscal policy ($\partial GDP/\partial G$) fell by 18.5% between 2000 and 2009, the effectiveness of monetary policy ($\partial GDP/\partial$Money) fell by 34% between 2007 and 2012,

---

[1]Whereas Chapters 3–5 give the quarterly results, Table 9.1 is based on annual averages of the quarterly results. By taking annual averages, the seasonal fluctuations that are very prominent in the quarterly results of many of the countries examined are eliminated.

[2]$\partial GDP/\partial$(Money Supply) was not estimated for the countries using the euro because they have no individual control over the supply of euros.

[3]Of the 49 multiplier series estimated, there were no cases where the multiplier continuously rose or stayed constant for 1981 to 2012.

Table 9.1: The Maximum then Minimum Annual Averages of the ∂GDP/∂G, ∂GDP/∂X, and ∂GDP/∂Money Results: 1981–2012

Annual Average	∂GDP/∂G Year		∂GDP/∂G Value			∂GDP/∂X Year		∂GDP/∂X Value			∂GDP/∂Money Year		∂GDP/∂Money Value		
	From	To	From	To	%Δ	From	To	From	To	%Δ	From	To	From	To	%Δ
Japan	1990	2012	7.358	4.777	−0.351	1994	2007	10.997	5.583	−0.492	1991	2012	3.855	0.854	−0.778
United Kingdom	1998	2009	5.603	4.262	−0.239	1988	2011	4.249	3.061	−0.280	1992	2005	9.395	7.720	−0.178
USA	2000	2009	6.962	5.673	−0.185	1986	2012	13.087	7.058	−0.461	2007	2012	10.756	7.055	−0.344
Brazil	1992	2012	5.751	4.723	−0.179	1996	2004	15.248	6.131	−0.598	1993	2007	11.493	3.728	−0.676
Russian Federation	1999	2009	6.791	4.886	−0.281	1997	2000	3.900	2.237	−0.426	2000	2012	1.485	0.612	−0.588
Austria	2007	2009	5.426	4.943	−0.089	1993	2008	2.772	1.612	−0.419					
Belgium	1990	2009	4.499	3.880	−0.138	1995	2008	1.265	1.058	−0.164					
Cyprus	2008	2009	4.450	4.053	−0.089	2009	2012	2.157	2.037	−0.055					
Estonia	2006	2009	6.279	4.587	−0.269	2009	2012	1.484	1.044	−0.297					
Finland	1989	2009	4.701	3.879	−0.175	1991	2008	4.248	2.069	−0.513					
France	1989	2010	4.305	3.867	−0.102	1987	2000	4.653	3.305	−0.290					
Germany	2007	2009	5.493	4.891	−0.110	1993	2012	2.952	1.511	−0.488					
Greece	2006	2009	4.799	4.137	−0.138	2009	2012	3.200	1.982	−0.381					
Ireland	2006	2009	5.176	4.090	−0.210	2006	2012	1.110	0.809	−0.271					
Italy	1995	2009	5.503	4.643	−0.156	1991	2012	5.350	3.309	−0.381					
Luxembourg	2007	2009	6.474	5.465	−0.156	2003	2008	0.512	0.438	−0.144					
Malta	2000	2012	5.020	4.468	−0.110	2005	2012	1.257	0.959	−0.237					
Netherlands	2000	2009	4.458	3.442	−0.228	1993	2012	1.354	1.011	−0.253					
Portugal	1987	2009	6.926	4.518	−0.348	1993	2011	4.296	2.796	−0.349					
Slovak	2007	2009	6.102	5.285	−0.134	2009	2012	1.220	0.916	−0.249					
Slovenia	2007	2011	5.472	4.562	−0.166	2003	2012	1.440	1.120	−0.222					
Spain	1986	2010	6.114	4.618	−0.245	1991	2012	5.886	3.072	−0.478					
Mean			5.621	4.530	−0.186			4.211	2.414	−0.339			7.397	3.994	−0.513

and the effect of an increase in exports ($\partial GDP/\partial X$) fell by 46% between 1986 and 2012. In Brazil (Row 4, Table 9.1), the effectiveness of fiscal policy ($\partial GDP/\partial G$) fell by 18% between 1992 and 2012, the effectiveness of monetary policy ($\partial GDP/\partial Money$) fell by 68% between 1993 and 2007, and the effect of an increase in exports ($\partial GDP/\partial X$) fell by 60% between 1996 and 2004. In Germany (Row 12, Table 9.1), the effectiveness of fiscal policy ($\partial GDP/\partial G$) fell by 11% between 2007 and 2009 and the effect of an increase in exports ($\partial GDP/\partial X$) fell by 49% between 1993 and 2012. In Spain (penultimate line, Table 9.1), the effectiveness of fiscal policy ($\partial GDP/\partial G$) fell by 24.5% between 1986 and 2010 and the effect of an increase in exports ($\partial GDP/\partial X$) fell by 48% between 1991 and 2012. Every single row in Table 9.1 tells a similar story: $\partial GDP/\partial G$, $\partial GDP/\partial X$, and $\partial GDP/\partial Money$ have fallen noticeably in all the countries examined.

In addition to the major result reported above, Table 9.1 contains some important patterns. The first column of each set of columns in Table 9.1 shows that for a few countries, the decline in the multipliers began with the 2007–2009 crisis.[4] However, for most countries, the decline started long before the current crisis. This implies that we need to look deeper than the events of the current crisis when analyzing the world's current economic woes.

For a majority of the countries studied, $\partial GDP/\partial Exports$ fell through the year 2012 (Column 7, Table 9.1) meaning that, as of the end of my data set, we do not know if $\partial GDP/\partial Exports$ has bottomed out for those countries. The same is true for $\partial GDP/\partial (Money\ Supply)$ for Japan, the USA, and the Russian Federation. However, except for Japan, Brazil, and Malta, $\partial GDP/\partial (Government\ Consumption)$ appears to have bottomed out before 2012. The partial rebound[5] in $\partial GDP/\partial G$ is not good news for Greece,

---

[4] $\partial GDP/\partial(G)$ began falling in 2007 or 2008 for Austria, Cyprus, Germany, Luxembourg, Slovakia, and Slovenia. However for the other 16 countries, it began falling before 2007. $\partial GDP/\partial Exports$ began falling in 2009 for Cyprus, Estonia, Greece, and Slovakia. However for the other 18 countries, it began falling before 2007. $\partial GDP/\partial(Money\ Supply)$ began falling in 2007 for the USA, but it began falling before 2007 for Japan, the United Kingdom, Brazil, and the Russian Federation.

[5] For all the multipliers that rebounded, the amount of the rebound can be seen by comparing Table 9.1 with Tables A5.1–A5.3 in Appendix 5. However, in none of the cases did the rebound exceed or equal the fall documented in Table 9.1. The case of $\partial GDP/\partial G$ for Cyprus

Ireland, Italy, Portugal, Slovenia, and Spain because in these countries, the rebound in ∂GDP/∂G corresponds to a fall in government consumption.[6] The rebound in ∂GDP/∂G in these countries might primarily be due to declines in GDP due to cuts in government spending hurting GDP more than increases in government spending helped GDP. Furthermore, the rebound in ∂GDP/∂G for the USA, the UK, the Russian Federation, Austria, Estonia, France, Germany, the Netherlands, and Slovakia corresponds to noticeable slowdowns in the growth of government consumption.[7] The only countries that had rebounds in ∂GDP/∂G with a steady increase in government consumption were Belgium, Cyprus, Finland, and Luxembourg and those countries had some of the weakest rebounds of all countries studied.[8]

The primary empirical conclusion from Chapters 3–5 (which is summarized in Table 9.1) is that ∂GDP/∂(Money Supply), ∂GDP/∂(Government Consumption), and ∂GDP/∂Exports have fallen noticeably over time and that these declines have occurred in all 22 of the countries studied.[9] A Keynesian Macroeconomic model would predict that the decrease in income equality documented in Chapter 8 would cause declining multipliers. As the rich gain an increasing share of income, the percent of income saved increases and the percent consumed decreases. As the marginal propensity to consume decreases, so does the multiplier effect of changes in the money supply, government consumption, or exports. The reason that most of the multipliers shown in Table 9.1 were falling long before the 2007–2008 crisis is that income inequality began rising long before the 2007–2008 crisis.

Production increasing investment requires two things — saving to fund the investment and consumption to buy what the investment produces.

---

was the closest to a full rebound. For Cyprus, ∂GDP/∂G fell from 4.450 in 2008 to 4.053 in 2009 for an 8.92% fall. ∂GDP/∂G then rose to 4.442 in 2012 for a relatively small net fall (from 4.450 to 4.442) between 2008 and 2012.

[6]See Figures 4.8–4.10, A2.9, A2.11, and 4.11 where the figures that start with "A2" are in Appendix 2.

[7]See Figures 4.2, 4.3, 4.5, 4.7, A2.1, A2.3, A2.5, A2.8, and A2.10. The figures that start with "A2" are in Appendix 2.

[8]See Figures 4.6, A2.2, A2.4, and A2.6 where the figures that start with "A2" are in Appendix 2.

[9]Furthermore, the time periods of these declines include the 2007–2008 crisis years for most (but not all) the countries studied.

As income has become less equal, saving has increased and consumption has fallen leading to a surplus of saving. Governments, wanting to stay in power, have responded to this situation by increasing government consumption. Government consumption is a substitute for private consumption, and, thus, it can keep the economy growing. However, a consequence of substituting government consumption for private consumption is increasing government deficits and debt. Many economic experts (especially those in the European Union and IMF) and political leaders believe that current government debt levels are unsustainable in the long run. This belief has led to austerity measures that include increases in taxes (usually on the lower and middle classes) and cuts in government spending, resulting in deepening recessions.

For any economic plan to succeed, there must be sufficient demand to purchase what is produced. Rising income inequality, the current recession, and austerity measures are reducing consumption. Government spending is falling as governments attempt to reduce their government deficits and debts. Investment is a derived demand that depends on someone purchasing what the investment produces. The only source of demand left is foreign demand or exports.

Many scholars[10] argue that countries using the euro are at a disadvantage during severe recessions because they cannot devalue their currencies in order to increase exports. Allowing a currency to fall to its natural equilibrium value would most likely help in a recession; however, many countries try to augment this effect by forcing their currencies below their natural equilibrium values. Countries can force their currencies below their equilibrium values by printing more of their domestic currencies and exchanging it for foreign reserves (usually US dollars). However, the country with the artificially devalued currency must continue to accumulate more foreign reserves every month for as long as they employ this strategy. If they ever stop accumulating foreign reserves, their exchange rates will rise and their exports fall. However, if ∂(Exports $-$ Imports)$/\partial$(Foreign Reserves) is **greater** than the value of the foreign reserves accumulated than this perpetual accumulation of foreign reserves (which will not be used) might

---

[10]For example, see Tierean and Tierean (2013).

produce a net gain for society.[11] This was the hope of "Export Driven Growth Models" that employed suppressed currencies. However, Chapter 6 shows that ∂(Exports − Imports)/∂(Foreign Reserves) is **less** than the value of the foreign reserves for the countries studied, implying that "Export Driven Growth via the accumulation of foreign reserves" does not create a net gain for society.[12] Therefore, even though the euro using countries cannot devalue their currencies by printing more of their currencies and exchanging it for foreign reserves, this lost option would not have worked any way.

Unable to devalue their individual currencies, euro using countries have turned to "internal devaluations." "Internal devaluation" is a euphemism for reducing wages and labor power[13] (Blanchard *et al.*, 2013) so that the cost of production will decrease causing exports to become more competitive internationally. However, in a world of insufficient consumption, countries using internal devaluations are pitted against each other — the country that can decrease its wages the most will increase its exports at everyone else's expense.[14] Meanwhile, by cutting wages, that country is making the fundamental global problem worse — in a world of insufficient consumption, they are employing policies that will reduce consumption more (Stockhammer, 2008). An export-driven growth model via the suppression of wages is an extremely bad idea in a world with a surplus of savings. Yet this is exactly what the IMF is trying to create.

The fact that ∂GDP/∂Exports (see Table 9.1) for a majority of the countries studied has not started rebounding by 2012 should be very disturbing for countries that hope to revive their economies by increasing exports.

---

[11]Whether or not there is a net gain depends upon the ∂GDP/∂(Export − Import) multiplier and the opportunity costs of employing this strategy.

[12]A dollar's worth of foreign reserves is forced to lie idle, and the country is not even getting a dollar's worth of exports–imports out of it. That dollar could be used better elsewhere.

[13]I have no problem with austerity measures aimed at increasing the flexibility of labor so that efficiency can be improved. However, I am against the cutting of wages due to the macroeconomic implications of wage cuts.

[14]This can be compared to competitive devaluations where several countries fight a price war by all of them trying to reduce their exchange rates more than the others reduce theirs. Price wars devastated part of the gasoline selling industry in the USA in the 1960s. Competitive internal devaluations would dramatically reduce wages, reducing the consumption needed to justify productive investment.

The solution to the world's current economic problems does not lie in employing market distortions to increase exports. It is very important that the reader understands that there are real gains from FREE trade. However, trying to increase those gains by artificially driving down wages or accumulating foreign reserves is not going to work in a world suffering from excess saving.

The solution to the world's problems is the direct opposite of what the IMF is forcing on crisis countries. The solution is to increase the income going to labor which would (1) provide a reason to invest savings in the expansion of production instead of the savings sitting idle or seeking a return from rent or a return from deception, (2) reduce the surplus of savings, (3) increase consumption and the standard of living, and (4) increase the multiplier effect from changes in government spending, the money supply, and exports. China has the right idea with its switch from an "Export Driven Growth Model" to a "Domestic Consumption Driven Growth Model." However, as Chapter 7 shows, China has a long way to go before it successfully implements consumption-driven growth.

Unfortunately, population dynamics are making the current situation worse in China and key economic developed countries. Greying populations in China, Europe, Japan, and the USA will soon need to be supported by a labor force that constitutes a shrinking proportion of the total population. The dependency ratio is the number of people that are either too old or too young to work divided by the working age population. China's dependency ratio is projected to climb from 39% in 2010 to 69% in 2050 (Naughton, 2007). This means that in 2010, every worker needed to produce enough for his or her own self and 39% of another person. By 2050, each worker will need to produce enough for his or her self and 69% of another person. China's decision to relax its one child policy in November 2013 will change these projections and is a welcomed policy shift that should help in the long run (once the additional children born become of working age).[15] Likewise, Japan's decision to better integrate women into the Japanese economy may help (Abe, 2013). During the 1950s, the Japanese government actively

---

[15]However, until the resulting increase in children become of working age, the dependency ratio will increase. Furthermore, this policy shift is too late for the many women in China who were sterilized when they had their first, and only, child.

encouraged greater equality and Japan enjoyed several waves of domestic consumption-driven growth (Ozawa, 1985).

Winning a war can sometimes[16] pull an economy out of recession. One of the dangers with the current situation is that when "Export Driven Growth" fails (and it will), then some desperate leaders may try "War Driven Growth," arguing that WWII got the world out of the Great Depression. Such a strategy would be horrible. Usually after a major war, the warring countries go into recession due to the fall in the demand for everything that goes with war: falling demand for bombs, bullets, aircraft carriers, submarines, etc. WWII was an exception precisely because the huge savings accumulated during the war were spent almost immediately after the war. If the world can figure out a way to spend the current surplus of savings, without going to war, then the world economy can prosper again. What the world needs is more consumption which would increase the effectiveness of fiscal, monetary, and trade policies.

The first step toward solving the world's current economic woes is to realize what the core problem is — a global surplus of savings that is sitting idle, funding speculative bubbles, or seeking a return from rent or deception. This savings is not being invested in expanding production because there is insufficient consumption to justify such investment. The next step toward a solution is to find the best ways to increase consumption and reduce the surplus of savings. In an effort to initiate a discussion of the next step, I offer the following ideas which I hope will be examined in much more depth than is offered here.

First any effort to gain a return from deception should be prosecuted in a severely punitive manner. As China's leader, Xi Jinping, has said corruption at all levels needs to be rooted out whether it comes from "flies or tigers." Pyramid schemes, deceptive derivatives, and melamine added to watered-down milk should not be allowed. People need to be able to trust their governments and the products they purchase. Where trust does not exist, people will hoard and save.

Rules and regulations should be changed so that it is harder to deceive. As mentioned in Chapter 2, those who originate mortgages should be

---

[16]The destruction of capital and the killing of labor might overwhelm the gains from increased demand and, thus, cause a net fall in GDP.

required to hold those mortgages. Allowing commercial banks to sell mortgages on a secondary market, where the buyers have much less information, makes deception too easy. Furthermore, in a world plagued by a surplus of savings, it makes no sense for the US Federal Reserve System to be paying interest to commercial banks for their deposits of excess reserves. Instead, the Federal Reserve should be taxing commercial banks for any excess reserves they hold.

Sales taxes reduce consumption, take a higher percent of the income of the poor than they do of the rich,[17] and encourage saving. All countries should eliminate sales taxes. I understand Shinzo Abe's (Japan's prime minister) desire to reduce Japan's extremely large government debt; however, reducing that debt by increasing sales taxes, as he is planning to do in 2014, will make the world's economic problems worse. When the world is suffering from insufficient consumption and a surplus of savings, additional tax revenues should be raised by taxing savings, property, or wealth — not by taxing consumption. Furthermore, reducing taxes on wage income, while increasing taxes on rents and savings, would encourage consumption and reduce savings.

Holding everything else constant, the taxing of profits would probably reduce production expanding investment.[18] However, increasing taxes on any retained earnings that are not invested in expanding production would encourage such investment. Furthermore, the sharing of profits with labor should be explored. If labor received bonuses based on the profits of a firm, then labor would have a greater incentive to innovate and to produce. In Japan, many companies give their employees large bonuses which, at least partially, are based on the profits of the firm. The connection between profits and bonuses could be strengthened, extended to all employees, and applied globally. If profit sharing with labor is not possible, then the effects of raising the minimum wage should be explored.

Since the fundamental problem is a *global* problem, the best solutions will be global. Some of the above proposals are more likely to be successful

---

[17]This is because the poor, out of necessity, spend a larger part of their income than the rich spend. It is because of this fact that sales taxes are viewed as one of the most unfair taxes.

[18]However, if taxes on wages are lowered, causing demand to increase, while taxes on profits are raised then it is possible that production expanding investment will increase.

if they are implemented on a global scale.[19] However, it is very difficult to get all countries to agree. Therefore, on a very pragmatic level, I recommend that the leaders of each individual country find the policies that are most likely to decrease savings and increase consumption in their countries while protecting themselves from the global surplus of savings by employing capital controls.[20] When consumption increases, the effectiveness of monetary, fiscal, and trade policies will improve.

---

[19] If only Japan eliminated all sales taxes, then Japan would benefit from consumers in other countries traveling to Japan for the purpose of shopping. In contrast, Japan increasing taxes on rent would probably not have an effect through the international market since rental property cannot be moved from one country to another. However, only Japan raising the minimum wage might result in Japanese businesses moving to other countries that do not have minimum wages.

[20] In general, greater freedom results in efficiency gains. However, if the global community cannot find a solution to the global surplus of savings, then the risk of that surplus of savings destabilizing the economies of individual countries is too great. Thailand was devastated by the entry and exit of foreign savings in the 1990s. Furthermore, Thailand continues (as of December 2013) to have major political problems 20 years after opening itself to foreign capital flows. See Chapter 2 for more details on the Thai case.

Appendix 1

REITERATIVE TRUNCATED PROJECTED
LEAST SQUARES[1]

Introduction

When omitted variables affect the relationship between the dependent variable and included explanatory variables the estimated coefficients are hopelessly biased and all statistics are inaccurate.[2] To be specific, if equation (1) is estimated without considering that the true slope, β_1, is affected by other variables (equation (2)), then a slope estimate is found that is a constant, in contrast to the true slope which varies with q.

$$Y = \alpha_0 + \beta_1 X + u \tag{1}$$

$$\beta_1 = \alpha_1 + \alpha_2 q \tag{2}$$

$$Y = \alpha_0 + \alpha_1 X + \alpha_2 Xq + u. \tag{3}$$

Equation (3) is produced by substituting equation (2) into equation (1). Equation (3) shows that a convenient way to model the omitted variables

---

[1]Reiterative Truncated Projected Least Squares (RTPLS) can be conducted by interfacing a regression program, a spreadsheet program, and a linear programming — frontier program; however, this is very time consuming. Thus, I am extremely grateful to Tomoo Inoue who wrote a computer program that produces RTPLS estimates in seconds. He also did all the simulations in this appendix.

[2]If the true relationship is $Y = \alpha_0 + \alpha_1 X_1 + \alpha_2 X_2$ and if X_2 is omitted from the analysis, but X_2 has no relationship with X_1, and thus does not affect the true slope — $\partial Y/\partial X_1$ — then X_2 acts as a source of additional random variation which (in large samples) does not change the numerical value of the estimated slope (α_1); however, it will affect the estimated level of statistical significance.

problem is to use an interaction term, $\alpha_2 Xq$. Equations (1) through (3) demonstrate that this modeling approach captures the omitted variables problem in its most general form.

When equation (1) is estimated without considering equation (2), a constant slope estimate equal to $(\alpha_1 + \alpha_2 E[q])$ is found for β_1 and the actual error is equal to $\alpha_2 X(q - E[q]) + u$ as shown by equation (5) which is derived from equation (4).

$$Y = \alpha_0 + \alpha_1 X$$

$$+ \alpha_2 X\{E[q] + q - E[q]\} + u \quad \text{adding 0 to equation (3)} \quad (4)$$

$$Y = \alpha_0 + (\alpha_1 + \alpha_2 E[q])X$$

$$+ \alpha_2 X(q - E[q]) + u \quad \text{rearranging equation (4).} \quad (5)$$

The use of instrumental variables or proxies is the standard approach to dealing with the omitted variables problem. To correctly use instrumental variables or proxies, the researcher must be able to correctly model (1) the omitted variable's relationship with the dependent variable and (2) the relationship between the omitted variables and the instruments. Furthermore, instrumental variables must be ignorable (not add any explanatory value independent of their correlation with the omitted variable) and they must be so highly correlated with the omitted variable that they capture the entire effect of the omitted variable on the dependent variable. These requirements are often impossible to meet (Bound *et al.*, 1995) since most researchers cannot even produce a comprehensive list of all the omitted variables that could affect the true slope. The omitted variables problem is a well-recognized problem in regression analysis. For examples, see Angrist and Imbens (1995), Baiocchi *et al.* (2010), Geronimus *et al.* (1996), Heller *et al.* (2009), Mare (1980), Moral-Benito (2012), O'Malley (2012), Pesaran *et al.* (2011), Rosenbaum (2010), and Zubizarreta *et al.* (2012).

The technique used in this book, RTPLS, recognizes that the relative vertical position of each observation captures the combined influence of all omitted variables and uses this intuition to produce a separate reduced form estimate for $\partial Y/\partial X$ for each observation. In other words the vertically highest observations (those at the top of a scatter plot) will be associated with values for the omitted variables that increase Y the most and the vertically lowest observations (those at the bottom) will be associated with omitted variable values that increase Y the least. By exploiting this intuition, RTPLS does not have to resort to instruments or proxies and thus does not have to make the strong (and usually impossible to meet) assumptions underlying the standard approach to omitted variables.

Section 2 of this appendix provides an intuitive explanation of the fourth generation of RTPLS and briefly surveys the literature leading up to it. Section 3 provides simulation results that show that, when the importance of the omitted variable is 10 times the size of measurement and round-off error, Ordinary Least Squares (OLS) produces 3.7 times the error as RTPLS. When the importance of the omitted variables is 100 times the size of measurement and round-off error, then OLS produces 30 times the error of RTPLS. When there is no measurement and round-off error than OLS error relative to RTPLS error approaches infinity as the sample size increases. Section 4 uses several individual simulations to show how RTPLS handles some more complex situations and relates those situations to specific RTPLS estimations made in this book. Section 5 examines how random error affects RTPLS estimates theoretically.

An intuitive explanation of RTPLS and literature survey

Initially, I will assume that all variation from the best fit line is due to omitted variables. Recall equation (5) which showed that when OLS is used to estimate equation (1) while ignoring the omitted variables problem, the "error" for the ith observation is $\alpha_2 X_i(q_i - E[q]) + u_i$. Thus, when researchers incorrectly assume that there are no omitted variables, they are assuming that $\alpha_2 X(q - E[q]) = 0$ and that $u \neq 0$; I am merely making the opposite assumption: $\alpha_2 X(q - E[q]) \neq 0$ and that $u = 0$. I believe that my initial assumption that all "error" is due to omitted variables is much more reasonable in most applications than the typical assumption that there are no omitted variables and, thus, that all "error" is just random. The simulation tests for RTPLS, which are included in this appendix, re-introduced random error ($u \neq 0$) and Section 5 examines the effects of random error theoretically.

The key to understanding RTPLS is Figure A1.1. To construct Figure A1.1, two series of random numbers, X and q, which ranged from

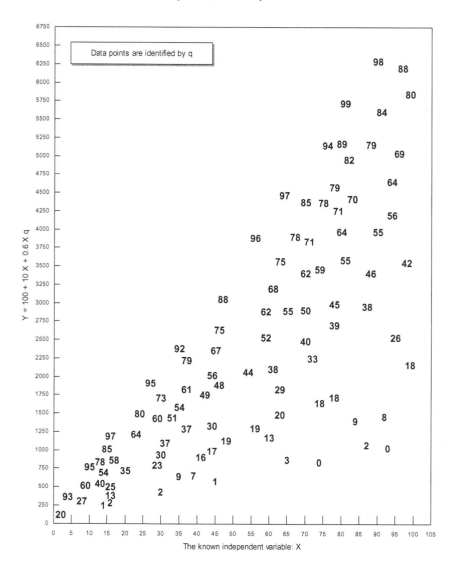

Figure A1.1:   The Intuition Behind RTPLS

0 to 100, were generated. I then defined

$$Y = 100 + 10X + 0.6qX. \tag{6}$$

Thus, the true value for $\partial Y/\partial X$ equals $10 + 0.6q$. Since q ranges from 0 to 100, the true slope will range from 10 (when $q = 0$) to 70 (when

$q = 100$). Thus, q makes a 700% difference to the slope. In Figure A1.1, I identified each point with that observation's value for q. Note that the upper edge of the data corresponds to relatively large qs — 93, 95, 97, 97, 99, and 98. The lower edge of the data corresponds to relatively small qs — 20, 1, 1, 0, and 0. This makes sense since as q increases so does Y, for any given X. For example, when X is between 44 and 47, reading the values of q from top to bottom produces 88, 75, 67, 56, 48, 30, 17, and 1. Thus, the relative vertical position of each observation is directly related to the values of q.[3]

An alternative way to view Figure A1.1 is to realize that, since the true value for $\partial Y / \partial X$ equals $10 + 0.6q$, the slope, $\partial Y / \partial X$, will be at its greatest value along the upper edge of the data where q is largest and the slope will be at its smallest value along the bottom edge of the data where q is smallest. This implies that the relative vertical position of each observation, for any given X, is directly related to the true slope.

Now imagine that we do not know what q is and that we have to omit it from our analysis. In this case, OLS produces the following estimated equation: $Y = -11.15 + 42.94X$ with an R-squared of 0.5574 and a standard error of the slope of 3.8655. On the surface, this OLS regression looks successful, but it is not. Remember that the true equation is $Y = 100 + 10X + 0.6qX$. Since q ranges from 0 to 100, the true slope (true derivative) ranges from 10 to 70 and OLS produced a constant slope of 42.94. OLS did the best it could, given its assumption of a constant slope — OLS produced a slope estimate of approximately $10 + 0.6E(q) = 10 + 0.6(50.57) = 40.34$. However, OLS is hopelessly biased by its assumption of a constant slope when, in truth, the slope is varying.

Although OLS is hopelessly biased when there are omitted variables that interact with the included variables, Figure A1.1 provides us with a very important insight — even when we do not know what the omitted variables are, even when we have no clue how to model the omitted variables or measure them, and even when there are no proxies for the omitted variables. Figure A1.1 shows us that the relative vertical position of each observation

---

[3]If, instead of adding $0.6qX$ in equation (1), we had subtracted $0.6qX$, then the smallest qs would be on the top and the largest qs on the bottom of Figure A1.1. Either way, the vertical position of observations captures the influence of the omitted variable q.

contains information about the combined influence of all omitted variables on the true slope. RTPLS exploits this insight.

RTPLS draws a faceted frontier between the top data points in Figure A1.1. It then projects all the data vertically up to this frontier. By projecting the data to the frontier, all the data would correspond to the largest values for q. However, there is a possibility that some of the observations will be projected to an upper right-hand side horizontal section of the frontier. For example, the 88 and 80 which are closest to the upper right-hand corner of Figure A1.1 would be projected to a horizontal section of the frontier. This horizontal section does not show the true relationship between X and Y and it needs to be eliminated (truncated) before a second stage regression is run through the projected data. This second stage regression (OLS) finds a truncated projected least squares (TPLS) slope estimate for when q is at its most favorable level and this TPLS slope estimate is then appended to the data for the observations that determined the frontier.

The observations that determined the frontier are then removed from the rest of the data set and the procedure repeated. We can visualize this removal as "peeling away" the upper frontier of the data points. As the process is iterated, we peel away the data in successive layers, working downward through the set of data points. The first iteration finds a TPLS slope estimate for when the omitted variables cause Y to be at its highest level, *ceteris paribus*. The second iteration finds a TPLS slope estimate for when the omitted variables cause Y to be at its second highest level, etc. This process is stopped when an additional regression would use fewer than 10 observations (the remaining observations will be located at the bottom of the data). It is important to realize that the omitted variable, q, in this process will represent the combined influence of all forces that are omitted from the analysis. For example, if there are 100 forces that are omitted where 60 of them are positively related to Y and 40 are negatively related to Y, then the first iteration will capture the effect of the 60 variables being at their largest possible levels and the 40 being at their lowest possible levels.

Just as the entire data set can be peeled down from the top, the entire data set also can be peeled up from the bottom. Peeling up from the bottom would involve projecting the original data downward to the lower boundary of the data, truncating off any lower left-hand side horizontal region, running an OLS regression through the truncated projected data to find a TPLS estimate for the observations that determined the lower boundary of the data, removing the observations that determined the lower boundary from the rest of the data set, and then reiterating this process until there are fewer than 10 observations left at the top of the data. By peeling the data from both the top to the bottom and from the bottom to the top, the observations at both the top and the bottom of the data will have an influence on the results. Of course, some of the observations in the middle of the data will have two TPLS estimated slopes associated with them — one from peeling the data downward and the other from peeling the data upward. The TPLS estimates (with the corresponding values for Y and X) from peeling the data down are stacked on top of the TPLS estimates from peeling the data up. This stacked data is used in a final regression as explained below.

Consider the following derivation:

$$Y = \alpha_0 + \alpha_1 X + \alpha_2 Xq \qquad \text{(Equation (3) repeated, assuming } u = 0)$$
$$(7)$$

$$\partial Y/\partial X = \alpha_1 + \alpha_2 q \qquad \text{(Derivative of equation (7))} \qquad (8)$$

$$Y/X = \alpha_0/X + \alpha_1 + \alpha_2 q \quad \text{(Dividing equation (7) by } X) \qquad (9)$$

$$\alpha_1 + \alpha_2 q = Y/X - \alpha_0/X \quad \text{(Rearranging equation (9))} \qquad (10)$$

$$\partial Y/\partial X = Y/X - \alpha_0/X \qquad \text{(From equations (8) and (10))} \qquad (11)$$

$$\partial Y/\partial X - Y/X = -\alpha_0/X \quad \text{(Rearranging equation (11))} \qquad (12)$$

Equation (11) tells us that we can calculate the true slope by subtracting α_0/X from Y/X. However, α_0 must be estimated. To estimate α_0, we use the TPLS slope estimates of $\partial Y/\partial X$ minus Y/X as the dependent variable and $1/X$ as the independent variable in a final regression (see equation (12)). We then plug the resulting estimate of α_0 and the data for Y and X for each observation into equation (11) to calculate a separate slope estimate for each observation.

To understand the role of the final regression, consider Figure A1.1 again. If all the observations on the upper frontier had been associated with exactly the same omitted variable values (perhaps 97), then the resulting TPLS estimate would perfectly fit all of the observations it was associated with. However, Figure A1.1 shows that the observations on the upper frontier were associated with omitted variable values of 93, 95, 97, 97, 99, and 98. The resulting TPLS slope estimate would perfectly fit a q value of approximately 96.5 (the mean of 93, 95, 97, 97, 99, and 98). When a TPLS estimate for a q of 96.5 is associated with qs of 93, 95, 97, 97, 99, and 98, some random variation, both positive and negative, remains. By combining the results from all iterations when peeling down and up, and then conducting this final regression, this random variation is eliminated. Realize that Y is co-determined by X and q. Thus, the combination of X and Y should contain information about q. This final regression exploits this insight in order to better capture the influence of q.

The mathematical equations used to calculate the frontier for each iteration of RTPLS are as follows: Denote the dependent variable of observation "i" by Y_i, $i = 1, \ldots, I$, and the known independent variable of that observation by X_i, $i = 1, \ldots, I$. Consider the following variable returns to scale, output oriented Data Envelopment Analysis (DEA) problem, which is used when peeling the data downward:

$$\max \Phi$$
$$\text{subject to} \quad \sum_i \lambda_i X_i \leq X^o$$
$$\Phi Y^o \leq \sum_i \lambda_i Y_i$$
$$\sum_i \lambda_i = 1; \quad \lambda_i \geq 0, \quad i = 1, \ldots, I. \quad (13)$$

The ratio of maximally expanded dependent variable to the actual dependent variable (Φ) provides a measure of the influence of unfavorable omitted variables on each observation. This problem is solved I times, once for each observation in the sample. For observation "o" under evaluation, the problem seeks the maximum expansion of the dependent variable Y^o consistent with best practice observed in the sample, i.e., subject to the constraints in the problem. In order to project each observation upward to the frontier, its Y value is multiplied by Φ. In Figure A1.2, Φ for the marked observation is distance "B" divided by distance "A".

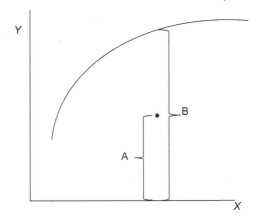

Figure A1.2:   Projecting to the Upper Frontier

The variable returns to scale, input-oriented DEA problem[4] used when projecting the data to the lower frontier and then peeling the data upward is:

$$\min \Phi$$

$$\text{subject to} \quad \sum_k \lambda_k Y_k \geq Y_i$$

$$\Phi X_i \geq \sum_k \lambda_k X_k$$

$$\sum_i \lambda_i = 1; \lambda_k \geq 0, \quad k = 1, \ldots, I. \qquad (14)$$

Figure A1.3 depicts how a given data point is projected to the lower frontier of the data.

Again Φ is distance "B" divided by distance "A". Multiplying the Y value for the marked observations by B/A would project that observation down to the lower frontier. It is important to realize that RTPLS uses linear

---

[4]In this case, the "input" for the "input"-oriented DEA problem is the dependent variable and the output is the independent variable. Thus, to think about this from the DEA perspective involves switching the items on the axes from Figure A1.2. Figure A1.3 does not make this switch, because making such a switch would add more confusion than it is worth for some non-DEA specialists.

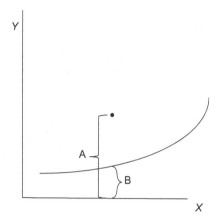

Figure A1.3:   Projecting to the Lower Frontier

programing (DEA) solely to construct and project to the upper and lower frontiers. All estimations are conducted with OLS.

The RTPLS process is similar to Two Stage Least Squares (2SLS) which is used to eliminate simultaneous bias. In 2SLS, all right-hand side endogenous variables are regressed by all exogenous variables. The data is plugged back into the resulting equation to construct instruments for the right-hand side endogenous variables. These instruments are then used to estimate the desired equations. In essence, 2SLS throws away all the variation in the right-hand side endogenous variables that is not explained by the exogenous variables. In a similar manner, by projecting the data to the frontier, RTPLS is removing (for a given iteration) the variation in the dependent variable due to omitted variables. However, after each iteration, and the elimination of the observations that determined the frontier in that previous iteration, RTPLS returns to the original (non-projected data) in order to create and project to the next frontier. Thus, unlike 2SLS, the reiterative process in RTPLS of peeling the data down and then up, iteration by iteration, does not permanently throw away the unexplained variation; instead, it captures the whole range of variation due to omitted variables.

RTPLS generates reduced form estimates that include all the ways that X and Y are correlated. Thus, even when many variables interact via a system of equations, a researcher using RTPLS does not have to discover and justify that system of equations. In contrast, traditional regression analysis theoretically must include all relevant variables in the estimation and the resulting slope estimate for $\partial Y/\partial X$ is for the effects of just X — holding all other variables constant. RTPLS' reduced form estimates are not substitutes for traditional regression analysis' partial derivative estimates. Instead, RTPLS and traditional regression estimates are compliments which capture different types of information. RTPLS has the disadvantage of not being able to tell the researcher the mechanism by which X affects Y. On the other hand, RTPLS has the advantage of not having to model and find data for all the forces that can affect Y in order to estimate $\partial Y/\partial X$. Both RTPLS and traditional regression techniques find "correlations." It is impossible for either one of them to prove "causation."

In this book, I created confidence intervals for specific RTPLS estimates by grouping the estimate with the two estimates before and after it and then using equation (15), which is based on the Central Limit Theorem.

$$99\% \text{ confidence interval} = \text{mean} \pm (s/\sqrt{n})t_{n-1,\alpha/2} \qquad (15)$$

In equation (15), "s" is the standard deviation, "n" is the number of observations which is 5, and $t_{n-1,\alpha/2}$ is 4.032 as taken off the standard t table. By always considering a given estimate and the two estimates before and after it, I am able to create a moving confidence interval (much like a moving average) for a given set of RTPLS estimates. This 99% confidence interval can be interpreted as meaning that there is only a 1% chance that the true average for a given RTPLS estimate with the two RTPLS estimates before it and the two RTPLS estimates after it will lie outside of the given range. Given this interpretation, it is possible for a given RTPLS estimate to lie outside of its confidence interval if the other four estimates around it are all noticeably above or below the given RTPLS estimate. However, such a situation is unusual.

A brief survey of the literature leading up to RTPLS is now provided. Branson and Lovell (2000) introduced the idea that by drawing a line around the top of a data set and projecting the data to this line, one can eliminate variations in Y that are due to variations in omitted variables. The first generation of this paper's technique (RTPLS1) was created when Leightner (2002a) added to Branson and Lovell's idea truncating off any horizontal section of the frontier, a peeling downward reiterative process, and running a final regression into which the data was then plugged to get a separate slope estimate for each observation. Leightner and Inoue (2007) ran simulation tests which show that RTPLS1 produces (on average) less than half the error of OLS when there are omitted variables that interact with the included variables under a wide range of conditions. Leightner and Inoue (2007) also explain how situations where Y is negatively related to X can be handled, how omitted variables that can change the sign of the slope can be handled, and how the influence of additional right-hand variables can be eliminated before conducting RTPLS (see Section 4 for more information on these issues).

Leightner (2008) created the second generation of the technique (RTPLS2) when he introduced a process that peeled the data from both the top and from the bottom. RTPLS1 and RTPLS2 used the TPLS estimates as the dependent variable and a constant, Y/X, and $1/X$ as the independent variables in the final regression. Leightner and Inoue (2012b) created the third generation (RTPLS3) when they discovered that eliminating the constant from the final regression noticeably improved the results. They also provided an informal proof that RTPLS3 is unbiased. Recall that RTPLS (the fourth generation which is used in this book) uses the TPLS estimates minus Y/X as the dependent variable and just $1/X$ as the independent variable in the final regression. The only difference between RTPLS3 and RTPLS is that the RTPLS3 coefficient for Y/X is forced to equal one in the final regression in RTPLS which is consistent with equation (11). This one change produced an enormous improvement in the results. Leightner (2010c) shows how the central limit theorem can be used to generate confidence intervals for groups of BD-RTPLS estimates.

Inoue *et al.* (2013) show that substituting β_0 for α_0, β_1 for $\alpha_1 + \alpha_2 E[q]$ and v for $\alpha_2 X(q - E[q]) + u$ in equation (5) produces

$$Y = \beta_0 + \beta_1 X + v \quad \text{where } v \sim N\left(0, \sigma_v^2\right) \quad \text{where } \sigma_v^2 = \alpha_2^2 X^2 \sigma_q^2 + \sigma_u^2 \tag{16}$$

According to Aitken (1935), equation (16) implies that Generalized Least Squares (GLS) produces the Best Linear Unbiased Estimate (BLUE) of equation (3)'s α_0. Furthermore, if $u = 0$, we know that this BLUE estimate of α_0 can be used to calculate a BLUE estimate of $\partial Y/\partial X$ by using equation (11). However, Inoue *et al.* (2013) also provide simulation evidence that using GLS in this manner produces two to three times the error of RTPLS when sample sizes of 250 observations are used and all error is due to omitted variables. They hypothesize that RTPLS is "better than BLUE" because it can better handle cases where omitted variables cause non-linear effects on the slope. Published studies that used RTPLS1, RTPLS2, RTPLS3, or RTPLS include Leightner (2013a; 2012; 2011; 2010c; 2010d; 2008; 2007a; 2005a; 2005b; 2002a) and Leightner and Inoue (2012a; 2012b; 2009; 2008a; 2008b; 2007).

Simulations[5]

The simulations are based on computer generated values of X and q which are uniform random numbers $Z \sim U[0, 10]$, where 0 is the lower bound of the distribution and 10 is the upper bound. Measurement and round-off error, e, is generated as a normal random number whose standard deviation is adjusted to be 0%, 1%, or 10% of variable X's standard deviation. We consider 36 cases — all the combinations where (1) the omitted variable (q) makes a 10%, 100%, or a 1,000% difference in $\partial Y/\partial X$, (2) where measurement and round-off error are 0%, 1%, or 10% of X, and (3) where 100, 250, 500, or 1,000 observations are used. Equations (17)–(19) are used to model when the omitted variable makes a 10%, 100%, and 1,000% difference in $\partial Y/\partial X$ respectively.

$$Y = 10 + 1.0X + 0.01qX + e \tag{17}$$

$$Y = 10 + 1.0X + 0.1qX + e \tag{18}$$

$$Y = 10 + 1.0X + 1.0qX + e, \tag{19}$$

$\partial Y/\partial X$ for equation (18) would be $1 + 0.1q$; since q ranges from 0 to 10, the true slope will range from 1 (when $q = 0$) to 2 (when $q = 10$). Thus, for equation (18), the omitted variable, q, makes a 100% difference to the true slope. For similar reasons, q makes a 10% difference to the real slope in equation (17) and approximately a 1,000% difference in equation (19). Total error for the ith observation would equal the error from the omitted variable plus the added measurement and round-off error.

---

[5]Tomoo Inoue wrote the computer program that ran these simulations and he personally did these simulations. He deserves the credit for producing the results I explain in this section. These simulations assume that q is uniformly distributed; Inoue *et al.* (2013) contains similar simulations that assume that q is normally distributed.

Tables A1.1 and A1.2 present the mean of the absolute value of the error and the standard deviation of the error for 36 sets of 5,000 simulations each where the error from OLS and from RTPLS are defined by equations (20) and (21) respectively. In these equations, "OLS" refers to the OLS estimate of $\partial Y/\partial X$ when q is omitted and "True" refers to the true slope as calculated by plugging each observation's data into the derivatives of equations (17)–(19).

$$\text{Define } E_i^{OLS} = (\text{OLS} - \text{True}_i)/\text{True}_i \tag{20}$$

$$\text{Define } E_i^{RTPLS} = (\text{RTPLS} - \text{True}_i)/\text{True}_i. \tag{21}$$

The mean absolute value of the percent OLS error (Table A1.1, Panel A) was calculated from equation (22) where "n" is the number of observations in a simulation and "m" is the number of simulations.

$$\sum_{j=1}^{m} \left[\left(\sum_{i=1}^{n} |E_i^{OLS}| /n \right) \right] \Big/ m. \tag{22}$$

Equation (23) was used to calculate the standard deviation of OLS error (Table A1.2, Panel A) where $E(E_i^{OLS}) = $ the mean of $E_i^{OLS} = \left(\sum_{i=1}^{n} E_i^{OLS} \right)/n$.

$$\left\{ \sum_{j=1}^{M} \left[\left(\sum_{i=1}^{n} (E_i^{OLS} - E\left(E_i^{OLS}\right))^2 \right) \Big/ (n-1) \right]^{1/2} \right\} \Big/ m. \tag{23}$$

The absolute value of the mean error (Table A1.1) and the standard deviation (Table A1.2) of RTPLS error (Panel B) were calculated with equations (21)–(23), respectively where "E_i^{RTPLS}" was substituted for "E_i^{OLS}."

The results when 100, 250, 500, and 1,000 observations are used in each simulation are shown in Rows 1 through 4 respectively of each panel. Columns 1–3, 4–6, and 7–9 correspond to when there is 0%, 1%, and 10% measurement and round-off error respectively. The omitted variable makes a 1,000% difference in $\partial Y/\partial X$ for Columns 1, 4, and 7; a 100% difference in $\partial Y/\partial X$ for Columns 2, 5, and 8; and a 10% difference in $\partial Y/\partial X$ for Columns 3, 6, and 9.

Table A1.1, Panels A and B, Row 1, Column 1 show that the mean error under OLS and RTPLS were 71% and 4% respectively when the omitted

Table A1.1: The Mean |e|, 5,000 Simulations for Each Case

Column		1	2	3	4	5	6	7	8	9
Importance of omitted q (%)		1,000	100	10	1,000	100	10	1,000	100	10
Size of measurement e (%)		0	0	0	1	1	1	10	10	10
A. %OLS error										
	$N = 100$	0.71430	0.17787	0.02398	0.71430	0.17787	0.02399	0.71430	0.17794	0.02494
	$N = 250$	0.71172	0.17706	0.02389	0.71172	0.17706	0.02389	0.71170	0.17707	0.02428
	$N = 500$	0.71110	0.17685	0.02386	0.71110	0.17685	0.02387	0.71111	0.17688	0.02405
	$N = 1,000$	0.71183	0.17682	0.02385	0.71183	0.17682	0.02385	0.71182	0.17683	0.02394
B. %RTPLS error										
	$N = 100$	0.04056	0.00787	0.00101	0.04129	0.01463	0.01483	0.06163	0.10784	0.14727
	$N = 250$	0.01871	0.00335	0.00043	0.02015	0.01349	0.01736	0.05073	0.12618	0.17339
	$N = 500$	0.00990	0.00172	0.00023	0.01203	0.01397	0.01886	0.04993	0.13725	0.18857
	$N = 1,000$	0.00518	0.00089	0.00012	0.00824	0.01524	0.02087	0.05309	0.15175	0.20870
C. OLS/RTPLS										
	$N = 100$	1,023.93	1,014.77	1,030.48	110.09	30.88	3.82	28.05	3.82	0.39
	$N = 250$	1,696.36	2,496.56	4,470.49	178.66	35.83	3.79	33.67	3.80	0.38
	$N = 500$	4,646.15	5,274.84	4,616.82	234.66	37.17	3.78	36.20	3.78	0.38
	$N = 1,000$	7,738.87	11,187.17	19,560.14	288.09	37.36	3.75	37.02	3.75	0.38

Table A1.2: The Standard Error of $|e|$, 5,000 Simulations for Each Case

Column		1	2	3	4	5	6	7	8	9
Importance of omitted q (%)		1,000	100	10	1,000	100	10	1,000	100	10
Size of measurement e (%)		0	0	0	1	1	1	10	10	10
A. OLS										
	$N = 100$	1.09175	0.20975	0.02751	1.09175	0.20975	0.02751	1.09175	0.20975	0.02751
	$N = 250$	1.09412	0.20964	0.02753	1.09411	0.20964	0.02753	1.09410	0.20962	0.02752
	$N = 500$	1.09442	0.20966	0.02753	1.09442	0.20966	0.02753	1.09443	0.20967	0.02754
	$N = 1,000$	1.09642	0.20974	0.02754	1.09642	0.20974	0.02754	1.09642	0.20974	0.02753
B. RTPLS										
	$N = 100$	0.11849	0.02017	0.00252	0.12103	0.03936	0.04026	0.18810	0.29672	0.40083
	$N = 250$	0.07490	0.01209	0.00153	0.08180	0.05157	0.06575	0.21781	0.48377	0.65710
	$N = 500$	0.05187	0.00830	0.00107	0.06455	0.06770	0.09003	0.27712	0.66549	0.90013
	$N = 1,000$	0.03534	0.00568	0.00074	0.05807	0.09544	0.12914	0.37513	0.95043	1.29140
C. OLS/RTPLS										
	$N = 100$	1.4042	1.4042	1.4042	1.5031	1.6935	1.7328	1.6669	1.7341	1.7466
	$N = 250$	1.4092	1.4092	1.4092	1.5833	1.7506	1.7563	1.7366	1.7564	1.7613
	$N = 500$	1.4114	1.4114	1.4114	1.6472	1.7668	1.7669	1.7630	1.7671	1.7684
	$N = 1,000$	1.4133	1.4133	1.4133	1.7093	1.7737	1.7735	1.7726	1.7738	1.7744

variable made 1,000% difference to the true slope, when 100 observations are used, and there is no measurement and round-off error. Under the same conditions, except 1,000 observations are used, OLS's error remains 71% but RTPLS's error falls to 0.5% (Row 4). When the omitted variable makes 100% difference to the true slope, 100 observations are used, and there is no measurement and round-off error, then OLS and RTPLS produce 18% and 0.8% error respectively (Table A1.1, Panels A and B, Row 1, Column 2). When the sample size is increased to 1,000, and the same conditions apply, OLS's error remains 18% while RTPLS's error falls to 0.09% (Row 4).

Panel A of Tables A1.1 and A1.2 shows that neither the sample size nor the amount of measurement and round-off error noticeably affects the mean and the standard deviation of the error when OLS is used, *ceteris paribus*. However, increasing the importance of the omitted variable from 10 to 100% increases the mean error from OLS by a factor of approximately 7.4 and the standard error by a factor of approximately 7.6 (dividing the numbers in Columns 2, 5, and 8 by the numbers in Columns 3, 6, and 9). Increasing the importance of the omitted variable from 100 to 1,000% increases the mean error from OLS by a factor of approximately 4 and the standard error by a factor of approximately 5 (dividing the numbers in Columns 1, 4, and 7 by the numbers in Columns 2, 5, and 8).

Note the slight increase in the mean error from OLS when omitted variables make a 1,000% difference to the true slope when going from 500 observations to 1,000 observations (Table A1.1, Panel A, Rows 3 and 4, Columns 1, 4, and 7). Furthermore, Table A1.2 shows that the standard error of the error for OLS increases slightly when going from 250 to 500 to 1,000 observations when the omitted variable makes a 100% or 1,000% difference to the true slope (Table A1.2, Panel A, Rows 2–4, Columns 1, 2, 4, 5, 7, and 8). The fact that an increase in the sample size does not cause the mean error and the standard deviation of that error from OLS to fall when omitted variables at least double the true slope, implies that OLS is not consistent[6] under those conditions.

---

[6]An estimation technique has the statistical property of "consistency" if an increase in the sample size results in the estimates become more accurate and the variance of the estimates falling.

Tables A1.1 and A1.2, Panels A and B, Columns 1–4 show that the mean error and standard error from RTPLS noticeably fall as the sample size increases. This provides simulation evidence that RTPLS is consistent when there is no measurement or round-off error (Columns 1–3) or when the importance of the omitted variable is 1,000 times the size of measurement and round-off error (Column 4).[7] However, when the importance of the omitted variable is only 100 times or 10 times the size of measurement and round-off error (Columns 5–9), the simulations show that RTPLS is not consistent.

When comparing the relative absolute value of the mean error (Table A1.1) and standard deviation (Table A1.2) of OLS error to RTPLS error by observation, "Ln($|E_i^{OLS}|/|E_i^{RTPLS}|$)" was substituted for $|E_i^{OLS}|$ in equation (22) and for E_i^{OLS} in equation (23) and then the anti-log of the result was found (Panels C of Tables A1.1 and A1.2 respectively). The natural log of the ratio of OLS to RTPLS error had to be used in order to center this ratio symmetrically around the number one. Consider a two observation example where the OLS/RTPLS ratio is 4/1 for one observation and 1/4 for the other observation. In this example, the mean OLS/RTPLS ratio is 2.12 making OLS appear to have 2.12 times as much error as RTPLS, when (in this example) OLS and RTPLS are performing the same on average. Taking the natural log solves this problem. Ln(4) = 1.386 and Ln(1/4) = −1.386 and their average would be 0 and the anti-log of 0 is 1, correctly showing that OLS and RTPLS are performing equally well in this example.

Panel C of Tables A1.1 and A1.2 provides the OLS/RTPLS ratios for the mean error and the standard error. If these ratios are greater than 1, then an observation by observation comparison of OLS and RTPLS produced a higher mean error and a higher mean standard error for OLS than it did for RTPLS. Table A1.2, Panel C, shows that the OLS/RTPLS ratio for the mean standard error is greater than 1.4 for all the cases examined. Table A1.1, Panel C, Column 9, Rows 1–4 show that OLS produced approximately

---

[7]Inoue *et al.* (2013) contain similar simulations, except they assumed that q is normally distributed in contrast to this appendix assuming that q is uniformly distributed. When q is normally distributed, the RTPLS simulation results do not support consistency. However, they also find that RTPLS produces much more accurate results than alternative approaches when all error is due to omitted variables and q is normally distributed.

0.39% of the error of RTPLS when the importance of the omitted variable and the size of measurement and round-off error are the same. When the importance of the omitted variable is 10 times the size of measurement and round-off error (Columns 6 and 8), OLS produces between 3.75 and 3.82 times the error of RTPLS. When the importance of the omitted variable is 100 times the size of measurement and round-off error (Columns 5 and 7), OLS produces between 28 times and 37 times the error of RTPLS. Furthermore, as the sample size increases, the OLS/RTPLS ratio appears to be converging to approximately 38 in this case (10 times the ratio given in Columns 6 and 8 and 100 times the ratio given in Column 9). When the importance of the omitted variable is 1,000 times the size of measurement and round-off error, then OLS produces between 110 and 288 times the error of RTPLS.

When there is no measurement and round-off error (Columns 1–3) and 100 observations are used, the OLS/RTPLS error ratio always exceeds 1,000 (Table A1.1, Panel C). When 1,000 observations are used, the OLS/RTPLS error ratio ranges between 7,700 and 19,500. This implies that OLS produces between 7,700 and 19,500 times the error of RTPLS when there is no measurement and round-off error. I believe that these huge numbers imply that as the sample size increase when there is no measurement and round-off error, the OLS/RTPLS error ratio will converge to infinity.

An Additional Simulation Showing Some More Complex Situations

In order to investigate what happens in some more complex situations, I generated five series of random numbers $\sim[0, 100]$ for X_1, X_2, X_3, q_1, q_2 and one series $\sim[0, 10]$ for random error (e). I generated 800 observations. I defined the dependent variable Y:

$$Y = 2{,}500 + 50X_1 + 2q_1X_1 - q_2X_1 + 10X_2 + 40X_3 + e. \qquad (24)$$

This problem illustrates at least three things: (1) what happens when there is more than one omitted variable that interact with X_1, (2) what happens when there are additional shift factors (X_2, X_3), and (3) what happens when omitted variables could change the slope from positive to negative (when q_1 is 0 and q_2 is 100, the true slope will be -50). First, consider our usual justification for the final regression equation for this case:

$$Y = \alpha_0 + \alpha_1 X_1 + \alpha_2 q_1 X_1 - \alpha_3 q_2 X_1 + 10 X_2 + 40 X_3 + e \tag{25}$$

$$\partial Y / \partial X_1 = \alpha_1 + \alpha_2 q_1 - \alpha_3 q_2 \qquad \text{(Derivative of 25)} \tag{26}$$

$$Y / X_1 = 1 / X_1^* [\alpha_0 + \alpha_1 X_1 + \alpha_2 X_1 q_1 - \alpha_3 X_1 q_2$$
$$+ 10 X_2 + 40 X_3 + e] \, (25 / X_1) \tag{27}$$

$$\alpha_1 + \alpha_2 q_1 - \alpha_3 q_2 = Y / X_1 - \alpha_0 / X_1 - 10 X_2 / X_1 - 40 X_3 / X_1$$
$$\text{(Rearranging 27)} \tag{28}$$

$$\partial Y / \partial X = Y / X_1 - \alpha_0 / X_1 - 10 X_2 / X_1 - 40 X_3 / X_1$$
$$\text{(From 26 and 28)} \tag{29}$$

Clearly, X_2 and X_3 affect the slope. In this case, it is best to purge the data of the influence of X_2 and X_3 as described in Leightner and Inoue (2007) before conducting RTPLS. This purging is done by running a normal OLS regression between Y and X_1, X_2, and X_3. If this OLS regression produced coefficients for X_2 and X_3 of $\beta_2^{\wedge}$ and $\beta_3^{\wedge}$, then $Y^{\wedge}$ is calculated as

$$Y^{\wedge} = Y - \beta_2^{\wedge} X_2 - \beta_3^{\wedge} X_3. \tag{30}$$

RTPLS can now be used with $Y^{\wedge}$ as the dependent variable. Consider Figures A1.4 and A1.5. Figure A1.4 is the normal RTPLS explanation graph based on equation (24) where only the first 100 observations are shown and the data points are identified by their omitted variable value. In this case, the omitted variable value is $2q_1 - q_2$. Note that Figure A1.4 is not as "nice" as my usual explanation graph. For example, consider the column of numbers for $2q_1 - q_2$ immediately above $X_1 = 30$: 125, 80, 173, 112, 20, -35, -7. The 173, 80, and the -7 are out of order; however, the higher numbers are still at the top and the lower numbers are at the bottom. When we ran an OLS regression using all 800 observations between Y and X_1, X_2, and X_3, we got $R^2 = 0.4045$ and:

$$Y = 2,304.306 + 95.34791 \; X_1 + 14.35823 \; X_2 + 42.9407 \; X_3. \tag{31}$$

$$(4.46177) \qquad (4.4034) \qquad (4.4976)$$

Using this estimate, I purged the data on Y of the influence of X_2 and X_3 (using equation (30) to get $Y^{\wedge}$) and then plotted the first 100 observations

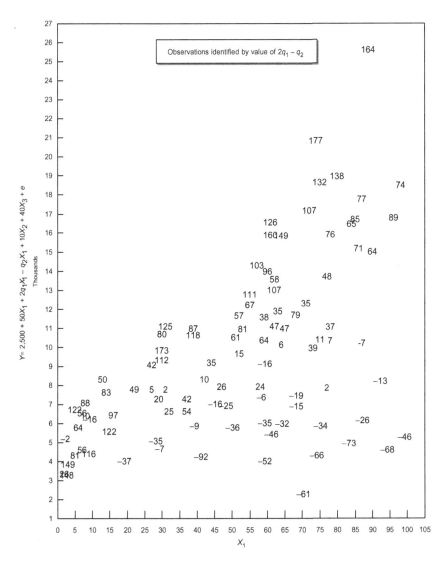

Figure A1.4:   The First 100 Observations: A Single More Complex Simulation

of $Y^{\wedge}$ versus X_1 in Figure A1.5. Note that Figure A1.5 looks similar to the normal RTPLS explanation diagram — for any given value of X_1, the value for $2q_1 - q_2$ is close to a strictly decreasing order as expected.

I ran simulations using the exact same data set for all the combinations for 100, 200, 400, and 800 observations when (1) just q_1 and q_2 are omitted,

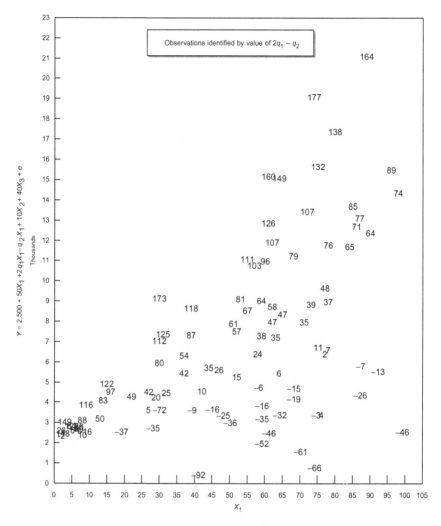

Figure A1.5: The First 100 Observations after Eliminating Effect of X_2 and X_3: The Elimination of the Effect of X_2 and X_3 Based on OLS Using All 800 Observations

(2) q_1, q_2, and X_2 are omitted, (3) q_1, q_2, and X_3 are omitted, and (4) q_1, q_2, X_2, and X_3 are omitted. The 800 observation data set contained some negative values for Y; however, equations (13) and (14) cannot handle negative values for Y or X. When negative values occur for Y (or X), then a constant is added to all values of Y (or X) sufficient to make all Ys (or Xs) positive. This added constant merely shifts the X (or Y) axis without

Table A1.3:   A More Complex Simulation

A. mean $|e|$ Omitted	q_1, q_2		q_1, q_2, x_2		q_i, q_2, x_3		q_1, q_2, x_2, x_3	
	OLS	RTPLS	OLS	RTPLS	OLS	RTPLS	OLS	RTPLS
$n = 100$	51.50	30.93	51.51	33.28	51.25	61.97	51.26	63.57
$n = 200$	52.82	10.90	52.81	17.75	52.78	54.32	52.78	54.94
$n = 400$	53.91	6.69	53.92	16.79	53.91	55.39	53.91	56.63
$n = 800$	54.25	8.11	54.28	15.13	54.37	58.85	54.40	61.21

B. variance $|e|$ Omitted	q_1, q_2		q_1, q_2, x_2		q_i, q_2, x_3		q_1, q_2, x_2, x_3	
	OLS	RTPLS	OLS	RTPLS	OLS	RTPLS	OLS	RTPLS
$n = 100$	1,224	3,232	1,225	3,686	1,218	14,227	1,218	13,706
$n = 200$	1,241	539	1,240	1,039	1,236	12,906	1,236	11,484
$n = 400$	1,253	319	1,253	2,073	1,254	20,036	1,254	23,728
$n = 800$	1,235	528	1,236	1,780	1,241	29,995	1,243	32,178

C. OLS/RTPLS Omitted	q_1, q_2	q_1, q_2, x_2	q_i, q_2, x_3	q_1, q_2, x_2, x_3
$n = 100$	2.80	2.63	1.42	1.39
$n = 200$	8.26	4.80	1.81	1.74
$n = 400$	18.32	7.60	1.83	1.78
$n = 800$	15.10	7.73	1.96	1.96

changing the slope.[8] The value 300 was added to all Y values in order to use RTPLS for this simulation. Table A1.3, Panel A shows the average mean of the absolute value of the error for each of these simulations, Panel B shows the variance of that error, and Panel C shows the mean OLS/RTPLS ratio for each simulation Table A1.3, Panel A shows that the mean error for OLS increases as the number of observations increase for all cases implying that OLS is inconsistent when there are omitted variables. In contrast, the mean error for RTPLS fell as the number of observations increased from 100 to 400 when just q_1 and q_2 are omitted and when just q_1, q_2, and X_2 are omitted.

---

[8]It is very important to realize that the shifted values for Y (or X) must be used in equations (11) and (12) when calculating RTPLS estimates, not the original values.

Table A1.3, Panel C shows that RTPLS outperformed OLS in all cases when the OLS/RTPLS ratio is calculated for each observation. When only 100 observations are used and q_1, q_2, X_2, and X_3 are omitted, the OLS/RTPLS ratio is 1.39. This was the worst case and OLS produced 39% more error (in absolute value terms) than RTPLS. In the best case (800 observations and only q_1 and q_2 are omitted), the OLS/RTPLS ratio was 15.100. However, Column 9 of Table A1.1 implies that if the importance of omitted shift factors equals the importance of the omitted variables that affect the slope, then OLS will outperform RTPLS.

Table A1.3 clearly implies that eliminating the influence of variables that merely shift the dependent variable up and down increases the accuracy of RTPLS. However, if two independent variables shift the dependent variable up and down and affect each other's slopes, then eliminating the influence of one of these variables to use RTPLS with the other variable may destroy the accuracy of RTPLS. For example, in equation (32) both X and q shift Y and affect each other's slopes.

$$Y = \alpha_0 + \alpha_1 X + \alpha_2 Xq + \alpha_3 q. \tag{32}$$

For equation (32), $\partial Y/\partial X = \alpha_1 + \alpha_2 q$ and $\partial Y/\partial q = \alpha_3 + \alpha_2 X$. To show what could happen if a researcher incorrectly tries to eliminate the shifting influence of q before using RTPLS to estimate $\partial Y/\partial X$ for equation (32), I used 800 observations, qs and Xs that were randomly generated between 0 and 100, and equation (33) where α_3 was set equal to 2, 4, and 6.

$$Y = 100 + 10X - 0.3Xq + \alpha_3 q. \tag{33}$$

For all three of these estimations, OLS produced an average value of |error| for the $\partial Y/\partial X$ estimates of approximately 7.63 whether or not q was included in the estimation. When the shifting influence of q was eliminated before conducting RTPLS, then RTPLS produced an average value for |error| for the $\partial Y/\partial X$ estimates of approximately 24.35 when α_3 was set equal to 2, 4, and 6. For all three of these cases, the OLS/RTPLS error ratio[9] was approximately 0.696 implying that using OLS while ignoring the effects of omitted variables on $\partial Y/\partial X$ produces 69.6% of the error of RTPLS. In other words, in this case, if a researcher tried to incorrectly eliminate the

---

[9]Calculated by observation, using the natural log and anti-log as explained above.

shifting influence of q which also affects the true slope, then RTPLS is worse than OLS in spite of OLS's omitted variables problem. However, if that researcher correctly estimates $\partial Y / \partial X$ with RTPLS (without attempting to eliminate q's shifting affect), then the average RTPLS $|e|$ for $\partial Y / \partial X$ is 3.40, 6.78, and 9.98 when α_3 equals 2, 4, 6 respectively. Furthermore, the OLS/RTPLS error ratio is 5.04, 2.56, and 1.74 when α_3 equals 2, 4, and 6 respectively.

The above example illustrates the importance of figuring out when to eliminate the influence of shift variables and when not to. Fortunately, theory provides us with an answer to that question. First, the RTPLS error when a researcher attempts to eliminate the shifting influence of q from equation (34) will be derived. Second, the RTPLS error from using RTPLS on equation (34) without attempting to eliminate the influence of q will be derived. Then these two errors will be compared.

$$Y = \alpha_0 + \alpha_1 X + \alpha_2 X q + \alpha_3 q \tag{34}$$

$$Y = \alpha_0 + \alpha_1 X + \alpha_2 q X + \alpha_3 q + \alpha_2 q E[X]$$
$$- \alpha_2 q E[X] \quad \text{adding zero to (34).} \tag{35}$$

"$E[X]$" is the expected or mean value for X. Using the above described procedure to supposedly "eliminate" the shifting effect of q actually removes more than just the shift effect. Since the OLS estimate of dY/dq would equal approximately $\alpha_3 + \alpha_2 E[X]$, equation (35) becomes equation (36) after the attempt to remove q's shifting affect.[10]

$$Y = \alpha_0 + \alpha_1 X + \alpha_2 q X - \alpha_2 q E[X] \tag{36}$$

$$Y/X = \alpha_0/X + \alpha_1 + \alpha_2 q - \alpha_2 q E[X]/X \quad \text{dividing (36) by } X \tag{37}$$

$$(\partial Y/\partial X)^{\text{True}} = \alpha_1 + \alpha_2 q \quad \text{derivative of (34)} \tag{38}$$

$$Y/X - \alpha_0/X + \alpha_2 q E[X]/X$$
$$= \alpha_1 + \alpha_2 q = (\partial Y/\partial X)^{\text{True}} \quad \text{(37) rearranged} \tag{39}$$

---

[10]This statement is based on equations (4) and (5).

$$Y/X - \alpha_0/X + \alpha_2\{q + E[q] - E[q]\}E[X]/X$$
$$= (\partial Y/\partial X)^{\text{True}} \qquad\qquad \text{adding 0 to (39)} \qquad (40)$$

$$Y/X - \alpha_0/X + \alpha_2 E[q]E[X]/X + \alpha_2\{q - E[q]\}E[X]/X$$
$$= (\partial Y/\partial X)^{\text{True}}. \qquad\qquad\qquad\qquad\qquad (41)$$

When RTPLS assumes that α_0 is a constant, it produces a $(\partial Y/\partial X)^{\text{RTPLS}}$ of approximately $Y/X - \alpha_0/X + \alpha_2 E[q]E[X]/X$ where $(\partial Y/\partial X)^{\text{RTPLS}}$ is the RTPLS estimate of $\partial Y/\partial X$. Thus, equation (41) becomes (42).

$$(\partial Y/\partial X)^{\text{RTPLS}} + \alpha_2\{q - E[q]\}E[X]/X = (\partial Y/\partial X)^{\text{True}} \qquad (42)$$
$$(\partial Y/\partial X)^{\text{True}} - (\partial Y/\partial X)^{\text{RTPLS}} = \alpha_2\{q - E[q]\}E[X]/X. \quad \text{(42) rearranged}$$
$$(43)$$

Therefore, the difference between the true slope and the RTPLS estimate of the slope for observation "i" when a researcher attempts to eliminate the shift influence of q from equation (34) is approximately $\alpha_2\{q_i - E[q]\} E[X]/X_i$.

Now consider the difference between the true slope and the RTPLS estimate of the slope when a researcher does not attempt to eliminate the shift influence of q from equation (34).

$$Y/X = \alpha_0/X + \alpha_1 + \alpha_2 q + \alpha_3 q/X \qquad \text{dividing (34) by } X \quad (44)$$
$$Y/X - \alpha_0/X - \alpha_3 q/X$$
$$= \alpha_1 + \alpha_2 q = (\partial Y/\partial X)^{\text{True}} \qquad \text{(44) rearranged} \qquad (45)$$
$$Y/X - \alpha_0/X - \alpha_3\{q - E[q] + E[q]\}/X$$
$$= (\partial Y/\partial X)^{\text{True}} \qquad\qquad \text{(45) plus zero} \qquad (46)$$
$$Y/X - \alpha_0/X - \alpha_3 E[q]/X - \alpha_3\{q - E[q]\}/X$$
$$= (\partial Y/\partial X)^{\text{True}} \qquad\qquad \text{(46) rearranged.} \qquad (47)$$

When RTPLS assumes that α_0 is a constant, it produces a $(\partial Y/\partial X)^{\text{RTPLS}}$ of approximately $Y/X - \alpha_0/X - \alpha_3 E[q]/X$; thus, equation (47) becomes equation (48).

$$(\partial Y/\partial X)^{\text{RTPLS}} - \alpha_3\{q - E[q]\}/X = (\partial Y/\partial X)^{\text{True}} \tag{48}$$

$$(\partial Y/\partial X)^{\text{True}} - (\partial Y/\partial X)^{\text{RTPLS}} = -\alpha_3\{q - E[q]\}/X \quad \text{(48) rearranged.} \tag{49}$$

Thus, the difference between the true slope and the RTPLS estimated slope when a researcher does not try to eliminate the shift influence of q from equation (34) before estimating $\partial Y/\partial X$ with RTPLS is $-\alpha_3\{q - E[q]\}/X$. Therefore, the decision on whether or not to eliminate the shift influence of a variable before conducting RTPLS should be based on comparing $\alpha_2\{q - E[q]\}E[X]/X$ to $-\alpha_3\{q - E[q]\}/X$. Since, $\{q - E[q]\}/X$ is common to both of these expressions, the choice is reduced to a comparison of $\alpha_2 E[X]$ and $-\alpha_3$. If $|\alpha_3| > |\alpha_2 E[X]|$, then the shift influence of q should be eliminated from equation (34) before RTPLS is used to estimate $\partial Y/\partial X$. If $|\alpha_3| < |\alpha_2 E[X]|$, then the shift influence of q should not be eliminated from equation (34) before RTPLS is used to estimate $\partial Y/\partial X$.

The effects of changes in the money supply, government consumption, and exports will interact with each other via a worldwide macroeconomic model similar to (but much more complex than) the Mundell Fleming Model. However, the money supply, government consumption, and exports may also have independent shift effects on GDP. I chose not to eliminate the shift effects of the other two variables when estimating $\partial GDP/\partial$(money supply), $\partial GDP/\partial$(government consumption), and $\partial GDP/\partial$(exports) in Chapters 3–5 respectively because I believe that the shift effect is much less than the interaction effect times the expected values of these variables; in other words, I believe that $|\alpha_3| < |\alpha_2 E[X]|$. For example, the effectiveness of increasing government spending is greatly affected by the resulting change in interest rates (via the "crowding out" effect) and monetary policy affects the interest rate. Likewise, since exports and government spending are two substitute forms of final demand, they will interact with each other. Furthermore, the effectiveness of monetary policy depends on the forces that drive investment which include exports and government spending. Likewise, when I estimated ∂exports/∂(foreign reserves) and ∂(exports–imports)/∂(foreign reserves) in Chapter 6, there was no attempt to eliminate the influence of other shift factors because there are no shift factors that would not also affect the estimated slope and I believe that $|\alpha_3| < |\alpha_2 E[X]|$.

In contrast when estimating the effect on Gross Provincial Product (GPP) of labor's share of income relative to profits and rents ($w/(p+r)$) in Chapter 8, the effect of government consumption (G) was eliminated prior to using RTPLS. Since government consumption is measured in currency units and $w/(p+r)$ is an unit-less ratio, it is highly likely that government consumption shifts GPP without noticeably changing the estimated slope, $\partial GPP/\partial(w/(p+r))$. Thus, in this case, I believe that $|\alpha_3| > |\alpha_2 E[X]|$. Government consumption was picked because, in a world of insufficient consumption, government consumption is the most obvious substitute that is most controlled by domestic policies. Finally, the influence of only one shift factor was eliminated, instead of several shift factors, because that minimized the danger of accidentally eliminating part of the true relationship being estimated.

Using RTPLS to determine if savings (S) constrains investment (I) or consumption (C) drives investment in Chapter 8 produced some unique issues because consumption and savings are so strongly correlated with each other. This correlation is due to an increase in income causing both consumption and saving to rise. Thus, an RTPLS estimate of $\partial I/\partial C$ (or $\partial I/\partial S$) would have included how savings (consumption) affects investment. Both consumption and savings could not have been used as separate right-hand side variables that affect investment because clearly omitted variables would affect both of their corresponding slopes and RTPLS can handle only one included right-hand side variable whose slope is affected by omitted variables. These problems were solved by estimating $\partial I/\partial(C/S)$. If $\partial I/\partial(C/S)$ is positive, then consumption drives investment; if $\partial I/\partial S$ is negative, then savings constrains investment. This approach includes both the forces that fund and drive investment. There were no other obvious shift factors whose influence needed to be eliminated that did not function either through consumption or savings. For example, an increase in profits is likely to increase savings and be driven by an increase in demand or consumption. Therefore, even though profits may seem like an obvious explanatory variable, it is actually included when RTPLS estimates are made of $\partial I/\partial(C/S)$.

When $\partial GDP/\partial M$, $\partial GDP/\partial G$, $\partial GDP/\partial X$, $\partial X/\partial(\text{foreign reserves})$, and $\partial(X - M)/\partial(\text{foreign reserves})$ were estimated using RTPLS, a positive relationship was assumed because economic theory requires a positive relationship. However, the purpose of estimating $\partial GPP/\partial(w/(p+r))$ and $\partial I/\partial(C/S)$ was to determine if the estimated relationships were positive or negative. If they are positive, then redistributing income to labor and consumers would increase growth. If they are negative, then redistributing income to profits and rents and to those who save would increase growth. RTPLS can estimate negative relationships as explained below. RTPLS can even handle cases where omitted variables cause some observations to have a positive $\partial Y/\partial X$ and others to have a negative $\partial Y/\partial X$ (Leightner and Inoue, 2007). However, RTPLS must make one of the following two initial assumptions: (1) that a majority of the observations have a positive $\partial Y/\partial X$ or (2) that a majority of the observations have a negative $\partial Y/\partial X$. When estimating $\partial GPP/\partial(w/(p+r))$ and $\partial I/\partial(C/S)$, this initial assumption was made based on the sign for $\partial Y/\partial X$ in a preliminary OLS regression.[11] If OLS produced a negative $\partial Y/\partial X$, then a negative relationship was assumed; if OLS produced a positive $\partial Y/\partial X$, then a positive relationship was assumed.

When the preliminary OLS regression indicated a negative relationship, then that negative relationship had to be temporarily transformed into a positive relationship in order to use equations (13) and (14) which are essential to the RTPLS process. This temporary transformation is accomplished by multiplying all Y values by negative one and then adding a constant that would make them all positive.[12] This temporary transformation is illustrated in Figure A1.6. By multiplying all Ys by negative one, the negative slope is changed into a positive slope. However, equations (13) and (14) cannot handle negative numbers, therefore a constant had to be added to every Y that would make all Y's positive. Adding this constant shifts the X-axis downward without changing the slope. The data can now be used with RTPLS[13]; however, the estimated RTPLS slopes must be re-multiplied

---

[11] Since this OLS regression only uses a constant and the single X variable that will be used in the RTPLS estimate, $\partial Y/\partial X = dY/dX$ (in other words, the total derivative is equal to the partial derivative).

[12] Alternatively, all X values could be multiplied by negative one and then a constant added to them that was big enough to make them all positive.

[13] When using equation (11) to calculate an individual slope estimate for each observation, the shifted Y values must be used, not the original Y values, because the estimated α_0 is based on the shifted Y values.

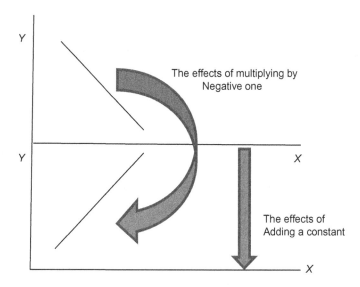

Figure A1.6:   Using RTPLS When $\partial Y/\partial X$ is Negative

by negative one in order to undo the temporary transformation. This is the procedure used to estimate equation (33).

How Random Error Affects RTPLS Theoretically

When this appendix began, I assumed that all error was due to omitted variables, thus I assumed no random error. However, the simulations reported in this appendix examined cases where random error was both added and not added. I will end the appendix by showing what happens theoretically when there is random error. Consider equation (50).

$$Y = \alpha_0 + \alpha_1 X + \alpha_2 Xq + u \tag{50}$$

$$(\partial Y/\partial X)^{\text{True}} = \alpha_1 + \alpha_2 q \qquad \text{Derivative of (50)} \tag{51}$$

$$Y/X = \alpha_0/X + \alpha_1 + \alpha_2 q + u/X \qquad \text{(50) divided by } X \tag{52}$$

$$\alpha_1 + \alpha_2 q = Y/X - \alpha_0/X - u/X \qquad \text{(52) rearranged} \tag{53}$$

$$(\partial Y/\partial X)^{\text{True}} = Y/X - \alpha_0/X - u/X \qquad \text{From (51) and (52)} \tag{54}$$

$$(\partial Y/\partial X)^{\text{True}} = Y/X - \alpha_0/X$$

$$- \{u - E[u] + E[u]\}/X \qquad \text{Adding zero to (54)} \quad (55)$$

$$(\partial Y/\partial X)^{\text{True}} = Y/X - \alpha_0/X$$

$$- E[u]/X - \{u - E[u]\}/X \quad \text{(55) rearranged} \qquad (56)$$

$$(\partial Y/\partial X)^{\text{True}} = Y/X - \{\alpha_0 + E[u]\}/X$$

$$- \{u - E[u]\}/X \qquad \text{(56) rearranged.} \qquad (57)$$

In this case, the coefficient produced when estimating equation (12) is approximately $\{\alpha_0 + E[u]\}$ because equation (12) assumed a Y intercept that is a constant. Thus, the RTPLS estimate that results from using equation (11) is approximately $Y/X - \{\alpha_0 + E[u]\}/X$. Therefore, equation (57) becomes equation (58).

$$(\partial Y/\partial X)^{\text{True}} = (\partial Y/\partial X)^{\text{RTPLS}} - \{u - E[u]\}/X. \qquad (58)$$

Therefore, the difference between observation i's RTPLS slope estimate and the true slope is $-\{u_i - E[u]\}/X_i$. If random error has a zero mean (as is usually assumed), this expression becomes $-u_i/X_i$. If the random error is small relative to the size of the explanatory variables (as is reasonable for most applications), then this difference between the true slope and the RTPLS estimate of the slope is small. Finally, as the size of measurement error falls and as the size of the explanatory variables rise, the RTPLS estimate will converge to the true slope.

Appendix 2

ADDITIONAL FIGURES FOR CHAPTER 4

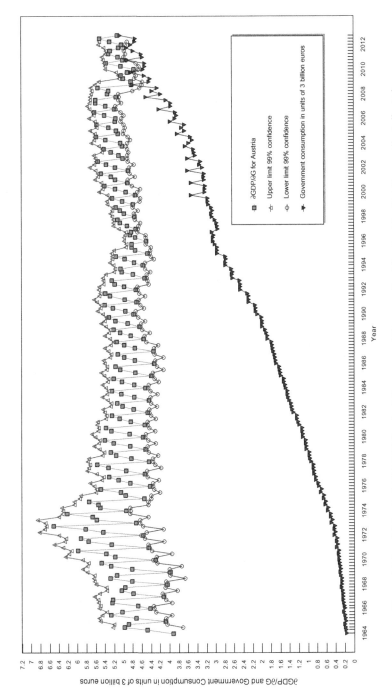

Figure A2.1:   ∂(Nominal GDP)/∂(Nominal Government Consumption) for Austria: Not Seasonally Adjusted

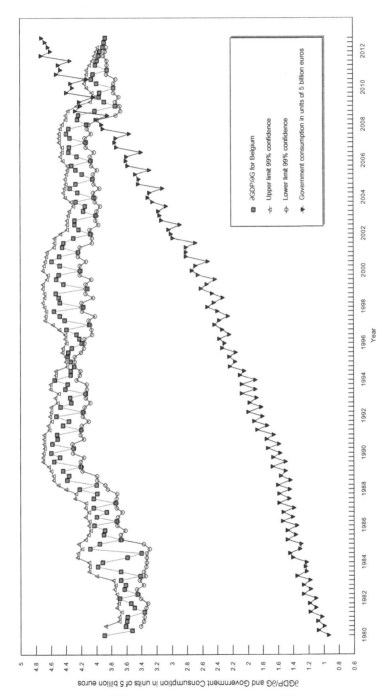

Figure A2.2:   ∂(Nominal GDP)/∂(Nominal Government Consumption) for Belgium: Not Seasonally Adjusted

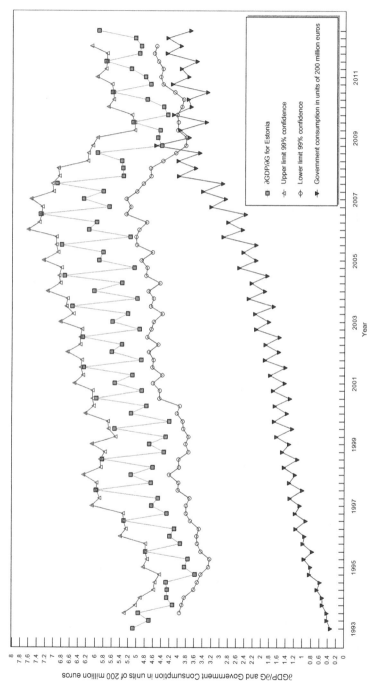

Figure A2.3:   ∂(Nominal GDP)/∂(Nominal Government Consumption) for Estonia: Not Seasonally Adjusted

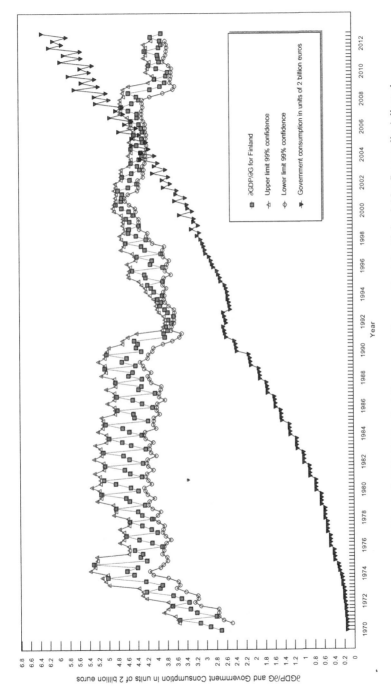

Figure A2.4: ∂(Nominal GDP)/∂(Nominal Government Consumption) for Finland: Not Seasonally Adjusted

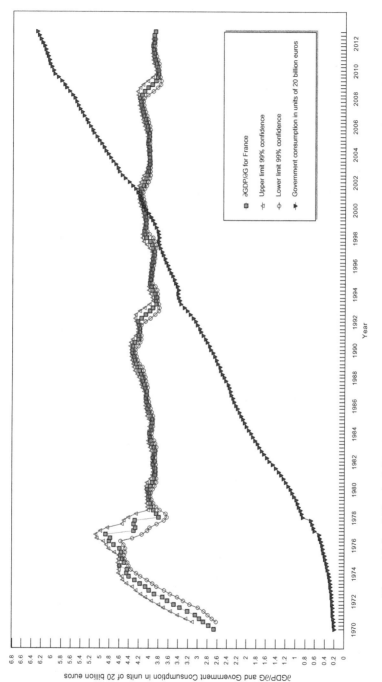

Figure A2.5: ∂(Nominal GDP)/∂(Nominal Government Consumption) for France: Seasonally Adjusted

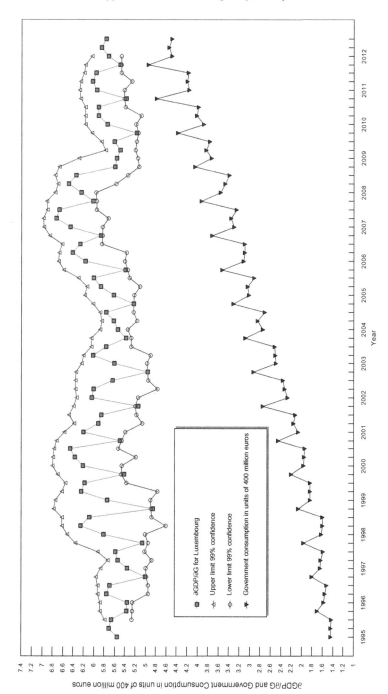

Figure A2.6: ∂(Nominal GDP)/∂(Nominal Government Consumption) for Luxembourg: Not Seasonally Adjusted

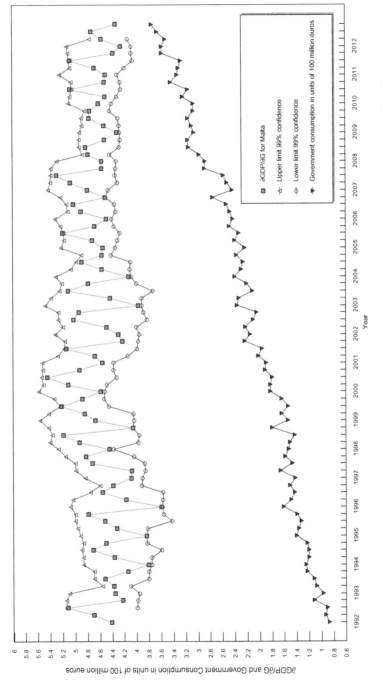

Figure A2.7: ∂(Nominal GDP)/∂(Nominal Government Consumption) for Malta: Not Seasonally Adjusted

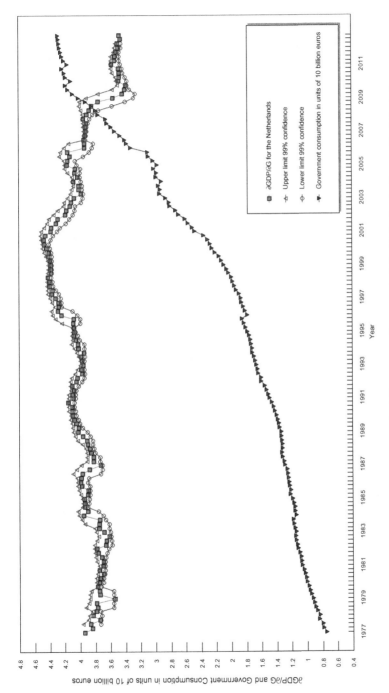

Figure A2.8: ∂(Nominal GDP)/∂(Nominal Government Consumption) for Netherlands: Seasonally Adjusted

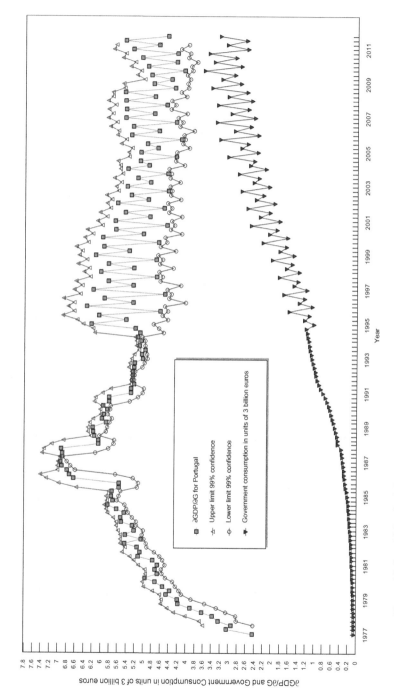

Figure A2.9: ∂(Nominal GDP)/∂(Nominal Government Consumption) for Portugal: Not Seasonally Adjusted

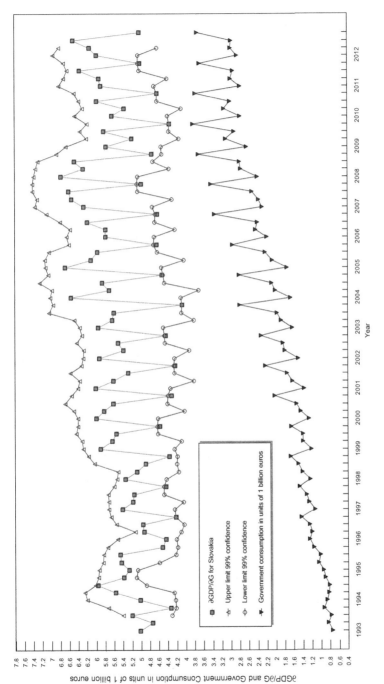

Figure A2.10: ∂(Nominal GDP)/∂(Nominal Government Consumption) for Slovakia: Not Seasonally Adjusted

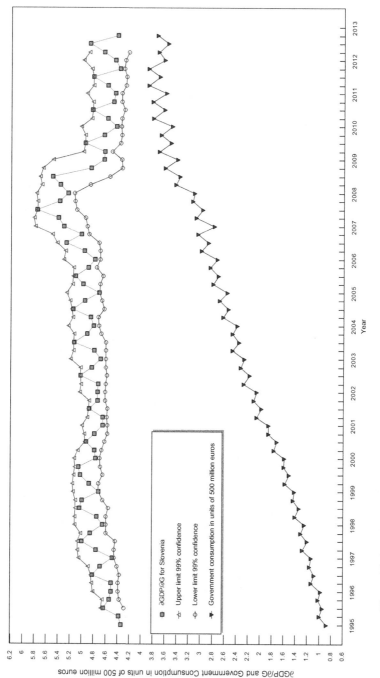

Figure A2.11: ∂(Nominal GDP)/∂(Nominal Government Consumption) for Slovenia: Not Seasonally Adjusted

Appendix 3

ADDITIONAL FIGURES FOR CHAPTER 5

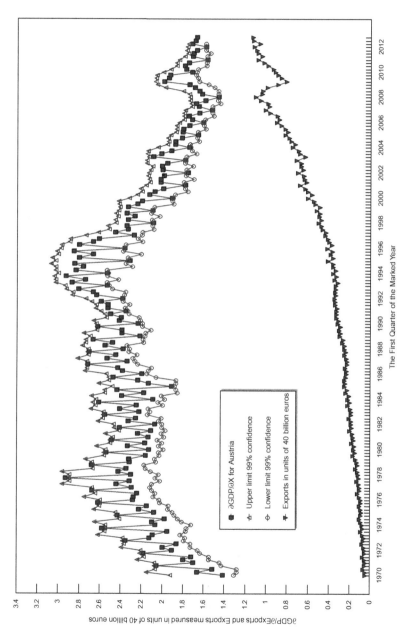

Figure A3.1:   ∂GDP/∂Exports for Austria: Not Seasonally Adjusted

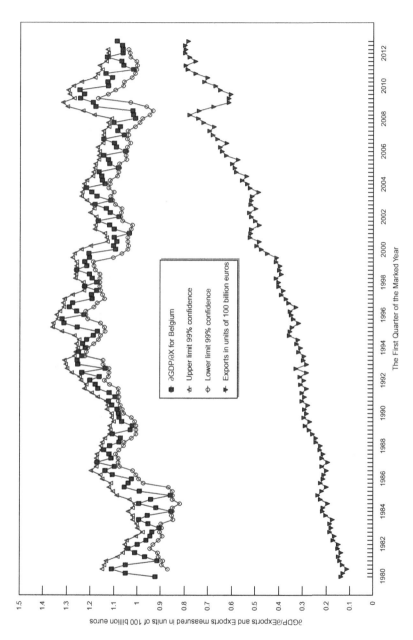

Figure A3.2:   ∂GDP/∂Exports for Belgium: Not Seasonally Adjusted

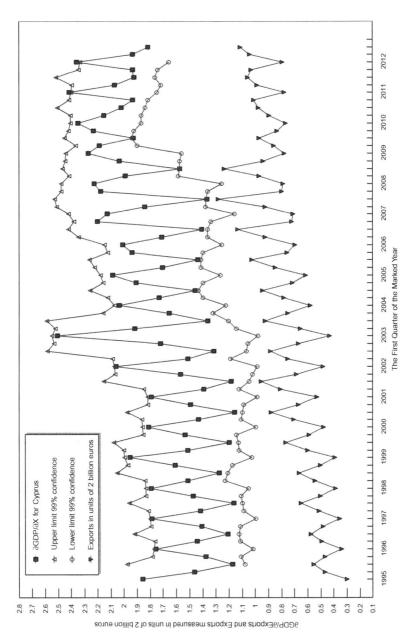

Figure A3.3:   ∂GDP/∂Exports for Cyprus: Not Seasonally Adjusted

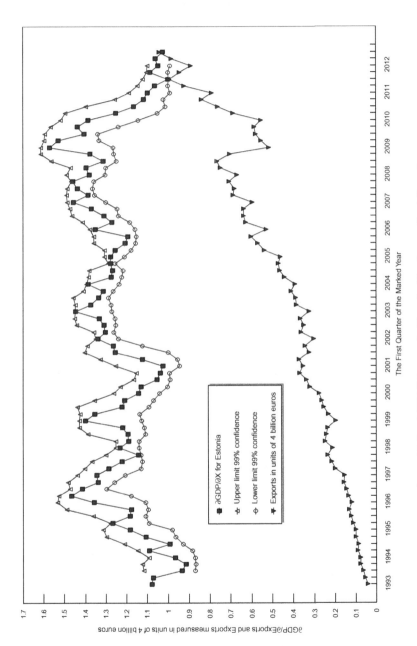

Figure A3.4: ∂GDP/∂Exports for Estonia: Not Seasonally Adjusted

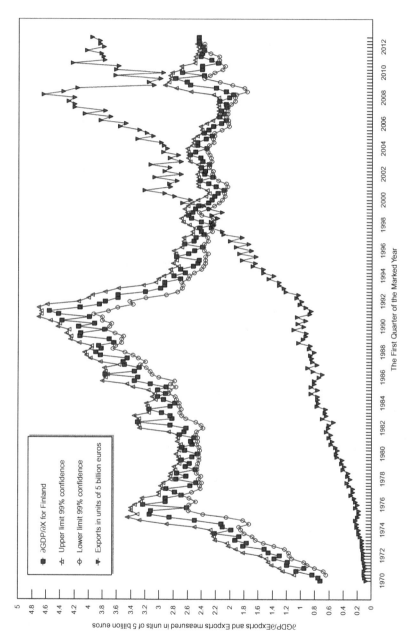

Figure A3.5:   ∂GDP/∂Exports for Finland: Not Seasonally Adjusted

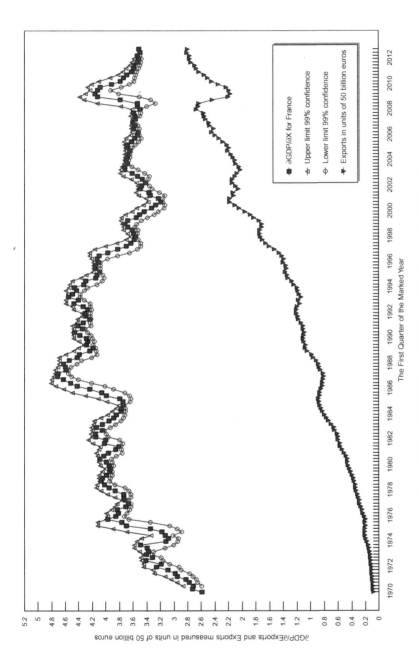

Figure A3.6:   ∂GDP/∂Exports for France: Not Seasonally Adjusted

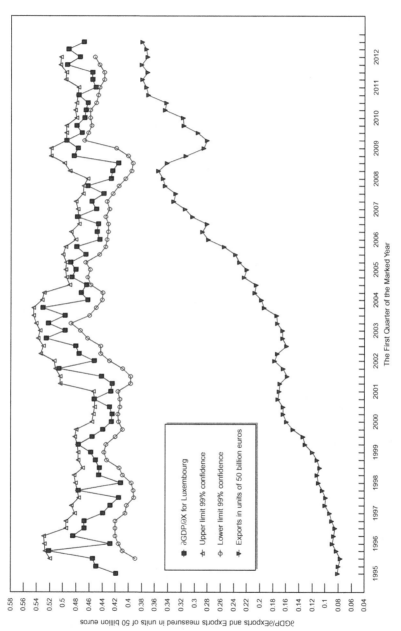

Figure A3.7:   ∂GDP/∂Exports for Luxembourg

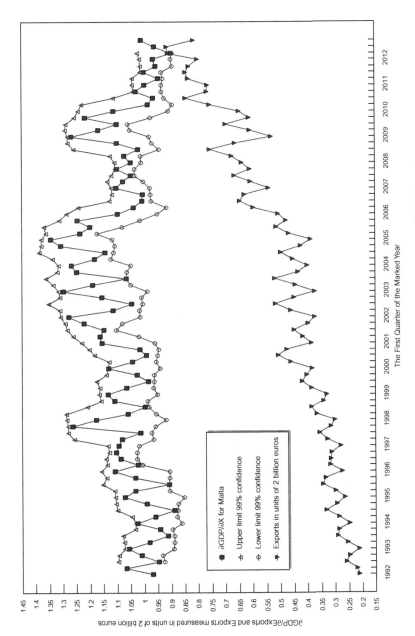

Figure A3.8: $\partial GDP/\partial Exports$ for Malta: Not Seasonally Adjusted

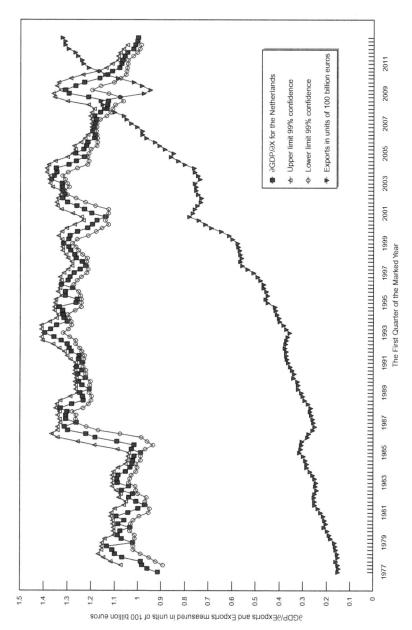

Figure A3.9: ∂GDP/∂Exports for the Netherlands

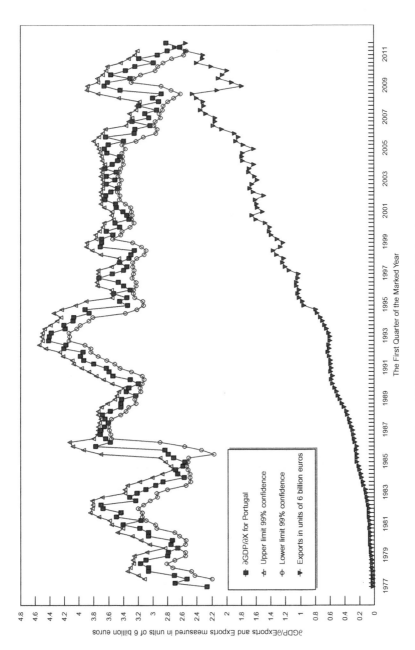

Figure A3.10: ∂GDP/∂Exports for Portugal

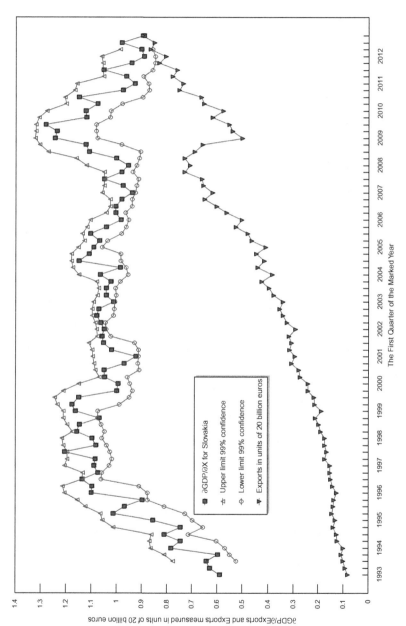

Figure A3.11:   ∂GDP/∂Exports for Slovakia: Not Seasonally Adjusted

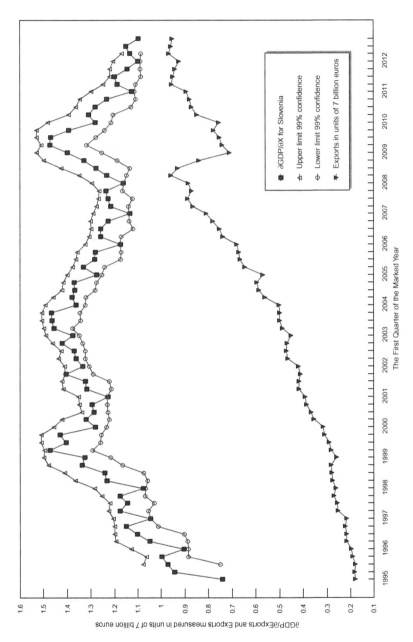

Figure A3.12: $\partial GDP/\partial$Exports for Slovenia

Appendix 4

ADDITIONAL INFORMATION FOR CHAPTER 8

It can be argued that the third steps of both the anti- and pro-equality arguments appear in Adam Smith's *Wealth of Nations*. The following passage is similar to the third step of the anti-equality argument:

> Whatever a person saves from his revenue he adds to his capital, and either employs it himself in maintaining an additional number of productive hands, or enables some other person to do so, by lending it to him for an interest, that is, for a share of the profits. As the capital of an individual can be increased only by what he saves from his annual revenue or his annual gains, so the capital of a society, which is the same with that of all the individuals who compose it, can be increased only in the same manner.
>
> Parsimony, and not industry, is the immediate cause of the increase of capital. Industry, indeed, provides the subject which parsimony accumulates. But whatever industry might acquire, if parsimony did not save and store up, the capital would never be the greater (p. 321).

In contrast to the above, *The Wealth of Nations* could be interpreted as emphasizing consumption's role in growth when it discusses the "extent of the market" which is identified with such domestic conditions as the size and density of the population. Of course, expanding this domestic market to international markets can be extremely important to growth according to Smith. The extent of the market is what limits the division of labor which drives growth. Furthermore, investment activity is an integral part of the division of labor. Paraphrasing and combining the above-mentioned views of Adam Smith could lead to the following conclusion, which resembles the third and fourth steps of the pro-equality argument: if consumption increases, the extent of the market increases (*ceteris paribus*), which causes the division of labor to increase (and thus investment), which drives growth (pp. 259–261).

Perhaps, the purest and most direct statement of the pro-equality argument is in A.F. Mummery and J.A. Hobson's book *The Physiology of Industry*. Mummery and Hobson argue that investment drives growth, demand drives investment, and consumption drives demand. The demand for investment goods is a "derived" demand in the sense that investments are made in order to increase the amount of consumption goods the economy can produce. If consumption demand dries up, then both production and investment would dry up.

Keynesian analysis also appears to have a pro-equality flavor. In the simplest form of Keynesian analysis, the "multiplier" is the inverse of the marginal propensity to save. If the marginal propensity to save declined, perhaps due to redistributing income to the poor, then the multiplier increases. Furthermore, any upward shift in the consumption function, caused perhaps by a redistribution of income to the poor, can be magnified by this Keynesian multiplier to obtain the total increase in output. Therefore, redistributing income to the poor may cause output to increase by shifting the consumption function up and by increasing the multiplier effect of such a shift.

The anti-equality argument, especially its third step, has a more extensive and entrenched history than the pro-equality argument. David Ricardo's *Principles of Political Economy* contains an anti-equality type of view stated in terms of the class divisions that separate capitalists and laborers. According to Ricardo, profits drive investment which, in turn, drives growth. As an economy grows, however, it expands onto more and more marginal land which causes rents to increase that also causes the wage bill to increase. The increasing wage bill and rising rents ultimately cause the profit rate to decrease which causes investment to decrease and, thus, growth to slow. Since profits are the income of the capitalists and the wage bill is the income of labor, Ricardo's views imply an anti-equality mechanism stated in terms of capitalists versus labor.

Karl Marx also had a capitalist/labor anti-equality view of growth in a capitalist economy. According to Marx, capitalism is class warfare. Capitalism grows as long as the capitalist class can increase its economic power relative to the labor class'. The capitalists increase their economic standing relative to labor in several ways. First, capitalists will attempt to increase the number of hours labor has to work in order to earn a subsistence level of income. When that tactic no longer works, capitalists will mechanize the production of wage goods and then of all goods. When mechanization will no longer increase the relative standing of the capitalists, then the greed of the capitalists will cause them to try to drive labor below the subsistence level of income. When this happens, labor either revolts or dies. Thus, according to Marx, a widening gap between capitalists and labor drives growth in a capitalist economy and when that gap can no longer be widened, then capitalism will fall.

Although W.W. Rostow mentions the influence of demand on growth, he focuses on how economic growth is financed. For economic growth to "take-off," the supply of loanable funds must increase. Furthermore, the supply of loanable funds increases when income is redistributed to those who save and to those who reinvest (see especially pp. 46–50).

W. Arthur Lewis' famous article on unlimited supplies of labor also contains a strongly state capitalist versus labor anti-equality argument. According to Lewis, "the central fact of economic development is rapid capital accumulation." Furthermore, for capital accumulation to occur, saving must increase. Therefore, "the central fact of economic development is that the distribution of incomes is altered in favor of the saving class. Practically, all saving is done by people who receive profits or rents" (p. 157). Lewis argues that capitalists are more reliable savers than landlords and, thus, growth "involves an increase in the inequality of incomes, as between capitalists and the rest" (1983, p. 159).

In a simple Domar growth model, the equilibrium growth rate is the marginal propensity to save divided by the capital/output ratio. If income is redistributed to the classes who save a larger proportion of their income than other groups, then the average marginal propensity to save will increase which, *ceteris paribus*, will cause the Domar growth rate to rise.

Table A4.1: Labor's Share of Income

	Australia	Austria	Belgium	Canada	Czech Rep.	Denmark	Estonia	Finland	France	Germany	Hungary	Iceland	Ireland	Israel	Italy	Japan
1970	0.64	0.62	0.52	0.63		0.69		0.60	0.69	0.67					0.73	0.48
1971	0.64	0.63	0.57	0.62		0.71		0.65	0.70	0.69					0.77	0.51
1972	0.63	0.64	0.58	0.61		0.71		0.66	0.70	0.70					0.77	0.52
1973	0.66	0.69	0.59	0.57		0.72		0.64	0.70	0.70		0.54			0.75	0.53
1974	0.68	0.70	0.62	0.55		0.76		0.60	0.73	0.70		0.71			0.72	0.57
1975	0.65	0.75	0.62	0.57		0.71		0.67	0.75	0.71		0.63			0.80	0.62
1976	0.63	0.75	0.69	0.58		0.73		0.70	0.75	0.70		0.56			0.75	0.60
1977	0.63	0.76	0.68	0.56		0.73		0.68	0.75	0.72		0.60			0.75	0.60
1978	0.61	0.77	0.67	0.55		0.73		0.63	0.74	0.71		0.65			0.75	0.57
1979	0.58	0.76	0.65	0.51		0.74		0.60	0.74	0.73		0.62			0.74	0.58
1980	0.58	0.76	0.66	0.51		0.72		0.62	0.74	0.75		0.60			0.70	0.57
1981	0.60	0.76	0.69	0.53		0.71		0.63	0.74	0.76		0.60			0.72	0.57
1982	0.59	0.73	0.67	0.56		0.67		0.63	0.75	0.75		0.61			0.71	0.57
1983	0.54	0.71	0.65	0.51		0.65		0.62	0.73	0.73		0.52			0.72	0.57
1984	0.53	0.71	0.64	0.48		0.65		0.61	0.72	0.73		0.48			0.69	0.56
1985	0.52	0.69	0.64	0.48		0.65		0.62	0.70	0.71		0.54			0.69	0.54
1986	0.54	0.69	0.63	0.53		0.66		0.63	0.69	0.71		0.51	0.57		0.69	0.55
1987	0.53	0.70	0.64	0.51		0.69		0.61	0.70	0.73		0.59	0.56		0.68	0.55
1988	0.54	0.69	0.62	0.51		0.70		0.60	0.68	0.73		0.58	0.55		0.69	0.55
1989	0.53	0.69	0.62	0.53		0.67		0.60	0.67	0.72		0.54	0.52		0.69	0.55
1990	0.54	0.68	0.63	0.54		0.67		0.65	0.67	0.73		0.54	0.51		0.72	0.55
1991	0.52	0.70	0.66	0.57		0.65		0.71	0.67	0.74	0.74	0.56	0.51		0.74	0.55
1992	0.51	0.71	0.66	0.58	0.50	0.64		0.65	0.68	0.77		0.57	0.49		0.74	0.56

(Continued)

Table A4.1: *(Continued)*

	Korea	Luxembourg	Mexico	Netherlands	N. Zealand	Norway	Poland	Portugal	Slovak Rep.	Slovenia	Spain	Sweden	Turkey	UK	USA
1970	0.51			0.65		0.67						0.74		0.75	0.71
1971	0.51			0.65	0.59	0.70						0.75		0.73	0.69
1972	0.48			0.64	0.62	0.70						0.76		0.74	0.69
1973	0.49			0.64	0.65	0.68						0.73		0.75	0.70
1974	0.51			0.63	0.69	0.66						0.69		0.79	0.70
1975	0.50			0.61	0.75	0.65						0.73		0.84	0.67
1976	0.51			0.58	0.65	0.65						0.80		0.79	0.67
1977	0.54			0.58	0.65	0.64		0.92				0.84		0.75	0.66
1978	0.58			0.59	0.65	0.60		0.88				0.84		0.74	0.67
1979	0.59			0.58	0.64	0.49		0.81				0.78		0.73	0.68
1980	0.60			0.55	0.65	0.42		0.81			0.61	0.77		0.69	0.67
1981	0.58			0.51	0.63	0.41		0.84			0.61	0.79		0.67	0.64
1982	0.57			0.52	0.59	0.40		0.85			0.60	0.75		0.65	0.65
1983	0.58			0.51	0.54	0.36		0.80			0.59	0.70		0.62	0.64
1984	0.57			0.47	0.52	0.34		0.72			0.56	0.67		0.60	0.63
1985	0.55	0.60		0.47	0.54	0.35		0.69			0.54	0.69		0.62	0.64
1986	0.55	0.58		0.53	0.53	0.48		0.70			0.54	0.66		0.64	0.67
1987	0.56	0.64	0.28	0.58	0.55	0.50		0.72			0.55	0.66	0.17	0.65	0.65
1988	0.60	0.59	0.32	0.58	0.53	0.53		0.63			0.55	0.67	0.16	0.66	0.63
1989	0.60	0.54	0.32	0.56	0.50	0.44		0.61			0.55	0.68	0.19	0.66	0.63
1990	0.61	0.56	0.32	0.56	0.51	0.41		0.62			0.59	0.70	0.23	0.69	0.63
1991	0.62	0.62	0.33	0.56	0.50	0.41		0.65			0.61	0.72	0.29	0.72	0.64
1992	0.62	0.64	0.35	0.59	0.49	0.42	0.51	0.64			0.65	0.72	0.28	0.67	0.65

(Continued)

Table A4.1:   *(Continued)*

	Australia	Austria	Belgium	Canada	Czech Rep.	Denmark	Estonia	Finland	France	Germany	Hungary	Iceland	Ireland	Israel	Italy	Japan
1993	0.49	0.72	0.67	0.55	0.54	0.65		0.59	0.69	0.79	0.74	0.53	0.48		0.73	0.57
1994	0.49	0.71	0.66	0.51	0.52	0.61		0.57	0.69	0.78	0.69	0.51	0.46		0.70	0.58
1995	0.51	0.67	0.65	0.49	0.52	0.62	0.66	0.55	0.68	0.78	0.68	0.53	0.42	0.68	0.68	0.58
1996	0.51	0.66	0.65	0.49	0.52	0.61	0.65	0.58	0.69	0.78	0.65	0.56	0.42	0.69	0.67	0.57
1997	0.49	0.65	0.64	0.49	0.54	0.59	0.64	0.56	0.68	0.76	0.59	0.55	0.38	0.67	0.68	0.57
1998	0.49	0.65	0.63	0.51	0.56	0.61	0.66	0.54	0.65	0.75	0.56	0.57	0.34	0.67	0.65	0.57
1999	0.48	0.64	0.65	0.47	0.54	0.60	0.63	0.55	0.66	0.75	0.57	0.64	0.32	0.65	0.66	0.57
2000	0.47	0.62	0.63	0.43	0.54	0.54	0.61	0.52	0.65	0.76	0.58	0.63	0.31	0.64	0.64	0.57
2001	0.46	0.61	0.66	0.45	0.55	0.57	0.58	0.53	0.66	0.76	0.58	0.54	0.30	0.68	0.64	0.59
2002	0.47	0.62	0.65	0.46	0.57	0.56	0.58	0.53	0.67	0.75	0.57	0.59	0.27	0.66	0.65	0.58
2003	0.46	0.62	0.66	0.45	0.59	0.57	0.57	0.54	0.67	0.75	0.55	0.64	0.29	0.63	0.67	0.57
2004	0.45	0.60	0.64	0.44	0.54	0.55	0.59	0.53	0.68	0.71	0.52	0.65	0.32	0.62	0.67	0.55
2005	0.42	0.60	0.63	0.43	0.54	0.52	0.58	0.55	0.68	0.70	0.53	0.74	0.34	0.60	0.68	0.54
2006	0.41	0.58	0.63	0.44	0.53	0.51	0.58	0.53	0.69	0.67	0.50	0.68	0.35	0.62	0.67	0.55
2007		0.57	0.63	0.43	0.52	0.53	0.58	0.50	0.68	0.65	0.52	0.71	0.33	0.62	0.66	0.53
2008		0.57	0.65	0.40	0.55	0.54	0.61	0.54	0.70	0.67	0.52	0.53	0.35	0.64	0.68	0.56
2009		0.62	0.69		0.52	0.60	0.63	0.63		0.77	0.49	0.43	0.31	0.66	0.72	0.57
2010		0.59	0.66		0.54	0.54	0.51	0.55		0.70	0.45			0.66	0.69	0.52
2011					0.55	0.55								0.69		0.58

(Continued)

Table A4.1: (Continued)

	Korea	Luxembourg	Mexico	Netherlands	N. Zealand	Norway	Poland	Portugal	Slovak Rep.	Slovenia	Spain	Sweden	Turkey	UK	USA
1993	0.61	0.65	0.36	0.59	0.48	0.41	0.52	0.63	0.49		0.67	0.64	0.26	0.65	0.65
1994	0.60	0.63	0.35	0.57	0.48	0.42	0.64	0.60	0.50		0.66	0.60	0.21	0.63	0.63
1995	0.62	0.63	0.28	0.55	0.49	0.40	0.61	0.58	0.46	0.82	0.63	0.56	0.17	0.61	0.61
1996	0.65	0.65	0.27	0.55	0.50	0.35	0.68	0.58	0.48	0.76	0.63	0.60	0.17	0.59	0.60
1997	0.61	0.62	0.29	0.56	0.49	0.35	0.69	0.57	0.56	0.70	0.63	0.60	0.18	0.59	0.60
1998	0.53	0.59	0.29	0.57	0.49	0.44	0.70	0.57	0.55	0.68	0.63	0.60	0.20	0.64	0.62
1999	0.51	0.60	0.30	0.58	0.47	0.38	0.68	0.57	0.49	0.66	0.63	0.58	0.27	0.64	0.61
2000	0.52	0.60	0.32	0.54	0.45	0.25	0.65	0.57	0.51	0.67	0.62	0.59	0.28	0.63	0.63
2001	0.55	0.62	0.34	0.54	0.46	0.27	0.65	0.57	0.50	0.66	0.62	0.62	0.27	0.63	0.64
2002	0.56	0.64	0.33	0.55	0.46	0.30	0.61	0.58	0.52	0.65	0.61	0.61	0.27	0.65	0.62
2003	0.55	0.62	0.33	0.54	0.48	0.29	0.56	0.57	0.49	0.63	0.61	0.60	0.26	0.66	0.62
2004	0.54	0.62	0.29	0.53	0.48	0.26	0.50	0.57	0.44	0.64	0.60	0.58	0.25	0.65	0.57
2005	0.57	0.63	0.29	0.49	0.47	0.23	0.51	0.58	0.44	0.65	0.59	0.57	0.24	0.64	0.55
2006	0.59	0.62	0.26	0.47	0.46	0.22	0.50	0.58	0.42	0.63	0.59	0.54	0.24	0.63	0.54
2007	0.58	0.52	0.24	0.46		0.24	0.50	0.56	0.43	0.62	0.59	0.55		0.62	0.53
2008	0.58	0.61	0.23	0.44		0.22	0.54	0.58	0.46	0.63	0.59	0.58		0.62	0.54
2009	0.56	0.82	0.25	0.51		0.29	0.49		0.49	0.68	0.60	0.62		0.69	0.54
2010		0.70		0.47		0.26			0.46	0.65		0.54		0.66	0.52
2011		0.66													0.51

Source: Data from OECD. http://stats.oecd.org/index.aspx?DatasetCode=ULC_QUA.

Table A4.2: ∂I/∂(C/S) Estimates

	Italy billions of euros	Spain billions of euros	UK billions of pounds	USA 10 billions of dollars	Estonia 100 millions of euros	Finland billions of euros	Germany 10 billions of euros
1980 Q1	53.74		22.60	97.97		0.246	
1980 Q2	54.30		23.53	94.57		0.252	
1980 Q3	51.23		23.09	93.21		0.107	
1980 Q4	50.54		24.50	100.08		0.009	
1981 Q1	46.35		23.20	102.76		0.164	
1981 Q2	50.53		21.28	102.69		0.199	
1981 Q3	48.45		21.14	110.29		0.068	
1981 Q4	48.43		22.53	108.46		−0.111	
1982 Q1	46.74		22.97	100.77		0.135	
1982 Q2	49.96		22.54	103.11		0.099	
1982 Q3	49.11		21.76	94.75		−0.024	
1982 Q4	45.92		22.24	82.99		−0.275	
1983 Q1	48.57		23.75	84.74		0.071	
1983 Q2	49.07		21.28	83.83		−0.011	
1983 Q3	50.60		23.32	82.31		−0.159	
1983 Q4	53.03		24.44	88.99		−0.383	
1984 Q1	50.12		24.62	98.50		−0.017	
1984 Q2	52.08		22.93	100.50		−0.047	
1984 Q3	52.48		23.57	102.70		−0.198	
1984 Q4	48.96		25.68	101.29		−0.410	
1985 Q1	50.02		23.48	96.87		−0.117	
1985 Q2	51.30		25.83	94.80		−0.147	
1985 Q3	50.11		24.26	89.00		−0.268	
1985 Q4	50.23		24.22	89.98		−0.544	
1986 Q1	49.29		22.72	90.43		−0.185	
1986 Q2	50.94		21.78	86.50		−0.157	
1986 Q3	52.75		22.08	80.55		−0.367	
1986 Q4	49.25		24.61	80.57		−0.591	
1987 Q1	49.21		23.53	84.21		−0.286	
1987 Q2	51.57		23.56	85.68		−0.333	
1987 Q3	48.69		25.25	88.31		−0.502	
1987 Q4	50.85		23.82	92.97		−0.750	
1988 Q1	51.34		23.71	92.36		−0.404	
1988 Q2	51.89		24.33	95.33		−0.493	
1988 Q3	51.21		26.22	96.10		−0.819	
1988 Q4	52.83		25.61	95.55		−0.998	
1989 Q1	50.37		26.96	97.94		−0.629	
1989 Q2	50.44		25.37	92.19		−0.890	
1989 Q3	49.43		26.24	90.51		−1.082	
1989 Q4	51.88		25.53	87.76		−1.400	

(*Continued*)

Table A4.2: (*Continued*)

	Italy billions of euros	Spain billions of euros	UK billions of pounds	USA 10 billions of dollars	Estonia 100 millions of euros	Finland billions of euros	Germany 10 billions of euros
1990 Q1	52.81		25.43	87.04		−0.936	
1990 Q2	53.47		24.91	88.83		−1.006	
1990 Q3	53.47		26.26	84.53		−1.079	
1990 Q4	46.88		23.05	83.96		−1.294	
1991 Q1	51.14		24.41	90.77		−0.774	0.691
1991 Q2	49.04		22.92	84.63		−1.028	0.337
1991 Q3	49.22		20.64	81.92		−1.820	0.165
1991 Q4	48.00		22.46	83.07		−1.442	−0.119
1992 Q1	48.52		22.50	81.46		−0.598	−0.668
1992 Q2	46.42		20.37	82.49		−0.749	−0.722
1992 Q3	44.37		19.29	76.92		−16.181	−0.512
1992 Q4	42.24		19.95	76.72		−1.100	−0.728
1993 Q1	46.30		20.37	77.98	0.442	−0.156	−0.452
1993 Q2	47.31		19.57	79.64	0.436	−0.405	−0.287
1993 Q3	46.54		19.69	77.15	0.327	−0.544	−0.529
1993 Q4	48.63		19.82	80.51	0.406	−0.654	−0.317
1994 Q1	47.21		21.27	84.36	0.371	−0.089	−1.192
1994 Q2	48.74		22.34	87.38	0.245	−0.216	−1.009
1994 Q3	48.49		22.85	87.56	0.357	−0.306	−1.260
1994 Q4	50.80		24.84	89.94	0.258	−0.549	−1.731
1995 Q1	55.43	23.57	23.41	94.64	0.218	−0.234	−1.448
1995 Q2	56.11	22.58	23.54	92.99	0.050	−0.416	−1.729
1995 Q3	57.84	22.03	24.31	94.58	0.031	−0.519	−1.656
1995 Q4	61.30	26.99	24.25	97.19	−0.082	−0.694	−1.674
1996 Q1	61.07	23.50	24.51	98.05	0.217	−0.312	−0.459
1996 Q2	56.65	22.46	25.46	100.34	−0.243	−0.555	−2.287
1996 Q3	61.72	23.38	24.47	103.10	−0.158	−0.742	−2.110
1996 Q4	57.68	26.96	23.47	105.19	−0.358	−0.897	−1.949
1997 Q1	61.33	26.24	25.54	107.85	−5.975	−0.401	−1.716
1997 Q2	57.67	24.75	26.42	112.79	−0.381	−0.643	−1.392
1997 Q3	58.47	22.79	27.33	114.98	−0.405	−0.787	−1.457
1997 Q4	61.56	28.20	26.99	114.08	−0.907	−0.987	−1.468
1998 Q1	59.56	25.61	28.30	118.71	−0.713	−0.559	−1.795
1998 Q2	58.60	25.76	28.53	118.18	−0.777	−0.744	−1.112
1998 Q3	56.29	26.43	30.75	120.31	−0.571	−1.074	−1.341
1998 Q4	57.47	28.95	28.95	117.52	−1.014	−1.168	−1.301
1999 Q1	60.54	26.99	26.10	123.24	−0.617	−0.866	−7.647
1999 Q2	56.49	29.53	23.59	118.34	−0.530	−0.970	−4.594
1999 Q3	55.86	27.26	25.52	115.87	−0.406	−0.928	−5.813
1999 Q4	56.63	32.16	25.37	117.02	−0.996	−0.898	−4.861

(*Continued*)

Table A4.2: (*Continued*)

	Italy billions of euros	Spain billions of euros	UK billions of pounds	USA 10 billions of dollars	Estonia 100 millions of euros	Finland billions of euros	Germany 10 billions of euros
2000 Q1	60.88	27.45	25.47	123.37	−0.522	−0.890	−4.994
2000 Q2	56.32	34.99	24.74	121.57	−0.633	−1.215	−6.280
2000 Q3	58.57	28.11	24.59	121.06	−0.680	−0.947	−11.534
2000 Q4	58.17	31.83	22.33	114.60	−1.015	−1.216	−6.716
2001 Q1	63.76	28.57	25.67	116.95	−0.719	−0.804	−6.835
2001 Q2	58.38	36.01	25.70	112.77	−0.732	−1.401	−8.837
2001 Q3	60.37	30.52	26.11	105.71	−0.984	−1.144	−7.732
2001 Q4	61.51	32.38	22.87	97.40	−1.684	−1.331	−4.893
2002 Q1	64.35	31.45	24.53	98.99	−1.102	−0.919	−6.703
2002 Q2	60.76	39.26	24.28	96.29	−1.225	−1.299	−4.054
2002 Q3	63.64	33.36	26.90	91.56	−1.516	−1.020	−2.608
2002 Q4	62.78	35.93	26.29	92.15	−2.168	−1.205	−4.648
2003 Q1	62.00	33.54	26.88	88.54	−1.537	−1.095	−6.569
2003 Q2	57.01	42.58	24.38	90.92	−1.602	−1.160	−10.463
2003 Q3	60.54	36.15	24.98	90.16	−1.955	−1.311	−3.807
2003 Q4	61.27	41.10	28.13	96.79	−2.655	−1.490	−2.836
2004 Q1	64.45	34.30	27.11	96.09	−1.385	−0.947	−1.637
2004 Q2	59.14	42.92	26.49	101.03	−2.416	−1.501	−1.403
2004 Q3	65.86	36.81	25.21	105.04	−1.917	−1.487	−1.580
2004 Q4	61.40	41.28	28.39	102.44	−5.044	−1.449	−1.388
2005 Q1	63.44	36.46	26.42	107.25	−1.908	−0.988	−1.571
2005 Q2	61.06	46.71	28.91	108.33	−2.234	−1.998	−1.372
2005 Q3	62.36	40.23	26.64	109.19	−2.497	−1.518	−1.814
2005 Q4	61.39	42.02	26.76	115.46	−3.457	−1.746	−1.954
2006 Q1	63.03	40.29	29.56	124.07	−2.915	−1.140	−1.656
2006 Q2	62.38	51.57	27.65	123.36	−3.061	−1.853	−2.180
2006 Q3	66.18	41.53	26.52	121.66	−3.581	−1.666	−2.237
2006 Q4	68.04	44.62	27.83	124.62	−5.349	−1.937	−2.614
2007 Q1	66.83	43.64	29.68	114.25	−4.640	−1.466	−2.221
2007 Q2	67.56	52.43	30.93	112.82	−4.147	−2.381	−2.253
2007 Q3	71.07	39.44	32.41	107.67	−3.907	−1.750	−2.295
2007 Q4	65.11	43.12	36.57	106.11	−4.983	−2.404	−2.739
2008 Q1	61.03	38.02	38.41	104.64	−7.693	−1.681	−2.790
2008 Q2	64.94	47.20	33.63	99.16	−3.819	−2.414	−2.557
2008 Q3	58.78	39.97	29.97	97.34	−3.270	−2.011	−2.934
2008 Q4	55.88	37.72	26.90	91.50	−3.951	−2.516	−3.459
2009 Q1	51.00	32.30	24.17	84.38	−3.204	−1.950	−3.709
2009 Q2	49.50	41.12	21.03	73.94	−2.284	−2.990	−3.179
2009 Q3	48.95	33.77	24.29	68.40	−1.801	−1.887	−2.176
2009 Q4	52.37	33.22	25.46	73.52	−1.787	−1.961	−2.298

(*Continued*)

Table A4.2:   (*Continued*)

	Italy billions of euros	Spain billions of euros	UK billions of pounds	USA 10 billions of dollars	Estonia 100 millions of euros	Finland billions of euros	Germany 10 billions of euros
2010 Q1	48.92	29.36	23.84	77.82	−1.929	−2.135	−2.649
2010 Q2	51.16	35.24	22.52	81.46	−1.692	−2.315	−2.943
2010 Q3	49.44	29.97	25.00	85.41	−1.520	−2.082	−3.197
2010 Q4	51.58	32.07	22.95	82.54	−2.165	−2.247	−2.747
2011 Q1	48.41	25.38	24.44	81.25	−2.121	−1.858	−3.677
2011 Q2	48.83	35.38	27.78	80.90	−1.627	−3.138	−3.729
2011 Q3	49.65	28.90	25.52	81.82	−1.847	−2.411	−3.846
2011 Q4	50.58	29.37	25.46	87.18	−2.680	−3.052	−4.280
2012 Q1	47.12	22.48	21.66	87.72	−2.093	−2.964	−4.017
2012 Q2	48.18	32.76	19.06	88.13	−2.187	−3.693	−3.714
2012 Q3	48.91	28.97	21.10	89.00	−2.782	−2.545	−3.726
2012 Q4		31.60	19.07	94.53		−3.541	−4.635

Data Source: IMF.

Appendix 5

ADDITIONAL TABLES FOR CHAPTER 9

Table A5.1: $\partial GDP/\partial G$ Annual Averages: 1981–2012

	Japan	UK	USA	Brazil	Russia	Austria	Belgium	Cyprus	Estonia	Finland	France
1981	6.829	4.401	5.970			4.926	3.498			4.656	3.890
1982	6.756	4.440	5.693			4.850	3.598			4.667	3.892
1983	6.640	4.483	5.756			4.877	3.686			4.618	3.949
1984	6.762	4.550	5.949			4.880	3.749			4.663	3.959
1985	6.967	4.719	5.831			4.844	3.855			4.488	3.988
1986	6.986	4.727	5.722			4.791	3.904			4.429	4.046
1987	6.956	4.870	5.786			4.805	3.951			4.397	4.089
1988	7.182	5.061	5.958			4.924	4.240			4.614	4.185
1989	7.280	5.147	6.050			5.007	4.421			4.701	4.305
1990	7.358	5.064	5.986			5.094	4.499			4.397	4.300
1991	7.298	4.837	5.879	3.998		5.089	4.380			3.819	4.204
1992	7.091	4.734	6.019	5.751		5.038	4.378			3.727	4.120
1993	6.837	4.905	6.181	5.686		4.855	4.318		4.714	3.915	3.883
1994	6.681	5.033	6.371	5.368	4.323	4.868	4.378		4.099	4.058	3.949
1995	6.461	5.154	6.479	4.748	5.134	4.709	4.354	3.629	4.087	4.210	3.965
1996	6.364	5.269	6.644	4.973	5.056	4.732	4.266	3.356	4.469	4.124	3.932
1997	6.376	5.521	6.802	5.023	4.718	4.962	4.383	3.123	4.941	4.270	3.946
1998	6.164	5.603	6.946	4.847	5.262	4.994	4.420	3.365	4.983	4.439	4.092
1999	5.964	5.451	6.946	4.923	6.791	4.949	4.394	3.406	4.692	4.504	4.085
2000	5.803	5.337	6.962	5.251	6.596	5.106	4.441	3.941	5.191	4.701	4.143
2001	5.539	5.219	6.736	5.143	6.090	5.202	4.356	3.829	5.455	4.683	4.174
2002	5.368	5.006	6.479	4.924	5.618	5.272	4.218	3.645	5.554	4.531	4.066
2003	5.366	4.867	6.331	5.212	5.683	5.201	4.145	3.529	5.591	4.389	4.011
2004	5.384	4.766	6.361	5.290	5.904	5.279	4.221	3.964	5.801	4.372	4.020
2005	5.351	4.690	6.372	5.103	5.941	5.302	4.203	4.133	5.933	4.316	4.026
2006	5.409	4.659	6.381	5.069	5.742	5.341	4.260	3.961	6.279	4.382	4.091
2007	5.429	4.768	6.317	4.988	5.694	5.426	4.308	4.332	6.096	4.532	4.164
2008	5.286	4.553	5.995	5.023	5.681	5.251	4.150	4.450	5.276	4.354	4.133
2009	4.919	4.262	5.673	4.768	4.886	4.943	3.880	4.053	4.587	3.879	3.880
2010	4.969	4.363	5.674	4.788	5.376	5.044	3.959	4.062	4.852	3.948	3.867
2011	4.793	4.502	5.837	4.905	5.610	5.201	3.947	4.064	5.170	4.014	3.928
2012	4.777	4.513	6.047	4.723	5.418	5.234	3.899	4.442	5.299	3.942	3.914

(*Continued*)

Table A5.1:   (*Continued*)

	Germany	Greece	Ireland	Italy	Luxemb.	Malta	Netherl.	Portugal	Slovak	Slovenia	Spain
1981	4.522			5.225			3.717	4.912			5.947
1982	4.573			5.241			3.680	5.265			5.973
1983	4.675			5.170			3.733	5.387			5.878
1984	4.724			5.256			3.928	5.657			6.035
1985	4.736			5.213			3.927	5.664			5.980
1986	4.793			5.317			3.954	6.772			6.114
1987	4.775			5.112			3.803	6.926			5.958
1988	4.850			5.012			3.906	6.120			6.051
1989	5.082			5.076			4.040	5.996			5.891
1990	5.262			4.869			4.111	5.856			5.772
1991	5.098			4.854			4.090	5.277			5.564
1992	4.954			4.909		4.615	4.005	5.239			5.297
1993	4.942			4.940		4.351	3.962	5.038	4.823		5.147
1994	4.990			5.158		4.344	4.042	5.125	5.487		5.325
1995	4.978			5.503	5.573	4.365	4.079	5.586	5.175	4.469	5.381
1996	4.920			5.412	5.456	4.179	4.270	5.514	4.635	4.629	5.417
1997	5.033		3.428	5.401	5.385	4.427	4.360	5.502	5.049	4.778	5.585
1998	5.088		4.055	5.459	5.756	4.655	4.395	5.457	4.919	4.860	5.646
1999	5.062		4.805	5.470	5.899	4.906	4.396	5.525	5.413	4.926	5.700
2000	5.133	4.069	5.111	5.419	6.137	5.020	4.458	5.288	5.435	4.826	5.723
2001	5.154	4.282	5.009	5.272	5.780	4.651	4.336	5.141	5.282	4.732	5.770
2002	5.087	4.154	4.999	5.207	5.667	4.689	4.146	5.071	5.313	4.835	5.735
2003	5.061	4.582	5.031	5.086	5.696	4.575	4.014	4.970	5.320	4.891	5.685
2004	5.168	4.630	5.044	5.035	5.543	4.536	4.053	4.917	5.659	4.953	5.550
2005	5.208	4.451	5.149	4.928	5.719	4.785	4.150	4.717	5.850	4.932	5.492
2006	5.337	4.799	5.176	4.975	6.178	4.732	3.928	4.879	5.595	5.016	5.496
2007	5.493	4.665	5.002	5.086	6.474	4.934	3.917	5.038	6.102	5.472	5.394
2008	5.361	4.627	4.443	4.957	6.172	4.673	3.835	4.991	6.069	5.249	5.077
2009	4.891	4.137	4.090	4.643	5.465	4.593	3.442	4.518	5.285	4.719	4.633
2010	5.010	4.554	4.332	4.703	5.739	4.680	3.471	4.620	5.403	4.586	4.618
2011	5.084	4.763	4.537	4.847	5.859	4.659	3.530	4.964	5.793	4.562	4.721
2012	5.040	4.578	4.745	4.846	5.784	4.468	3.471		5.912	4.600	4.922

Table A5.2:   ∂GDP/∂X Annual Averages: 1981–2012

	Japan	UK	USA	Brazil	Russia	Austria	Belgium	Cyprus	Estonia	Finland	France
1981	6.777	3.629	9.364			2.226	0.984			2.614	3.911
1982	6.863	3.688	10.562			2.304	0.961			2.902	4.092
1983	7.163	3.672	11.786			2.377	0.953			2.960	4.010
1984	6.652	3.443	12.109			2.277	0.929			2.922	3.783
1985	6.944	3.398	13.076			2.192	0.986			3.110	3.903
1986	8.815	3.817	13.087			2.434	1.092			3.435	4.455
1987	9.630	3.852	12.303			2.508	1.136			3.578	4.653
1988	10.046	4.249	10.891			2.520	1.094			3.812	4.496
1989	9.570	4.127	10.363			2.407	1.049			3.940	4.244
1990	9.529	4.067	10.021			2.392	1.101			4.113	4.370
1991	9.943	4.199	9.596	6.745		2.499	1.141			4.248	4.320
1992	10.063	4.155	9.564	9.055		2.625	1.186			3.542	4.346
1993	10.863	3.835	9.759	9.596		2.772	1.250		1.000	2.893	4.470
1994	10.997	3.681	9.466	9.972	3.036	2.745	1.216		1.040	2.674	4.307
1995	10.952	3.449	8.806	13.866	3.182	2.661	1.265	1.469	1.203	2.571	4.136
1996	10.225	3.359	8.726	15.248	3.650	2.611	1.263	1.454	1.393	2.525	4.078
1997	9.242	3.452	8.450	14.813	3.900	2.355	1.198	1.461	1.249	2.436	3.685
1998	9.187	3.722	8.938	14.466	3.436	2.265	1.208	1.548	1.209	2.458	3.611
1999	9.734	3.793	9.185	10.685	2.291	2.222	1.214	1.550	1.295	2.456	3.613
2000	9.106	3.581	8.859	10.058	2.237	2.029	1.097	1.475	1.090	2.196	3.305
2001	9.479	3.639	9.776	8.289	2.694	1.955	1.107	1.484	1.166	2.307	3.359
2002	8.815	3.779	10.344	7.723	2.813	1.934	1.129	1.654	1.320	2.366	3.471
2003	8.355	3.840	10.450	6.671	2.827	1.956	1.176	1.861	1.366	2.477	3.683
2004	7.510	3.892	9.818	6.131	2.909	1.833	1.154	1.785	1.301	2.411	3.674
2005	6.949	3.691	9.468	6.614	2.849	1.758	1.120	1.794	1.232	2.304	3.644
2006	6.132	3.429	8.916	7.001	2.951	1.685	1.098	1.833	1.325	2.120	3.554
2007	5.583	3.693	8.291	7.484	3.266	1.617	1.081	1.880	1.434	2.110	3.583
2008	5.633	3.338	7.608	7.483	3.238	1.612	1.058	1.956	1.365	2.069	3.586
2009	7.863	3.448	8.649	9.122	3.647	1.904	1.229	2.157	1.484	2.595	4.118
2010	6.521	3.258	7.723	9.251	3.443	1.763	1.125	2.114	1.230	2.422	3.783
2011	6.535	3.061	7.071	8.489	3.328	1.669	1.071	2.087	1.061	2.375	3.582
2012	6.768	3.139	7.058	8.018	3.425	1.671	1.072	2.037	1.044	2.439	3.511

(Continued)

Table A5.2: (*Continued*)

	Germany	Greece	Ireland	Italy	Luxemb.	Malta	Netherl.	Portugal	Slovak	Slovenia	Spain
1981	0.904			4.239			1.006	3.378			5.215
1982	0.953			4.345			1.042	3.481			5.076
1983	1.108			4.531			1.078	3.038			4.588
1984	1.141			4.410			1.024	2.633			4.149
1985	1.156			4.384			1.030	2.731			4.274
1986	1.358			4.970			1.254	3.677			4.954
1987	1.481			5.164			1.295	3.655			5.120
1988	1.549			5.292			1.270	3.531			5.279
1989	1.548			5.043			1.237	3.335			5.538
1990	1.654			5.029			1.246	3.411			5.876
1991	2.404			5.350			1.258	3.838			5.886
1992	2.696			5.210		1.000	1.320	4.188			5.749
1993	2.952			4.460		0.975	1.354	4.296	0.616		5.272
1994	2.922			4.164		0.967	1.322	3.984	0.771		4.602
1995	2.862			3.836	0.462	1.012	1.286	3.419	0.932	0.914	4.333
1996	2.770			4.021	0.462	1.081	1.298	3.476	1.101	1.052	4.118
1997	2.535		0.860	3.929	0.440	1.113	1.247	3.438	1.114	1.135	3.706
1998	2.459		0.834	3.962	0.438	1.086	1.280	3.398	1.116	1.221	3.656
1999	2.422		0.855	4.118	0.458	1.052	1.291	3.639	1.122	1.408	3.665
2000	2.150	1.318	0.819	3.706	0.433	1.046	1.183	3.412	1.015	1.295	3.373
2001	2.076	1.557	0.820	3.706	0.450	1.172	1.249	3.513	1.012	1.318	3.436
2002	2.036	2.022	0.893	3.906	0.484	1.148	1.319	3.579	1.065	1.372	3.592
2003	2.039	2.388	1.017	4.068	0.512	1.200	1.349	3.575	1.029	1.440	3.734
2004	1.911	2.312	1.027	3.967	0.472	1.225	1.285	3.524	1.077	1.370	3.794
2005	1.791	2.311	1.068	3.843	0.479	1.257	1.236	3.577	1.076	1.291	3.840
2006	1.646	2.481	1.110	3.591	0.455	1.036	1.191	3.202	0.993	1.228	3.752
2007	1.610	2.527	1.097	3.454	0.452	1.082	1.179	3.075	0.986	1.202	3.670
2008	1.590	2.591	1.048	3.506	0.438	1.060	1.153	3.061	1.047	1.250	3.733
2009	1.783	3.200	0.954	4.205	0.481	1.188	1.276	3.536	1.220	1.433	4.130
2010	1.638	2.699	0.856	3.768	0.468	1.023	1.123	3.199	1.081	1.275	3.637
2011	1.549	2.283	0.824	3.447	0.464	0.974	1.061	2.796	0.971	1.164	3.264
2012	1.511	1.982	0.809	3.309	0.478	0.959	1.011		0.916	1.120	3.072

Table A5.3: ∂GDP/∂Money Annual Averages: 1981–2012

	Japan	UK	USA	Brazil	Russia
1981	3.605	7.309	8.970		
1982	3.541	7.723	8.690		
1983	3.591	7.783	8.354		
1984	3.710	7.804	8.556		
1985	3.786	8.022	8.303		
1986	3.717	8.151	7.646		
1987	3.552	8.465	7.313		
1988	3.586	8.624	7.463		
1989	3.688	8.865	7.904		
1990	3.803	9.101	7.992		
1991	3.855	9.251	7.736	2.866	
1992	3.742	9.395	7.223	8.814	
1993	3.581	9.332	6.785	11.493	
1994	3.501	9.197	6.790	8.186	
1995	3.255	9.163	7.121	8.817	−0.042
1996	2.934	9.063	7.742	8.333	0.306
1997	2.779	8.969	8.448	5.832	0.514
1998	2.533	8.921	8.772	5.439	0.598
1999	2.257	8.638	9.107	5.353	1.319
2000	2.124	8.434	9.691	4.930	1.485
2001	1.911	8.190	9.516	4.602	1.337
2002	1.480	7.905	9.453	4.293	1.246
2003	1.188	7.846	9.247	4.654	1.082
2004	1.082	7.758	9.280	4.453	1.018
2005	1.033	7.720	9.683	4.350	0.969
2006	1.019	7.897	10.269	4.129	0.848
2007	1.027		10.756	3.728	0.699
2008	1.006		10.291	3.866	0.747
2009	0.937		8.915	3.810	0.720
2010	0.939		8.650	3.798	0.641
2011	0.872		7.796	3.964	0.633
2012	0.854		7.055	3.940	0.612

REFERENCES

Abe, S. (2013). Unleashing the Power of 'Womenomics,' *The Wall Street Journal*, September 26, 2013, A15.

Aitken, A.C. (1935). On Least Squares and Linear Combinations of Observations, *Proceedings of the Royal Society of Edinburgh*, 55, 42–48.

Alam, I.S. and J.E. Leightner (2001). The Impact of the Financial Crisis on the Productivity of Thailand's Financial Institutions, *Singapore Economic Review* 46(2), 153–177.

Alpert, L.I. (2013). Russia Denounces Deposit-Tax Plan, *The Wall Street Journal*, March 19, 2013, A8.

Angrist, J.D. and G.W. Imbens (1995). Two-Stage Least Squares Estimation of Average Causal Effects in Models with Variable Treatment Intensity, *Journal of the American Statistical Association* 90(430), 431–442.

Appleyard, D.R. and A.J. Field, Jr. (2014). *International Economics*, 8th edition (New York: McGraw-Hill Irwin).

Baiocchi, M., D.S. Small, S. Lorch and P.R. Rosenbaum (2010). Building a Stronger Instrument in an Observational Study of Perinatal Care for Premature Infants, *Journal of the American Statistical Association* 105(492), 1285–1296.

Batson, A. (2009). China Takes Aim at Dollar, *The Wall Street Journal*, March 24, 2009. Online version available at http://online.wsj.com/article/SB123780272456212885.html [accessed October 9, 2009].

Berg, A.G. and J.D. Ostry (2011). Inequality and Unsustainable Growth: Two Sides of the Same Coin? *IMF Staff Discussion Note*, April 8. SDN/11/08 available at http://www.imf.org/external/pubs/ft/sdn/2011/sdn1108.pdf [accessed December 8, 2013].

Bernanke, B. (2005). The Global Saving Glut and the US Current Account Deficit. *Remarks given at the Sandridge Lecture, Virginia Association of Economists*, Richmond, Virginia, March 10. Available at http://www.federalreserve.gov/boarddocs/speeches/2005/200503102/default.htm [accessed August 23, 2013].

Blanchard, O., F. Jaumotte and P. Loungani (2013). Labor Market Policies and IMF Advice in Advanced Economies During the Great Recession. *An IMF Discussion Note*. Available at http://www.imf.org/external/pubs/cat/longres.aspx?sk=40412 [accessed on April 2, 2014].

Blumenstein, R., A. Browne and D. McMahon (2010). China Deflects Pressure for Yuan Rise, *The Wall Street Journal*, September 1, 2010, A9, Cols. 1–6.

Bound, J., D.A. Jaeger and R.M. Baker (1995). Problems with Instrumental Variables Estimation when the Correlation between the Instruments and the Endogenous Explanatory Variable is Weak, *Journal of the American Statistical Association* 90(430), 443–450.

Bowen, R.M., III (2010). Testimony to Financial Crisis Inquiry Commission, April 7.

Branson, J. and C.A. Knox Lovell (2000). Taxation and Economic Growth in New Zealand. In *Taxation and the Limits of Government*, eds. G.W. Scully and P.J. Caragata, pp. 37–88 (Boston: Kluwer Academic).

Casselman, B. (2012). Cautious Companies Stockpile Cash, *The Wall Street Journal*, December 7, 2012, A2.

Chang, A. (2010). China Premier Wen Jiabao Says Japanese Companies' Wages Too Low, *Huffington Post*, August 29. Available at http://www.huffingtonpost.com/2010/08/29/wen-jiabao-china-wages-japanese-companies_n_698297.html [accessed September 1, 2010].

Chasan, E. (2013). Lots of Cash, Few Alternatives, *The Wall Street Journal*, April 23, 2013, B6.

Demos, T., S. Russolillo and M. Jarzemsky (2013). Firms Send Record Cash Back to Investors, *The Wall Street Journal*, March 8, 2013, A1 and A2.

Diamond, D.W. (2007). Banks and Liquidity Creation: A Simple Exposition of the Diamond-Dybvig model, *Federal Reserve Bank of Richmond Economic Quarterly* 93(2), 189–200.

Diamond, D.W. and P.H. Dybvig (1983). Bank Runs, Deposit Insurance, and Liquidity, *Journal of Political Economy* 91(3), 401–419. doi:10.1086/261155. Reprinted (2000) *Federal Reserve Bank of* **Minneapolis** *Quaterly Review* 24(1), 14–23.

Dvorak, P. and E. Warnock (2013a). Japan's Banks Find it Hard to Lend Easy Money, *The Wall Street Journal*, November 18, 2013, A1 and A14.

Dvorak, P. and E. Warnock (2013b). Suffering Japan Rolls Dice on New Era of Easy Money, *The Wall Street Journal*, March 21, 2013, A1 and A12.

Fidler, S. (2012). Firms' Cash Hoarding Stunts Europe, *The Wall Street Journal*, March 24–25, 2012, A10.

Flood, R.P. and P.M. Garber (1984). Collapsing Exchange-Rate Regimes: Some Linear Examples, *Journal of International Economics* 17, 1–13.

Frangos, A. (2013). Asia Wrestles with a Flood of Cash, *The Wall Street Journal*, May 9, 2013, C1 and C4.

Gara, T. (2012). S&P: US Companies Underinvest by Billions, *The Wall Street Journal*, December 12, 2012, B6.

Geronimus, A.T., J. Bound, and L. Neidert (1996). On the Validity of Using Census Geocode Characteristics to Proxy Individual Socioeconomic Characteristics, *Journal of the American Statistical Association* 91(434), 529–537.

Heller, R., P.R. Rosenbaum, and D.S. Small (2009). Split Samples and Design Sensitivity in Observational Studies, *Journal of the American Statistical Association* 104(487), 1090–1101.

Hilsenrath, J. and R. Simon (2011). Penitent Debtors Hobble Recovery in US, *The Wall Street Journal*, October 22–23, 2011, A1 and A14.

Inoue, T., P.L. de Micheaux, and J.E. Leightner (2013). Several Related Solutions to the Omitted Variables Problem and the Effectiveness of Quantitative Easing (unpublished manuscript).

Jenkins, H.W., Jr. (2013). Cyprus Bailout Revisted, *The Wall Street Journal*, May 8, 2013, A15.

Jittrapanun, T. and S. Prasartset (2009). *Hot Money and Capital Controls in Thailand. TWN Global Economy Series # 15* (Penang, Malaysia: Third World Network). Available at http://twnside.org.sg/title2/ge/ge15.pdf [accessed September 9, 2013].

Krugman, P. (1979). A Model of Balance of Payments Crises, *Journal of Money, Credit and Banking* 11(3), 311–325.

Lauricella, T., S. Reddy, and E. McCarthy (2012). Central Banks Flex Muscles, *The Wall Street Journal*, September 20, 2012, A1 and A12.

Legislature Proposes Narrowing the Gap in Wealth, *China Daily On Line*, August 24, 2010.

Leightner, J.E. (2013a). The Changing Effectiveness of Monetary Policy, *Economies*, 49–64. Available at http://www.mdpi.com/2227-7099/1/3/49 [accessed on April 3, 2014].

Leightner, J.E. (2013b). Chinese Protectionism. In *Prevention and Crisis Management: Lessons for Asia from the 2008 Crisis*, eds. S. Rosefielde, M. Kuboniwa and S. Mizobata, pp. 173–189 (Singapore: World Scientific Publishers).

Leightner, J.E. (1992). Technology Transfer and the Functional Distribution of Income in Japan: 1952–1980, *The International Trade Journal* 7(2), 221–254.

Leightner, J.E. (1999). Globalization and Thailand's Financial Crisis, *Journal of Economic Issues* 33(2), 367–373.

Leightner, J.E. (2000). Asia's Financial Crisis, Speculative Bubbles, and Underconsumption Theory, *Journal of Economic Issues* 34(2), 385–392.

Leightner, J.E. (2002a). The *Changing Effectiveness of Key Policy Tools in Thailand*. Institute of Southeast Asian Studies for East Asian Development Network, EADN Working Paper # 19(2002) x0219-6417.

Leightner, J.E. (2002b). The Domestic Effects of Tight Monetary Policy in the Wake of Thailand's Financial Crisis, *Journal of Asia Pacific Economy* 7(2), 242–266.

Leightner, J.E. (2005a). Fight Deflation with Deflation, Not With Monetary Policy, *The Japanese Economy: Translations and Studies* 33(2), 67–93.

Leightner, J.E. (2005b). The Productivity of Government Spending in Asia: 1983–2000, *Journal of Productivity Analysis* 23, 33–46.

Leightner, J.E. (2005c). Utility Maximization, Morality, and Religion, *Journal of Economic Issues* 39(2), 375–381.

Leightner, J.E. (2006). Returns to Market Power in Financial Institutions, *Journal of the Asia Pacific Economy* 11(3), 268–291.

Leightner, J.E. (2007a). Omitted Variables, Confidence Intervals, and the Productivity of Exchange Rates, *Pacific Economic Review* 12(1), 15–45.

Leightner, J.E. (2007b). Thailand's Financial Crisis: Its Causes, Consequences, and Implications, *Journal of Economic Issues* 41(1), 61–76.

Leightner, J.E. (2008). Omitted Variables and How the Chinese Yuan Affects Other Asian Currencies, *International Journal of Contemporary Mathematical Sciences* 3(14), 645–666.

Leightner, J.E. (2009). How the Crisis is Killing One Asian Development Model, While Birthing Another One (in Chinese). In *Transformation of Development Models and Reforms in the Post-Crisis Period*, eds. C. Fulin and Y. Zhongyi, pp. 134–144 (Beijing: Huawen Publishing Corporation).

Leightner, J.E. (2010a). Alternative Property Systems for China, *China: An International Journal* 8(2), 346–359.

Leightner, J.E. (2010b). Are the Forces that Cause China's Trade Surplus with the USA Good? *Journal of Chinese Economic and Foreign Trade Studies* 3(1), 43–53.

Leightner, J.E. (2010c). China's Fiscal Stimulus Package for the Current International Crisis: What Does 1996–2006 Tell Us? *Frontiers of Economics in China* 5(1), 1–24.

Leightner, J.E. (2010d). How China's Holdings of Foreign Reserves Affect the Value of the US dollar in Europe and Asia, *China & World Economy* 18(3), 24–39.

Leightner, J.E. (2011). Fiscal Stimulus for the US in the Current Financial Crisis: What does 1930–2008 tell us? *Applied Economic Letters* 18(6), 539–549.

Leightner, J.E. (2012). Chinese Overtrading. In *Two Asias: The Emerging Postcrisis Divide*, eds. S. Rosefielde, M. Kuboniwa and S. Mizobata (Singapore: World Scientific Publishers).

Leightner, J.E. and I.M.S. Alam (2002). Financial Crisis Hypotheses and the Productivity of Thailand's Financial Institutions. In *Productivity and Economic Performance in the Asia-Pacific Region*, eds. T.-T Fu, C.J. Huang and C.A. Knox Lovell, pp. 410–432 (Northampton, MA: Edward Elgar Publishing, Ltd.).

Leightner, J.E. and T. Inoue (2007). Tackling the Omitted Variables Problem Without the Strong Assumptions of Proxies, *European Journal of Operational Research* 178(3), 819–840.

Leightner, J.E. and T. Inoue (2008a). Capturing Climate's Effect on Pollution Abatement with an Improved Solution to the Omitted Variables Problem, *European Journal of Operational Research* 191(2), 539–556.

Leightner, J.E. and T. Inoue (2008b). The Effect of the Chinese Yuan on Other Asian Currencies During the 1997–1998 Asian Crisis, *International Journal of Economic Issues* 1(1), 11–24.

Leightner, J.E. and T. Inoue (2009). Negative Fiscal Multipliers Exceed Positive Multipliers During Japanese Deflation, *Applied Economic Letters* 16(15), 1523–1527.

Leightner, J.E. and T. Inoue (2012a). Is China Replacing the USA As an Engine for Global Growth? *International Economics & Finance Journal* 7(1), 55–77.

Leightner, J.E. and T. Inoue (2012b). Solving the Omitted Variables Problem of Regression Analysis Using the Relative Vertical Position of Observations, *Advances in Decision Sciences*. Available at www.hindawi.com/journals/ads/2012/728980 [accessed on April 3, 2014].

Leightner, J.E. and C.A. Knox Lovell (1998). The Impact of Financial Liberalization on the Performance of Thai Banks, *Journal of Economics and Business* 50(2), 115–131. Reprinted in Maximilian J.B. Hall, ed. (2001). The Regulation and Supervision of Banks. In *The International Library of Critical Writings in Economics*, series ed. Mark Blaug, Vol. 4 (Edward Elgar Publishing, Ltd.).

LeVine, S. (2009). China's Yuan: The Next Reserve Currency? *BusinessWeek*, May 26, 2009.

Lewis, A. (1983). Economic Development with Unlimited Supplies of Labour. In *Selected Economic Writings of W. Arthur Lewis*, ed. M. Gersovitz, pp. 311–364 (New York: New York University Press).

Lindsey, L.B. (2006). Yuan Compromise? *The Wall Street Journal*, April 6, 2006, A14.

Lyons, J. (2011). Dark Side of Brazil's Rise, *The Wall Street Journal*, September 13, 2011, A1 and A14.

Mare, R.D. (1980). Social Background and School Continuation Decisions. *Journal of the American Statistical Association* 75(370), 295–305.

Mead, J. and J. Hilsenrath (2013). Banks Rush to Ease Supply of Money, *The Wall Street Journal*, May 14, 2013, A7.

McCarthy, E., P. Natarajan and K. Inagaki (2013). Japan Triggers a Shift to Emerging Markets, *The Wall Street Journal*, April 15, 2012, C1 and C2.

Mill, J.S. (1967). On the Influence of Consumption on Production. In *Essays on Economics and Society*, Vol. 4 of *Collected Works* (Toronto: University of Toronto Press, 1967) as quoted in Richard T. Froyen, *Macroeconomics: Theories and Policies*, 10th edition, p. 32 (New York: Pearson, 2013).

Modigliani, F. and R. Brumberg (1954). Utility Analysis and the Consumption Function: An Interpretation of Cross-Section Data. In *Post Keynesian Economics*, ed. K.K. Kurihara, pp. 388–436 (New Brunswick, Rutgers University Press).

Modigliani, F. and S.L. Cao (2004). The Chinese Saving Puzzle and the Life-Cycle Hypothesis, *Journal of Economic Literature* 42(1), 145–170.

Molinski, D. (2007). Dollar Pummeled on Report by China Over its Reserves, *The Wall Street Journal*, November 8, 2007, C5.

Monga, V. (2011). Companies' $2 Trillion Conundrum, *The Wall Street Journal*, October 5, 2011, B5.

Moral-Benito, E. (2012). Determinants of Economic Growth: A Bayesian Panel Data Approach, *The Review of Economics and Statistics* 94(2), 566–579.

Mozur, P. and T. Orlik (2012). China's Migrant Workers Lingering in Cities, *The Wall Street Journal*, December 31, 2012, A16.

Mummery, A.F. and J.A. Hobson (1889). *The Physiology of Industry: Being an Exposure of Certain Fallacies in Existing Theories of Economics* (London: J. Murray: New York: Kelley and Millman Inc., 1956).

Naughton, B. (2007). *The Chinese Economy: Transitions and Growth* (Cambridge, Massachusetts: MIT Press).

Olivero, M.P., Y. Li, and B.N. Jeon (2009). Consolidation in Banking and the Lending Channel of Monetary Transmission: Evidence from Asia and Latin America. Available at http://faculty.lebow.drexel.edu/OliveroM/research/Consolidation%20paper%20OLJ.pdf [retrieved August 25, 2013].

O'Malley, A.J. (2012). The Analysis of Social Network Data: An Exciting Frontier for Statisticians, *Statistics in Medicine* 32(4), 539–555. doi:10.1002/sim.5630.

Orlik, T. (2013). Rising Wages Pose Dilemma for China, *The Wall Street Journal*, May 17, 2013. Available at http://online.wsj.com/news/articles/SB10001424 127887324767004578488233119290670 [accessed December 13, 2013].

Ozawa, T. (1985). Macroeconomic Factors Affecting Japan's Technology Inflows and Outflows: The Postwar Experience. In *International Technology Transfer: Concepts, Measures, and Comparisons*, eds. N. Rosenberg and C. Frischtak, pp. 222–254 (New York: Preager).

Persianis, M., M. Stevis and A. Granitsas (2013). Cypriots Try Getting By Without Credit, *The Wall Street Journal*, August 29, 2013, A11.

Pesaran, M.H., A. Pick and A. Timmermann (2011). Variable Selection, Estimation and Inference for Multi-period Forecasting Problems. *Journal of Econometrics* 164(1), 173–187.

Prasad, E.S. (2009). Rebalancing Growth in Asia. Available at http://www. nber.org/papers/w15169 [accessed August 3, 2009]. An earlier version of the paper was presented at the NIPFP-DEA conference in New Delhi in March of 2009.

Ricardo, D. (1817). *On the Principles of Political Economy and Taxation* (London: John Murray, Albemarle-Street, Cambridge: Cambridge University Press, 1951).

Rosenbaum, P.R. (2010). Design Sensitivity and Efficiency in Observational Studies, *Journal of the American Statistical Association* 105(490), 692–702.

Rosenberg, S. (2003). *American Economic Development Since 1945* (New York: Palgrave MacMillan).

Rostow, W.W. (1951). *The Stages of Economic Growth: A Non-communist Manifesto*, 2nd edition (Cambridge: Cambridge University Press).

Shelley, M. (1818). *Frankenstein: Or the Modern Prometheus* (London: Lackington, Hughes, Harding, Mavor, & Jones). Reprinted (New York: W.W. Norton & Company, 1996).

Sidel, R. (2013). Wads of Cash Squeeze Bank Margins, *The Wall Street Journal*, January 11, 2013, C1.

Smith, A. (1937). *The Wealth of Nations* (New York: The Modern Library).

Somerville, R.A. (2007). Housing Tenure in Ireland, *The Economic and Social Review* 37, 107–134 as cited in Whelan (2013).

Stevis, M., A. Granitsas and S. Bouras (2013). Cyprus Plays for Time, *The Wall Street Journal*, March 19, 2013, A1 and A8.

Stockhammer, E. (2008). Wage Flexibility or Wage Coordination? Economic Policy Implications of the Wage-Led Demand Regime in the Euro Area, *Intervention* 5(1), 54–62.

Tierean, O.M. and S.H. Tierean (2013). The Disadvantages of Joining the Euro: Lessons for Romania, *Bulletin of the Transilvania University of Brasov* 6(55) Series V: Economic Sciences, 163–168. Available at http://webbut.unitbv. ro/Bulletin/Series%20V/BULETIN%20V%20PDF/27%20tierean%20o%20s. pdf [accessed December 13, 2013].

US Senate, Permanent Subcommittee on Investigations (2011), *Wall Street and the Financial Crisis: Anatomy of a Financial Collapse* (also known as: *The Senate Financial Crisis Report*). Available at http://hsgac.senate.gov/public/_ files/Financial_Crisis/FinancialCrisisReport.pdf [retrieved August 25, 2013].

Wei, L. and R. Davis (2011). China Stumbles in Yuan Grand Plan, *The Wall Street Journal*, July 15, 2011.

Whelan, K. (2013). Ireland's Economic Crisis: The Good, the Bad and the Ugly UCD Centre for Economic Research Working Paper presented at Bank of Greece conference on the Euro Crisis in Athens May 24, 2013. Available at http://www.ucd.ie/t4cms/WP13_06.pdf [accessed September 7, 2013].

Wines, M., K. Bradsher and M. Landler (2009). China's Leader Says He is 'Worried' Over US Treasuries, *The New York Times On-Line*, March 14, 2009. Available at http://www.nytimes.com/2009/03/14/world/asia/14china. html?_r=1&pagewanted=print [accessed May 1, 2009].

Zhiming, X. (2008). Transfer Payments Set to Rise, *China Daily*, April 17, 13.

Zhou, X. and F. Li (2013). PBOC says no longer in China's interest to increase reserves, *Bloomberg News*, November 20, 2013.

Zheng, X., "Coping with global inflation," *China Daily*, July 14, 2011. Available at http://www.chinadaily.com.cn/opinion/2011-07/14/content_12898687.htm [accessed July 14, 2011].

Zubizarreta, J.R., M. Neuman, J.H. Silber and P.R. Rosenbaum (2012). Contrasting evidence within and between institutions that provide treatment in an observational study of alternative forms of anesthesia. *Journal of the American Statistical Association* 107(499), 901–915.

INDEX

Argentina, 13, 172
austerity, 1, 9, 19, 55, 58, 61, 171, 191, 192
Australia, 172, 174, 258, 260
Austria, 36, 38–42, 50, 75–79, 90, 93, 95, 97, 111–120, 126, 129, 130, 172, 175, 188–190, 230, 242, 258, 260, 268, 270

banking, 2, 8, 11, 15–18, 20, 28, 166, 275, 279
Belgium, 36, 38–42, 75–79, 90, 93–95, 97, 111–120, 126, 129, 130, 172, 175, 188, 190, 231, 243, 258, 260, 268, 270
Bernanke, 28, 97, 100, 273
Bolivia, 172
Brazil, 6, 8, 13, 24–26, 30, 32, 36, 38–42, 46, 49, 50, 52, 75–79, 83, 90, 92, 97, 110–120, 126, 127, 134, 136, 140, 188, 189, 268, 270, 272, 278
bubbles, 1, 2, 18, 21, 22, 34, 35, 46, 137, 141, 166, 167, 169, 177, 194, 277
Bulgaria, 172

Cambodia, 17
Canada, 18, 104, 121, 172, 174, 258, 260
capital, 7, 18, 19, 21, 64, 104, 109, 137, 138, 164, 166, 167, 173, 177, 194, 196, 255–257, 275
Chile, 13, 172
China, 1, 2, 5, 6, 8, 9, 17, 18, 24, 64, 69, 70, 72–74, 90, 101–104, 107–110, 137–143, 149, 155, 160–169, 171, 172, 186, 193, 194, 273–280
Chinese saving, 278
consumption, 2, 7, 8, 17, 30, 34–37, 44–49, 51–61, 70–74, 97, 109, 110,

137, 138, 140–143, 147–151, 155–163, 165, 167–169, 173, 176–185, 187, 189–196, 223, 224, 255, 256, 277, 278
corruption, 2, 73, 162, 194
Croatia, 172
currency policy, 97, 137
Cyprus, 17, 20, 36, 38–42, 50, 52, 53, 73, 75–79, 90, 93, 95, 188–190, 244, 268, 270, 275, 280
Czech, 174, 258, 260

deception, 2, 15, 17, 34, 35, 46, 137, 169, 177, 193–195
Denmark, 172, 174, 258, 260

Ecuador, 171, 172
El Salvador, 172
England, 64
Estonia, 36, 38–42, 46, 50, 75–79, 90, 93–95, 97, 111–120, 126, 129, 130, 172, 175, 178, 181, 184, 185, 188–190, 232, 245, 258, 260, 262–265, 268, 270
Europe, 1–3, 8, 18, 20, 21, 24, 36, 70, 73, 74, 98, 108, 109, 129, 130, 137, 142, 160, 162, 166–168, 173, 185, 193, 275, 276
European Union, 185, 191
exchange rate, 9, 17, 19, 23, 65, 67, 73, 74, 90, 91, 95, 98, 100–106, 108–110, 121, 123, 125, 126–128, 131–136, 138–141, 168, 191, 192, 275, 276
exports, 1, 2, 8, 9, 24, 36, 64, 65–75, 80–95, 97–103, 104, 108–111, 116, 121–143, 155, 167, 168, 184, 185, 187, 189–194, 223

FED, 24, 28
Federal, 164, 195, 274
federal reserve, 273
Finland, 36, 38–42, 50, 75–79, 90, 93, 97,
    111–120, 126, 129, 130, 172, 175, 178,
    182, 184, 185, 188, 190, 233, 246, 258,
    260, 262–265, 268, 270
fiscal policy, 35, 36, 137, 173, 187, 189
France, 36, 38–42, 45, 75–79, 93, 97,
    111–121, 126, 129, 130, 171, 172, 175,
    188, 190, 234, 247, 258, 260, 268, 270

German, 93, 94
Germany, 36, 38–42, 52, 54, 55, 75–79,
    85, 90, 93–95, 97, 111–121, 126, 129,
    130, 172, 175, 178, 183–185, 188–190,
    258, 260, 262–265, 269, 271
Gini coefficients, 139, 171, 172
Greece, 36, 38–42, 45, 50, 52, 55, 56, 70,
    73, 75–79, 86, 93, 94, 126, 172, 188,
    189, 269, 271
Greek, 20

Hong Kong, 13, 104
Hungary, 172, 174, 258, 260

Iceland, 172, 174, 258, 260
IMF, 8, 19, 20, 24, 30, 35, 55, 65, 67, 70,
    92, 110, 123, 178, 191–193, 273, 274
imports, 37, 64–70, 74, 90, 97–103, 110,
    116, 126, 130–136, 140–142, 152, 155,
    164, 168, 191, 192, 223
income distribution, 7, 9, 11, 43, 65, 139,
    140, 160, 171, 173, 176, 177, 186
India, 13, 24, 140
Indonesia, 13, 92, 140
interest rates, 3, 12, 18, 19, 21, 22, 34–36,
    37, 108, 109, 162, 164–167, 223
internal devaluations, 1, 2, 67, 70, 72–74,
    93, 95, 185, 186, 192
Ireland, 17, 21, 22, 36, 38–42, 52, 55, 57,
    58, 70, 73, 75–79, 87, 90, 91, 93–95,
    172, 175, 188, 190, 258, 260, 269, 271,
    280
Israel, 172, 174, 258, 260

Italy, 1, 36, 38–42, 52, 58, 59, 73, 75–79,
    88, 90, 93, 95, 97, 111–120, 126, 129,
    130, 172, 175, 178, 180, 184, 188, 190,
    258, 260, 262–265, 269, 271

Japan, 3, 5–8, 13, 18, 24–26, 28–30, 36,
    38–46, 73, 75–80, 91, 92, 97, 109–122,
    133, 136, 138, 140, 142, 160, 162, 163,
    172–174, 187–189, 193–196, 258, 260,
    268, 270, 272, 274, 276–279

Korea, 6, 13, 64, 73, 92, 140, 172, 174,
    259, 261

labor, 1, 8, 21, 36, 37, 64, 65, 70, 72, 73,
    137–139, 141, 160, 161, 163, 171,
    173–176, 185, 192–195, 224, 225,
    255–258, 274
Laos, 17
Latvia, 70, 172
Lithuania, 171, 172
Luxembourg, 36, 38–42, 50, 75–79, 90,
    91, 94, 95, 172, 175, 188–190, 235,
    248, 259, 261, 269, 271

Macedonia, 172
Malaysia, 13, 17
Malta, 36, 38–42, 75–79, 90, 93–95, 188,
    189, 236, 249, 269, 271
Mexico, 13, 140, 171, 172, 174, 259, 261
monetary policy, 23, 24, 30, 34, 35, 173,
    186, 187, 189, 223, 275–277
Myanmar, 17

Netherlands, 36, 38–42, 45, 46, 75–79, 90,
    93–95, 97, 111–120, 126, 129, 130,
    172, 175, 188, 190, 237, 250, 259, 261,
    269, 271
New Zealand, 173, 174, 259, 261, 274
North Korea, 64
Norway, 173, 174, 259, 261

Peru, 13
Poland, 173, 174, 259, 261

Portugal, 36, 38–42, 50, 52, 64, 70, 73, 75–79, 90, 93, 95, 97, 111–120, 126, 129, 130, 173, 175, 188, 190, 238, 251, 259, 261, 269, 271

rent, 2, 5, 7, 20, 34, 35, 46, 137, 142–144, 147–151, 169, 177, 193–196, 224, 225, 256, 257
renter, 5
reserves, 3–6, 19, 97, 99–111, 116, 121–136, 138, 140–142, 155, 164–167, 168, 191–193, 195, 223, 224, 276, 278, 280
return, 193, 194
Romania, 70, 173, 280
Russia, 6, 20, 24–26, 30, 36, 38–42, 51, 52, 75–79, 84, 90–93, 95, 97, 109–120, 126, 128, 135, 136, 268, 270, 273
Russian, 8, 33, 36, 50, 84, 90–93, 95
Russian Federation, 188–190

Saudi Arabia, 6
saving, 2, 5, 8, 12, 13, 15–18, 20–22, 24, 34, 35, 43, 45, 46, 61, 65, 72–74, 97, 100, 101, 110, 137, 140, 141, 161, 162, 167, 169, 177–185, 190–196, 224, 257, 273, 278
Singapore, 13
Slovakia, 36, 38–42, 50, 75–79, 90, 93–95, 173, 175, 188–190, 239, 252, 259, 261, 269, 271
Slovenia, 36, 38–42, 75–79, 90, 93–95, 173, 175, 188–190, 240, 253, 259, 261, 269, 271
South Korea, 142
Spain, 1, 2, 9, 36, 38–42, 52, 58, 60, 61, 73, 75–79, 89, 90, 93, 95, 97, 111–120,

126, 129, 130, 171, 173, 175, 178, 180, 184, 188–190, 259, 261–265, 269, 271
Sudan, 167
Sweden, 140, 173, 174, 259, 261
Switzerland, 6
Syria, 64

Taiwan, 73, 173
tax, 1, 37, 108, 191, 195, 196, 273
taxation, 274, 279
Thailand, 8, 12, 17–21, 68, 92, 104–107, 137, 140, 166, 273, 275–277
trade policy, 8, 9, 63, 164, 176, 194, 196
Turkey, 174, 259, 261

unemployment, 1, 37
United Kingdom, 1, 3, 8, 24–26, 30, 31, 36, 38–42, 46, 47, 75–79, 81, 90, 92, 95, 97, 110–121, 123, 125, 126, 132, 136, 173, 174, 178, 179, 184, 188–190, 259, 261–265, 268, 270, 272
United States, 1–8, 13–15, 17, 18, 21, 24–27, 30, 36, 38–42, 46, 48, 58, 64, 73–79, 82, 90, 92, 97–102, 105–121, 123, 124, 131, 136, 138, 140–142, 155, 160–164, 166–168, 171, 173, 174, 178, 179, 184, 185, 187–193, 259, 261–265, 268, 270, 272, 273, 275, 276, 280
US Federal, 24, 164, 195

Venezuela, 171, 173
Vietnam, 17, 18

wages, 1, 2, 8, 17, 18, 65, 67, 69–74, 90, 91, 137, 138, 141–144, 147–151, 160, 192, 193, 195, 196, 274, 279

Printed in the United States
By Bookmasters